Revisiting the Nomadic Subject

Radical Cultural Studies

Series Editors: Fay Brauer, Maggie Humm, Tim Lawrence, Stephen Maddison, Ashwani Sharma and Debra Benita Shaw (Centre for Cultural Studies Research, University of East London, UK)

The Radical Cultural Studies series publishes monographs and edited collections to provide new and radical analyses of the culturopolitics, sociopolitics, aesthetics and ethics of contemporary cultures. The series is designed to stimulate debates across and within disciplines, foster new approaches to Cultural Studies and assess the radical potential of key ideas and theories.

Other Titles in Series

Sewing, Fighting and Writing: Radical Practices in Work, Politics and Culture, Maria Tamboukou

Radical Space: Exploring Politics and Practice, edited by Debra Benita Shaw and Maggie Humm

Science Fiction, Fantasy and Politics: Transmedia World-Building Beyond Capitalism, Dan Hassler-Forest

EU, Europe Unfinished: Europe and the Balkans in a Time of Crisis edited by Zlatan Krajina and Nebojša Blanuša

Postcolonial Interruptions, Unauthorised Modernities, Iain Chambers

Austerity as Public Mood: Social Anxieties and Social Struggles, Kirsten Forkert

Metamodernism: Historicity, Affect, Depth edited by Robin van den Akker, Alison Gibbons and Timotheus Vermeulen

Affect and Social Media: Emotion, Mediation, Anxiety and Contagion, Edited by Tony D. Sampson, Stephen Maddison and Darren Ellis

Gender, Sexuality, and Space Culture, Kat Deerfield

Work That Body: Male Bodies in Digital Culture, Jamie Hakim

Writing the Modern Family: Contemporary Literature, Motherhood and Neoliberal Culture, Roberta Garrett

Revisiting the Nomadic Subject: Women's Experiences of Travelling Under Conditions of Forced Displacement, Maria Tamboukou

Revisiting the Nomadic Subject

Women's Experiences of Travelling Under Conditions of Forced Displacement

Maria Tamboukou

ROWMAN & LITTLEFIELD
Lanham • Boulder • New York • London

Published by Rowman & Littlefield
An imprint of The Rowman & Littlefield Publishing Group, Inc.
4501 Forbes Boulevard, Suite 200, Lanham, Maryland 20706
www.rowman.com

86-90 Paul Street, London EC2A 4NE

Copyright © 2021 by Maria Tamboukou

All rights reserved. No part of this book may be reproduced in any form or by any electronic or mechanical means, including information storage and retrieval systems, without written permission from the publisher, except by a reviewer who may quote passages in a review.

British Library Cataloguing in Publication Information Available

Library of Congress Cataloguing-in-Publication Data

Names: Tamboukou, Maria, 1958- author.
Title: Revisiting the nomadic subject : women's experiences of travelling under
   conditions of forced displacement / Maria Tamboukou.
Description: Lanham : Rowman & Littlefield, [2021] | Series: Radical Cultural Studies |
   Includes bibliographical references and index.
Identifiers: LCCN 2021036318 (print) | LCCN 2021036319 (ebook) |
   ISBN 9781538142622 (Cloth : acid-free paper) | ISBN 9781538142639
   (Paperback : acid-free paper) | ISBN 9781538142646 (ePub)
Subjects: LCSH: Women refugees. | Internally displaced persons. | Forced migration. |
   Feminist theory.
Classification: LCC HV640 .T36 2021 (print) | LCC HV640 (ebook) |
   DDC 305.42—dc23
LC record available at https://lccn.loc.gov/2021036318
LC ebook record available at https://lccn.loc.gov/2021036319

♾️™ The paper used in this publication meets the minimum requirements of American National Standard for Information Sciences—Permanence of Paper for Printed Library Materials, ANSI/NISO Z39.48-1992.

To Sebastian

Contents

Acknowledgements	ix
Introduction	1
1 Mobility Assemblages and Geographies of Nomadism	9
2 Who Are you? The Art of Listening	21
3 Crossing Borders and Inhabiting Borderlands	55
INTERLUDE I: NADIA'S STORY	**77**
4 Feminist Genealogies of Labour under Conditions of Forced Displacement	91
INTERLUDE II: SOMI'S STORY	**115**
5 Thinking with Antigone: Political Narratives of Agonistic Humanism	129
INTERLUDE III: HANNA'S STORY	**147**
6 Education, Art and Radical Hope	155
7 Imagining the Non-Nomad	179
Conclusion: Decolonizing Feminist Theories	195
References	205
Index	221

Acknowledgements

I want to thank from the depths of my heart all those people who were entangled in the process of *Revisiting the Nomadic Subject and of course* the Leverhulme Trust for granting me a research fellowship in 2018–2019, that made the whole thing happen.

My deepest gratitude goes to the twenty-two amazing women who graciously offered me the gift of their stories. Thank you so much, Nadia, Somi, Hanna, Sima, Click, Christina, Elena, Derya, Melina, Awat, Dana, Mariam, Anna, Hanielle, Linda, Erika, Ilya, Zahra, Elina, Shachnaz, Warda and Tanya! You know who you are as you have chosen your 'other names'. I still cannot believe it that you shared with me your experiences and memories of *errance*. I feel so lucky to have met you; you have opened unknown vistas in the ways I see and understand the world.

My thanks also go to the wonderful people that opened the gates of the field and introduced me to my participants: Ariagni Adam, Thodoris Zeis and Efi Stathopoulou from Refugee Legal Support (RLS-Athens); Maria Liapi from Diotima Centre; Maria Doukakarou from the Observatory of the Refugee and Migration crisis in the Aegean at the University of the Aegean; Maritina Koraki from Caritas Hellas, Lesvos; Elina Karagiorgi from the UN Refugee Agency (*UNHCR*-Lesvos); Konstantina Kalampoki from Iliaktida Lesvos; Kleio Chatzidaniil from the University of the Aegean. Thank you all so much for your gift of trust!

I was further supported by a group of academic colleagues and feminist friends, who showed me tracks and traces in a field that I had not treaded before, invited me to their classes, workshops and seminars and gave me wise advice: Akis Papataxiarchis from the Observatory of the Refugee and Migration crisis in the Aegean, Giannis Kallas and Panagiotis Grigoriou from the sociology department of the University of the Aegean, Alexandra

Chalkias from the sociology department of Panteion University, Efi Avdela and Alexandra Zavos from the University of Crete, Maria Preka from the 2nd General Lykeion of Nea Filadelfia, Myrto Tsilimpounidi from the *Feminist Autonomous Centre for Research,* Aggeliki Sifaki from the University of Newcastle; feminist author and journalist Aggelika Psara. Thank you, dear colleagues and friends, for helping me navigate the maze. Thanks also to artist Mato Ioannidou for generously allowing me to use the beautiful images of her exhibition *Genealogies* for the website and all presentations of the project.

Many of the ideas of this book were shared in conferences and seminars in the UK and around the world, and I am grateful for very useful comments and suggestions I got during this time of testing my ideas. Special thanks to my colleagues Erika Cudworth, Cigdem Esin, Maja Korac and Angie Voela, as well as my PhD students Graham Robertson and Emma Jones at the University of East London, for insightful discussions we had about some of the concepts of this project and particularly about my critique of nomadism. In bringing this book together, I was supported by the editors of the Rowman and Littlefield series *Radical Cultural Studies,* Debra Shaw and Stephen Maddison, who endorsed my publication proposal and offered very useful feedback and suggestions during the writing process.

As always, the people I love were around me, not only during the research project, but also throughout the writing of the book, which mostly happened during the darkest times of the pandemic. Thank you Mihali, Ariagni, Anna, Thodori, Stelio and Stephane. The making of this book run in parallel with a new joyful beginning in our lives: this is for you, Sebastian.

Introduction

The Making of a Book in Dialogue with the Real

On March 8, 2016, I felt uncomfortable in circulating something celebratory in the social media, on the occasion of women's international day. Instead, I shared an image from Mato Ioannidou's art series Genealogy, as a reminder of a day that did not seem to be so happy for many women. It was the beginning of a long process of 'revisiting the nomadic subject', the central theme of this book.

Throughout my work, I have repeatedly drawn on the nomadic subject as a useful configuration of female subjectivity.[1] Nomadism as a spatial concept denoting uncharted movements seemed to facilitate non-static ways of theorizing the subject and his/her relations to the world and to others. But it seems that the nomads of the real world and their torturing wanderings today have challenged the romance of unregulated movement and force us to radically rethink the very concept of nomadism itself.

Dorothea Lange's exhibition 'Politics of seeing' at the Barbican Centre,[2] which I visited in June 2018, was insightful in opening visual imageries of women's entanglement in the complex histories of forced displacement. I was particularly drawn to the caption of a photograph taken in Sacramento Shanty town on May 21, 1935: 'How can we go when we ain't no place to go to?'[3] The question of 'where you can go if you have nowhere to go to', was very much in my mind when I visited the *Wanderlust* exhibition[4] at the Old National Gallery in Berlin in the end of August 2018. I laughed bitterly at Ludwig Richter's depiction of the serene *Crossing of the Elbe*,[5] painted in around 1840 after his 1834 travel to Bohemia. Romantic, pensive and liberating, as they have been expressed in art, literature and philosophy, walking, travelling, sailing and crossing are social practices entangled within historical and political conditions that make them possible for some and impossible for others.

The question I, therefore, raise in this book is whether nomadism has become a *hybris*, a concept politically loaded and irreparably infected with the unbearable heaviness of those who are not able to move and cross borders and boundaries—the dark side of the moon of privileged mobility. To put it simply: Can we still use the nomadic subject in the era of the recent huge refugee waves that have uprooted millions of people across the globe and have forced them to take up nomadic paths as the only feasible way of going on living? When the majority of these forced nomads are reportedly today women and children, how can the feminist notion of the nomadic subject enable us to grasp the condition of refugee women on the move? In the light of feminist relational ethics, how do migrant and refugee woman on the move challenge our perception of the subject of feminism and force us to revise who we are and how we relate to ourselves and to others?

The book draws on a Leverhulme-funded research project,[6] which I conducted in 2018–2019. In initiating this research, I was intrigued by the fact that in January 2016, women and children on the move outnumbered adult men for the first time comprising 60 per cent of migrants crossing into Europe.[7] I was further puzzled by the way these women were represented and discussed in institutional and organizational reports, as well as in the media worldwide, as 'women travelling alone'. The case study of Farah in the initial assessment report of the United Nations Refugee Agency, the United Nations Population Fund and Women's Refugee Commission, published in January 2016, illustrates the language paradoxes used for the representation of 'women travelling alone': 'Farah is an Afghan refugee *travelling alone through Europe with her eight children*, seven of whom are girls under the age of 17'.[8]

What has been particularly striking for me when reading the various journalistic and institutional publications and reports around 'refugee women travelling alone' is that nearly all of them base their observations and draw their conclusions on stories elicited through interviews. There is an underlying consensus about the power of the voice of 'the refugee woman travelling alone', who stands up and offers her experience as a testament of a greater malaise: the phenomenon of sex and gender-based violence (SGBV). In this context, Oumo's story has been repeatedly cited in a number of blogs and newspaper articles that draw on the January 2016 report above to highlight the urgency of women refugee's condition:

> Oumo is a young woman from a conflict-affected sub-Saharan African country. She fled her country of origin a month before the team met her, due to the political persecution of her family, including the killing of her brother-in-law and the disappearance of her sister. Fearing for her life, she was travelling alone towards Germany. During her journey to Greece, Oumo was forced to engage

in transactional sex twice, the first time to access a fake passport and the second time to gain passage on a boat from Turkey.[9]

I do not want to downplay the importance of reports such as the above in raising awareness and calling for action vis-à-vis critical gender-based problems in situations and contexts of forced displacement. The scope of my research, however, was different. Taking up the force of narratives to respond to the real, rather than correspond with it (see Tamboukou 2010), I have asked migrant and refugee women to tell their story of being on the move. Following lines from Hannah Arendt's (1998) and Adriana Cavarero's (2000) philosophies, I have encouraged them to tell stories of *Who* they are, as unique and unrepeatable human beings, and not of *What* they are—objectified 'refugees', 'victims', 'stateless subjects'. My argument is that the existential experiences of women on the move create a rich archive that can challenge and transpose the way we think, understand and conceptualize the subject of feminism. Following Bonnie Honig's, important question about 'what problems might foreigners solve for us' (2001, 4), I have explored questions and issues that displaced and uprooted women pose to feminist theory and praxis, in times of crises. Having presented the concepts, figures, debates and facts that underpin the writing of this book, I now want to make a cartography of its moves and chapters.

This introductory chapter has set the context of the book in the light of global flows of mobility. Drawing on the unprecedented phenomenon of women and children having superseded the number of men for the first time in migration history, it has raised the question of whether the figuration of the nomadic subject needs to be revisited as part of the wider move to decolonize theory in feminist research and beyond.

An important notion that subsequently emerges in Chapter 1 is what I have called *mobility assemblages* drawing on Édward Glissant's (2010) take of Deleuze and Guattari's nomadology (1988). In further looking at feminist debates around the use and abuse of the nomadic subject (see Boer 1996; Gedalof 1996, 2000; Wuthnow 2002), I have put forward the argument of making cartographies of nomadism as a move to ground philosophical abstractions that seem to have lost sight of 'the real'.

In Chapter 2, I draw on my experiences of listening to migrant and refugee women's stories of displacement and explore questions around the ethics, aesthetics and politics of listening across borders and languages. In doing so, I particularly focus on the materiality of listening, the force of corporeal voices, the rhythms of embodied listening and their effects on understanding and making connections within the web of human relations. It is within the soundscapes of women's voices that the idea of the *interludes* emerged. Interludes in music are pieces played or sung between the parts of a longer composition, but are also taken as gaps, breaks and pauses. Given that this is a book on entanglements between narratives, voices and texts, a musical interlude seemed to be the most appropriate form to encompass three interventions in its theoretical analysis. Taken as both interruptions and disruptions, these three *interludes* that I will present below give space to women's voices to sound through the unfolding of their uninterrupted narrative and order of discourse. There is no question that since it is only the transcribed stories that the readers will have access to, women's voices will have succumbed to the monotones of the text, as I will further discuss in Chapter 2. Despite their dry prose form however, the three *Interludes* open dialogic spaces with different theoretical chapters, themes, concepts and figurations of the book.

Chapter 3 problematizes the notion of the border through *assemblage* analytics. In considering borders as components of *mobility assemblages*, I chart their diverse manifestations and practices on local and global levels. In transposing the question of 'What is a border?' to the question of 'What does a border do?' I chart discourses and practices revolving around borders, but I also focus on women's stories of surviving the borderlands. In doing so, I draw on a rich body of critical feminist poetics in dialogue with political theory and cultural anthropology.

Chapter 3 is interrupted by the first narrative *interlude*, Nadia's story: Nadia is a young Afghan woman who was separated from her family when she was fifteen years old at the Turkish–Greek borders and worked at the Istanbul textile industry for three years under conditions of modern slavery, before she was able to travel to Greece on her own and finally reunite with her family in Germany. This *interlude* is a narrative pathway to Chapter 4, where I consider entanglements between refugee and migrant women on the move, intense experiences of gendered labour, forces of radical solitude and affective encounters in crossing borders and following *lines of flight*. Nadia's *interlude* further makes connections with the concept of education as risk in Chapter 6, as well as with the notion of 'radical solitude' that is discussed in Chapter 7.

Somi's story comes as the second narrative *interlude* of the book: Somi is an Iranian woman who fled Iran when she was nineteen years old and spent sixteen years in a refugee camp in Iraq before she was transferred to Albania and then travelled to Greece. At the time of the interview, Somi was about to start her studies at a university in Athens, determined to rebuild her life in Europe. Somi's story has opened up insights in re-imagining Antigone, the theme of Chapter 5. Antigone is of course a figure that has inspired a range of readings and interpretations in feminist theory and beyond. But what has brought Antigone on the stage of narratives of displacement is migrant and refugee women's desire to rewrite the histories of their exclusion and affirm their determination for new beginnings. Somi's *Interlude* is also interwoven with ideas and debates in Chapters 3 and 6 revolving around borders and education, respectively.

Chapter 5 is followed by the third narrative *Interlude* of this book, Hanna's story: Hanna is a migrant woman from Sierra Leone, who has lived in Greece for over thirty years and has been involved in migrant women's agonistic politics for citizenship and labour rights. She is also a performance artist and founder of the United African Women's Organization in Greece (UAWO-Greece), which over the years has created a vibrant body of educational and cultural activities in Athens. This *Interlude* further interlaces with Chapter 4 in terms of Hanna's involvement in agonistic labour politics, as well as with Chapter 5 through the figure of Antigone.

Having been inspired by migrant and refugee women's simultaneous involvement in the educational and cultural politics of their new countries, in Chapter 6, I theorize entanglements between education and art as a plane of 'radical hope' (Lear 2008) Women's attachment to and belief in the power of education runs as a red thread through their narratives. Moreover, educational activities and practices have opened up heterotopic spaces in the dystopias of the refugee camps and have shattered the discourses and practices of the neoliberal university.

Chapter 7 revolves around Dana's story, a *bidun* woman from Kuwait. The biduns constitute a minority group (10 per cent) of the people in Kuwait and their name, *bidun*, carries the semantics of their condition: 'bidun jinsiyya', means 'without nationality' in Arabic. In thus tracing storylines of 'a real nomad', I follow Katerina Kolozova's deployment of principles of non-philosophy in theorizing female subjectivity. What I suggest in this chapter is a radical encounter between the nomad and 'uprooted women travelling alone'. What emerges from this encounter is the *non-nomad*, a figuration that retains the radical possibilities of unregulated and free movement while responding and reacting to the material conditions of displaced women's urgent precariousness.

In the concluding chapter, I weave together the analytical lines that I followed throughout the book to make the argument that what emerges from the encounter between theoretical abstractions and women's lived experiences is the need to decolonize feminist theories and make cartographies of *mobility assemblages*, wherein nomadism is a component of entangled relations and not a category or a figuration of a subject position. Recognizing migrant and refugee women's many and important differences instead of subsuming them under the label of 'the victim' is an important aspect of decolonization as I will argue throughout the book. Indeed, the twenty-two participants of this study create an exemplary cartography of differences on many levels, as the tables below powerfully demonstrate. But in writing this book, I have tried to follow trails of Chandra Mohanty's project of *feminism without borders*: 'I

Table 0.1 List of participants in Athens, Greece

Name	Personal Status	Language of interview	Ethnicity	Age	Educ.	Occupation	Date
Nadia	single	English	Afghan	20	HE	textile worker, HE student, NGO Volunteer and translator	25-7-2018
Somi	in a relation	Farsi (with interpreter)	Iranian	36	HE	HE student, NGO Volunteer	7-12-2018
Hanna	single mother	English	Sierra Leonean	50-60	HE	domestic worker, activist, actress	8-12-2018
Sima	married mother	Pashto (interpreter)	Afghan	40-50	PE	Housewife	13-12-2018
Click	widow, mother	English	Zimbabwean	60+	HE	freedom fighter, military officer, history teacher, bee-keeper, domestic worker, textile artist, dancer, singer	20-3-2019
Christina	divorced mother	Greek	Bulgarian	62	SE	domestic worker	13-4-2019
Elena	married, mother	English	Turkish	30	HE-graduate studies	physicist	17-4-2019
Derya	married mother	English	Turkish	30+	HE-graduate studies	civil servant	17-4-2019
Melina	married mother	English	Turkish	20-30	HE-graduate studies	teacher	18-4-2019
Awat	separated mother	Farsi (interpreter)	Kurd	35	PE	hairdresser	22-4-2019
Dana	mother, disappeared husband	Arabic (interpreter)	Kuwaiti	49	FE	farmer	23-4-2019

Table 0.2 List of participants in Lesvos, Greece

Name	Personal status	Language	Ethnicity	Age	Educ.	Occupation	Date
Mariam	single	French	Congolese	20+	SE	retail worker	5-4-2019
Anna	single mother	French	Congolese	20+	SE	domestic worker	8-4-2019
Hanielle	separated mother	French	Cameroonian	20+	SE	housewife	8-4-2019
Linda	married	Greek	Syrian	40	HE	translator	9-4-2019
Erika	married mother	Arabic (interpreter)	Somalian	20–30	SE	restaurant owner	10-4-2019
Ilya	married mother	Farsi (interpreter)	Iranian	30+	FE	housewife	10-4-2019
Zahra	divorced	Farsi (interpreter)	Afghan	23	HE	nurse	10-4-2019
Elina	divorced mother	Arabic (interpreter)	Syrian	22	HE	nurse	11-4-2019
Shachnaz	widow, mother	Pashto (interpreter)	Afghan	36	HE	teacher	11-4-2019
Warda	single	Arabic (interpreter)	Somalian	20+	SE	student	11-4-2019
Tanya	divorced	Farsi (interpreter)	Iranian	20+	SE	housewife	12-4-2019

want to speak of feminism without silences and exclusions in order to draw attention to the tension between the simultaneous plurality and narrowness of borders and the emancipatory potential of crossing through, with, and over these borders in our everyday lives.' (2003, 2)

NOTES

1. See Tamboukou 2002, 2003, 2004, 2009, 2010, 2012.
2. See https://www.barbican.org.uk/search?search=Dorothea+Lange&past_events=1, accessed December 1, 2019.
3. Dorothea Lange, *Notes from the Field'*, The DL Collection, Oakland Museum of California, A78.144.26.24, http://collections.museumca.org/?q=category/2011-schema/art/dorothea-lange, accessed December 1, 2019.
4. https://www.smb.museum/en/exhibitions/detail/wanderlust.html, accessed December 1, 2019.
5. https://curiator.com/art/adrian-ludwig-richter/crossing-the-elbe-at-aussig, accessed December 1, 2019.
6. See https://sites.google.com/view/revisiting-the-nomadic-subject
7. 'Human rights of refugee and migrant women and girls need to be protected', available at: http://www.coe.int/en/web/commissioner/-/human-rights-of-refugee-and-migrant-women-and-girls-need-to-be-better-protected [Acessed, May 16, 2016]
8. 'Initial Assessment Report: Protection Risks for Women and Girls in the European Refugee and Migrant Crisis', United Nations Refugee Agency (UNRA), United Nations Population Fund (UNPF) and Women's Refugee Commission (WRC), January, 20, 2016, p. 7. Available at: http://www.unhcr.org/uk/protection/operations/569f8f419/initial-assessment-report-protection-risks-women-girls-european-refugee.html [Accessed, May 6, 2016, my emphasis}
9. 'Initial Assessment Report' as above, p. 8.

Chapter 1

Mobility Assemblages and Geographies of Nomadism

'Crisis' is a debated and contested notion in current bodies of literature around migration.[1] It is a discursive formation that creates a sense of panic and uneasiness around human mobility, a sociopolitical context within which harsh bordering practices are being implemented, because 'society must be defended' (Foucault 2003). Historians of migration on the other hand have always viewed human movement as an ordinary part of human life, 'an almost universal human experience' (Gabaccia 1999, 1115). Stephen Castles has further maintained that conflict and forced migration form a continuum that is linked to the social transformations of globalization (2006, 7). In his analysis, the distinction between migration as voluntary movement and asylum as coercion does not stand, since migratory movements across the globe have historically been triggered by wars, regional conflicts, national and international politics, as well as local and global economic dynamics.

Taking Castle's 'migration/asylum nexus' further, Encarnación Guttiérez Rodríguez has developed the analytical framework of 'the coloniality of migration' (2018), looking into socioeconomic and political connections between asylum and migration in the process of their mutual constitution. In mapping 'the coloniality of migration' within relations of colonial power and racial capitalism, Rodríguez has also considered 'the coloniality of gender', Maria Lugones' (2008) notion, explicating how racial differences have been historically entangled with patriarchal relations and how this European oppressive regime was exported to the colonies from the fifteenth century onwards.

It is within such economic, political and colonial *assemblages* that I have mapped migrant and refugee women's experiences of travelling to Greece. What I argue is that their stories encompass components of what I have called *mobility assemblages*, a notion, which I now want to present and explicate as a useful lens for making sense of mobility under conditions of forced displacement.

MOBILITY ASSEMBLAGES

There is currently an increasing interest in *assemblages* in social analytics and beyond, but the notion is often used in a vague way and certainly not always within the philosophical context of its emergence, namely Deleuze and Guattari's philosophical work, *A Thousand Plateaus* (1988). This wide and diverse use of the term has led to many misconceptions to the point where anything can become an *assemblage* (see Kinkaid 2020, 459), but there are also approaches that claim that 'there is no single "correct" way to deploy the term, nor any one theoretical tradition or style hold an exclusive right to it' (Anderson and McFarlane 2011, 124). Given that *assemblage* analytics is often used to highlight material and symbolic entanglements of components through which provisional entities and relations emerge and intra-act, imposing conceptual boundaries upon the term would simply defeat the purpose of its use and deployment.

Although I concur with Anderson and McFarlane (2011) against the imposition of any orthodoxies around *assemblage* thinking, I also feel the need to chart my position in the field. In this context, my take of the *assemblage* draws on Deleuze and Guattari's concept of *agencement* (1984, 1988) that Brian Massumi has translated as *assemblage*. Unlike institutions, structural systems, identities and axes of difference – which are the usual terms deployed in analysing the social – *assemblages* do not have any fixed organization, structure or centre; they are rather networks of connections, always in flux, assembling and reassembling in different ways. *Assemblages* are, thus, emergent features of relationships and can only function as they connect with other *assemblages* in a constant process of becoming.

Assemblages are also related to two important notion in Deleuze and Guattari's analytics: territorialization and deterritorialization. Both notions derive from the Latin word terra, meaning earth and thus relate to processes of grounding or uprooting. In this light, processes of territorialization 'define or sharpen the spatial boundaries of actual territories' (DeLanda, 2006, 13), but they also work towards solidifying the often-moving grounds of the *assemblage* thus 'increasing its internal homogeneity' (2006, 13). Processes of territorialization are therefore always antagonistically related to processes of deterritorialization, which 'destabilize spatial boundaries' (2006, 13) and once again create earthquakes in the grounds of the *assemblage*. Here, the long history of women's desire to escape, get away and travel is an excellent example of this war of discourses and processes of territorialization and deterritorialization. It is this sensitivity to how orders change that *assemblage* thinking facilitates. Migrant and refugee women's stories of escaping patriarchal and war machines show that as Deleuze and Guattari have argued, society is not so much defined by its molar formations and their dialectic oppositions but rather by what has escaped them, not the molar sociocultural entities, but the molecular counter-formations, its *lines of flight*: 'There is always something that flows or flees, that escapes the binary organizations, the resonance apparatus and the overcoding machine: things that are attributed to a 'change in values', the youth, women, the mad, etc' (Deleuze & Guattari 1988, 216).

Moreover, *mobility assemblages* also include molecular formations and microrelations. In the case of this book, desire and affects that mobilize the movement of bodies, geographical proximities that facilitate border crossing, unexpected political developments as well as specific climate conditions. In the context of my research, migrant and refugee women talked about how they had to leave war-stricken countries, but their stories were also about escaping violent partners and domestic violence. In a way the disastrous war conditions they lived through, paradoxically also opened up escape paths. Their decision to travel was not always reactive or negative; they often expressed their desire for a better future. Tanya is a young Iranian woman in her early twenties, who I met through Iliaktida, a Greek civil non-profit company providing accommodation and protection for vulnerable asylum seekers,[2] and interviewed her in a flat in Mytilini Lesvos. She started her story saying that 'I left Iran because I wanted to develop my skills and that's why I wanted to come here'.[3] Although she added that fearing her ex-husband's violent behaviour was also a reason, she put her desire 'to develop herself first'. Sometimes a desire to leave was not targeted or specific: 'I don't know why, I just wanted to leave',[4] Linda told me. Linda is a Syrian woman in her early forties, who I met through a research student at the University of the Aegean and interviewed her at her flat in Mytilini. She fled the war and internal conflicts in Syria by seeking refuge to her brother's home in Turkey, but she didn't like it there, jumped in a boat and sailed to Greece.

Geography also played a role, the fact that the Greek islands are very close to the Turkish coast, so that getting on a boat did not seem such an impossible act, despite the many drownings that have also happened. What is actually surprising is how many women dared to get on a boat despite the horrific drownings they had definitely heard about. This is how Zahra, put it boldly in her story: 'we got on the boat and they told us, Greece is on the other side; they showed the operation of the boat to one of the passengers and they told him, "Can you see those lights on the other side? Just drive the boat there". It was terrifying.'[5] Zahra is a young Afghan woman in her early twenties who fled an abusive husband in Iran and travelled to Greece with her elderly mother and her young nephew. I met her in the Kara Tepe municipal refugee camp in Lesvos and interviewed her in the women's friendly centre there. While recounting her story, she also talked about how safe she felt in her first encounter with the port and border authorities of Greece, a country that at the time of their voyage had elected a left government with strong humanitarian pledges: 'I was wondering how I had not known for such a long time where humanity lies; the policeman was so kind', Zahra told me. I am not so sure how her experience would have been with the current conservative government in Greece whose hostile policies against refugees have radically changed the political terrain of their reception and treatment.[6] As Kelly Oliver has argued, 'we should critically consider how the uneasy alliance between humanitarian aid, human rights and military operations produce refugees as either security risks or charity cases' (2016, 2).

Drawing on some narrative moments from migrant and refugee women's stories of travelling to Greece, what I have tried to show is that *assemblages* encompass very diverse elements and stage unexpected encounters across multiple differences and contradictions. It is thus important to note here that *assemblages* are characterized by 'relations of exteriority', put it simply, relations that have autonomy from the terms related and vice versa. This idea of 'the exteriority of relations' may seem strange and yet it is absolutely fundamental in *assemblage* approaches. As Anderson and colleagues helpfully explain, when we think of relations we usually have in mind individuals, organizations, structures and other things that relate through some form of exchange or contact, but we also accept that individuals and other entities are fully determined by their relations to the point that when relations change, their components also change (2012, 177). By suggesting the idea of 'the exteriority of relations', Deleuze has argued that things are conditioned, but not determined by their relations, that relations may change without their constituent components changing and that finally entities are never fully realized within their relations (Deleuze and Parnet 1997, 41). In short, not only *assemblages* are never reducible to their parts, but also components are relatively autonomous to the point where 'a component part of the *assemblage* may be detached from it and plugged into a different *assemblage* in which its interactions are different' (DeLanda 2006, 10).

It is here that Barad's notions of 'entanglements' and 'intra-actions' become particularly important in my configuration of mobility assemblages. Drawing on atomic physics, Barad (2003, 2007) has introduced the neologism of 'intra-actions' as a theoretical juxtaposition to the usual notion of interactions. In doing this, she denotes a significant difference: while interactions occur between already established and separate entities, 'intra-actions' occur as relations between components. Entities – both human and non-human – actually emerge as an effect of these intra-actions, without having stable points or positions. It is important to note here that although *assemblages* are not part of Barad's conceptual vocabulary, her notions of *entanglements* and *intra-actions* constitute a significant contribution to *assemblage* thinking from the field of feminist science studies. As Anderson et al. (2012, 81) note however, in focusing on entangled intra-actions, Barad downplays the autonomy of the components that intra-act. Yet, her approach is important in how agency is theorized within *assemblage* thinking. Why is that? For Barad, it is 'phenomena' and not parts that are the primary ontological units. It is through their entanglement and intra-actions within the configuration of a particular phenomenon that things are constituted, words take up meaning and 'agential cuts' emerge. Her notion of 'agential cut' (2007, 348) is particularly illuminating in assemblage thinking: although within the intra-acting phenomena of relations, causality is inevitably rendered multiple and indeterminate, there are however recurrent 'cuts' to the assemblage, where strategic decisions and acts create disturbances in the *assemblage* in an attempt to mobilize an ethics of responsibility and critical politics.

Here it is important to remember that Barad's notion of 'agential cuts' emerge from the 'agential realism' of her thesis, namely the dynamism of matter in (re)configuring the world. In the context of agential realism, the objects of analysis are phenomena, that is 'a specific intra-action of "an object" and the "measuring agencies" [which] emerge from rather than precede the intra-action that produces them' (2007, 128). Transposing Barad's notion of agential realism in the field of narrative analysis, I have traced agential cuts within 'narrative phenomena'. In this way, I have argued that the meaning of the stories we research is enacted in entanglement with the spaces, feelings and temporalities within which we read and understand them (see Tamboukou 2016a).

In the milieu of 'narrative phenomena' then, Linda's story of her 'inexplicable' decision to leave the comfort of her brother's home in Turkey and go to Greece carries traces of multiple causalities and 'agential cuts'. When recounting her story of travelling to Greece, she talked about her strange anxiety in Turkey, the beauty of the Greek islands, her love of the Greek language, which she had studied at school, as well as the excitement of making a new beginning as an independent woman. Linda cannot fully explain what underpinned her decision to go to Greece; she cannot locate clear causes and effects. Her story is rich, full of visual images, impressions, desires, affects and feelings, as well as fears and anxieties. The phenomenon within which *lines of flight* and 'agential cuts' can be mapped encompasses components with material and expressive roles – the boat, the smuggler, the friend, the weather, the landscape, the language – as well as processes of territorialization and deterritorialization:

I didn't like Turkey. I didn't like the weather and I felt like a foreigner. I didn't feel secure, I didn't feel good. I was anxious all the time without knowing why. So, I talked with my brother and I told him that I wanted to leave. He asked me: 'where will you go?' I told him 'I will go to Greece'. He asked me 'how?' I said 'in a boat, like everyone else'. He said, 'you must be mad', I said, 'no, I am not mad, I want to leave'. He said 'no way', but I didn't listen to him. There was another lady from Syria when I left my country for Lebanon. She had told me, 'when you reach Turkey, I know a smuggler, who is good and if you want to go to Germany you can talk to him, this is his mobile number, you can talk to him'. Back then I had told her that I didn't want to leave Turkey, I was staying with my brother, but I didn't know then, that I wouldn't like Turkey. (Linda's story)

What are the implications of working with *assemblage* theories then? A central task of the analysis would be to make specific cartographies of situated phenomena and problems, trace the connections they make in order to configure emerging new formations, but also follow their lines of flight, through revisiting and problematizing the notion of nomadism.

CHALLENGING THE NOMADIC SUBJECT

Rosi Braidotti's figuration of 'the nomadic subject' has been a radical intervention in the way feminism has theorized subjectivity. Spaces, places, gendered bodies and movement are at the heart of the embodied and embedded conceptualization of 'the nomadic subject'. But while Braidotti has tried to ground and sex the abstract figure of the nomad in Deleuze and Guattari's philosophical work (1988), she has nevertheless created her own abstractions, as I will further argue in this section. In introducing her figuration, Braidotti has highlighted its mythical traits and has pointed to its connections to a Spinozist take of political imagination – imagining a different world so that social change can become an actuality: 'the nomadic subject is a myth, or a political action, that allows me to think through and move across established categories and levels of experience: blurring boundaries without burning bridges', she has written (2011, 26).

Despite its mythical and metaphorical traits however, the nomad acknowledges the real by pointing to the bodily, material and spatial roots of subjectivity. Nomadic subjects are subjects in transition. They are not characterized by homelessness, but by their ability to recreate their homes everywhere. As Deleuze and Guattari have put it 'the nomad has a territory; distributes himself [sic] in a smooth space; occupies, inhabits, holds that space' (1988, 380). Distributed in a smooth space, the nomadic subject is not permanent: it is constituted by continuous shifts and changes, which have their cycles of repetition and recurrence. The nomad is not unified but is not completely devoid of unity either. The nomad passes through, connects, circulates, moves on; she or he makes connections and keeps coming back (380). It is, however, in passing between these points that the nomad enjoys the freedom of movement. The life of the nomad is the going between, 'the intermezzo' (380). Nomadic subjects cannot be integrated into established social structures and react critically to the discourses and practices that have set the conditions of their existence in this world.

In the light of Deleuze and Guattari's nomadology (1988), Braidotti has thus imagined 'nomadic consciousness as a form of political resistance to hegemonic and exclusionary views of subjectivity', (2011, 58); she has further related it to the Foucauldian notion of counter-memory that has the possibility of enacting a rebellion of subjugated knowledges (60). Travelling is not essential in the condition of the nomad. As Deleuze and Guattari have put it, 'the question is what in nomad life is a principle and what is only a consequence' (1988, 380), and in this line of analysis the nomad's transition from point to point is indeed a consequence, 'a factual necessity', while 'it is false to define the nomad by movement'. Braidotti has therefore noted that 'it is the subversion of set conventions that defines the nomadic process, not the literal act of travelling', adding that 'some of the greatest trips can take place without physically moving from one's habitat' (2011, 26). In this light, nomadism is not a situation of being, but of becoming: 'nomadic shifts designate therefore, a creative sort of becoming, a performative metaphor that allows for otherwise unlikely encounters and unsuspected sources of interaction, of experience and of knowledge' (27).

Braidotti has stressed the interdependence of travelling and nomadism in an attempt to respond to certain critiques that have problematized the use of travel metaphors in contemporary social and cultural studies and in feminist theories in particular.[7] In addressing reservations about the romanticizing of the notions of deterritorialization and the nomad, Braidotti has argued that the 'radical nomadic epistemology Deleuze and Guattari propose is a form of resistance to microfascisms in that it focuses on the need for a qualitative shift away from hegemony, whatever its size and however "local" it may be' (2011, 26). Nomadism can thus be conceived as an *assemblage* of spatial tactics against borders and movement regulation.

Nomadic tactics keep erupting all over the globe today. Yet, while I can see the radicalness of nomadic theories, I think that critiques and reservations about the absence of specific historical and cultural context within which nomads should be situated and analysed are particularly pertinent today. As Braidotti herself has noted: 'what we need [. . .] is higher degrees of accuracy in accounting for both the external factors and the internal complexity of nomadic subjectivity' (2011, 4).

In thinking about the material, spatial and historical conditions of nomadism, I consider here Édward Glissant's reservations vis-à-vis the supposedly radical and anti-conformist aspects of nomadism in Deleuze and Guattari's configuration. 'Is the nomad not overdetermined by the conditions of his [sic] existence [. . .] is it not a form of obedience to contingencies that are restrictive?' Glissant has asked (2010, 12) In raising such questions, Glissant draws a distinction between 'circular' and 'invading, or arrow-like' nomadism. 'Circular nomadism' emerges out of necessity: Groups move when certain territories are exhausted and there is a need for new resources to be found. In this sense, 'circular nomadism' is not a spatial practice against settlement but rather a tactic of survival, Glissant notes (12). 'Invading nomadism' on the other hand has historically been an aggressive strategy 'whose goal was to conquer lands by exterminating their occupants' (12). 'Circular nomadism' is here juxtaposed to 'arrowlike nomadism', which does not oppose settlement, but is actually 'a devastating desire for settlement' (12). What both 'circular' and 'arrowlike' nomadisms share, however, is a defiance of 'roots'. According to Glissant, this is the conjunction that has made nomadism the enemy par excellence of the nation states of modernity.

Going against the root is indeed the core of *errance* [*errantry*], a notion that Glissant offers to denote spatial, cultural, existential and political wanderings. *Errance* in Glissant's configuration is interwoven with Deleuze and Guattari's notion of the rhizome: 'rhizomatic thought is the principle behind what I call the Poetics of Relation, in which each and every identity is extended through a relationship with the Other', he writes (Glissant 2010, 11). *Errance* then is a different mode of mobility and its trajectories are neither arrowlike, nor circular, as in the two forms of nomadism outlined above. Moreover, as a different mode of rootedness, *errance* is not idle roaming either: 'in errantry one knows at every moment where one is at every moment in relation to the other', Betsy Wing has commented (2010, xvi). *Errance* encapsulates the relationship between trauma, memory and movement, since in Glissant's poetics, the traumatic experience of crossing the sea in the slave ship becomes a material mnemonic trace that grounds and supports rising from the ruins and beginning again. 'The entire ocean, the entire sea gently collapsing in the end into the pleasures of sand, make one vast beginning, but a beginning whose time is marked by these balls and chains gone green', Glissant writes, reminding the reader of all those slaves, who were thrown into the sea, every time slave ships were being chased (2010, 6). *Errance* then 'lies between a notion of fixed identity, rooted in an ancestral past (the movement back to Africa) and a purely fluid subjectivity that precludes communities of affinity and shared horizons of meaning', Max Hantel has commented (2012, par.37). By going against totalitarian roots without rejecting rhizomatic connections, *errance* is entangled in Glissant's *Poetics of Relation* as movement and as a transformative mode of history.

As a notion emerging from the depths of Glissant's archipelagic thought – *la pensée archipelique* – *errance* is thus juxtaposed to the territorialities of nomadism – *la pensée continentale*; it is an image of thought surrounded by ambivalence and fragility, the ever-eluding feeling of the sea. But even when he uses the sea as the plane of consistency for his *errance,* Glissant makes differentiations: 'Compared to the Mediterranean, which is an inner sea surrounded by lands, a sea that concentrates [. . .] the Caribbean is in contrast, a sea that explodes the scattered lands into an arc', he writes (1997, 33). The nuances and subtleties of Glissant's analytics are a good example of the cartographic approach that Braidotti proposes in supporting the pragmatism of her nomadic thesis, but never really stages in her own work.

Moreover, it is interesting to note that although the *Poetics of Relation* was first published in France in 1990, there is not a single reference to Glissant in the first edition of the *Nomadic Subjects* in 1994, and only a quick reference in the second edition of 2011. In situating her analysis on a plane of thinking where race discourses have been contested, Braidotti argues that she follows Glissant in positing multilocality as a positive stance vis-à-vis the negativity of loss and pain (2011, 80). I think an important encounter could have happened between *errance* and *nomadism,* the archipelago and the continent, *la pensée archipelique* and *la pensée continentale,* but this relation is never taken up in Braidotti's analysis. This is despite her argument that rather than thinking about separate concepts we should consider processes: 'flows and interconnections' between them (2012, 14).

It is, therefore, in this lacuna, the in-between space of *errance* and nomadism that I have situated my analysis of stories of forced displacement. As I will further discuss in the following chapters, Glissant's mapping of different modalities of nomadism, always historically and geographically specific, grounds philosophical abstractions and figurations and opens up analytical paths for understanding migrant and refugee women's movement in the wilderness. But it is not only as a figuration within *la pensée continentale* that I interrogate 'the nomadic subject' in this book, but also as a name, a word, a descriptor. Even when the nomad is taken as a figuration or a metaphor, the constitutive power of myths, words and names should not be downplayed or bracketed.

Drawing on Wittgenstein's philosophy of language, Jane Baaten has argued that the naming of experience, which includes nomadic subjectivity in the case of this book, can be considered as 'an emergent language game' (2002, 187). Baaten has particularly highlighted Wittgenstein's exposition of the dynamically social character of meaning, arguing that there are powerful non-literalist components in Wittgenstein's philosophy of language that might be useful for a feminist radical critique of language. 'If Wittgenstein's concept of language games allows us to contrast actual usage with as yet unrealized language games, it could be useful in articulating the underlying philosophical commitments of the politics of naming' (181). It is, thus, the possibilities and constraints of emerging language games that I want to interrogate in this book, through problematizing the political salience of the nomad as a descriptor of a subject position, even if the latter is being transposed and/or in the process of becoming other.

Braidotti has noted that 'being a nomad, living in transition, does not mean that one cannot or is unwilling to create those necessarily stable and reassuring bases for identity that allow one to function in a community' (2011, 64). She has further added that nomadic consciousness is not about dispensing with identity altogether, but rather about 'not taking any kind of identity as permanent' (64). In doing so, she has pointed to moments when 'the nomadic subject' inhabits a subject position, even if this is only momentary and provisional. Moreover, in *Metamorphoses* Braidotti (2002) has extensively deployed the trope of the 'glue' – discursive, symbolic, imaginary, invisible and/or psychic – holding together the fragments of her nomadic subjects.

Given that 'the nomadic subject' does indeed emerge as a descriptor of a subject position in Braidotti's analysis, as well as in other takes of it in the relevant literature, including my own work (see Tamboukou 2002), challenging its power to name and, therefore, create the subjects of which it speaks is both important and urgent. If we follow Wittgenstein's suggestion that language is exclusively a social activity, as well as his proposed method of explaining meaning as use, the context within the nomadic subject is configured becomes crucial. What should, therefore, be interrogated is not only what the nomadic subject means, but also the practice of language: what the nomadic subject does

Virginia Woolf's famously statement that 'as a woman I have no country, as a woman I want no country, as a woman my country is the whole world' (1978, 109) has been flagged up in the rich body of feminist literature that has looked at dangerous liaisons between gender, place and all kinds of nationalisms. Braidotti has taken issue with this form of 'planetary exile' and celebration of 'homelessness, countrylessness, of not having a common anchoring point' (2011, 56). It is precisely in her attempt to embed female subjectivity in Adrian Rich's 'politics of location' that she has come up with the figuration of the nomadic subject. When, however, she uses 'the passport' to denote women's many possibilities for continuous movement and serial spatial, cultural and emotional attachments, the frame of reference, the mythic correlation or the metaphoric trait for even the feminist nomad, who 'has no passport – or has too many of them' (Braidotti 2011, 64) is mostly a white, Western, and privileged subject. Indeed, in the era of walls, iron fences, mass drownings and authoritarian travel bans, who can choose to have or not to have a passport, even if the nomad is taken as a figuration of the subject? As Braidotti has observed about mobility in the globalized network society of advanced capitalism, 'goods, commodities and data circulate much more freely than human subjects or in some cases, the less than human subjects, who constitute the bulk of asylum seekers and illegal inhabitants of the world' (2011, 6).

Following Arendt (1998), what I argue throughout the book is that stories have the power of grounding abstractions and making connections within the web of human relations. In this context, when recounting her experiences of escaping Sierra Leone to find a job in Greece, Hanna simply told me that she didn't even know about the requirement to have a passport in order to travel: 'the consul had told me that I needed a passport; where could I look for passports, [. . .] I didn't know how to do it with my government, I had never thought of it, you understand'.[8] The 'passport' in the context of Hanna's story was an unknown object until the moment she was told that she needed it and even when she learnt about its value and function she didn't have the knowledge or the money to obtain it. Moreover, when she eventually came to Greece, she deeply desired to acquire a fixed identity and claim citizenship rights. The nomad who 'never takes on fully the limits of one national, fixed identity' in Braidotti's analysis (2011, 64) is privileged in terms of survival and mobility. The archive of stories that underpins the writing of this book bursts with displaced women's desire to register as asylum seekers and get a legal status in the country they have managed to reach: 'without identity, you don't have any right, you are nothing', Nadia simply put it in her story.[9] Words and meanings circulate and translate differently; they always exceed the speaker's or writer's intentions, so we need to be more sensitive in how we deploy them and with what effects.

Moreover, figurations are always expressed in words and words taken as practices rather than linguistic signs can wound, as their use presupposes material, spatial and administrative conditions that are only available to some on the basis of the exclusion of many others. As Christine Koggel has noted, 'words have functions in purposeful activity in the same way that particular objects have functions' (2002, 237). Drawing on Ian Hacking's notion of 'dynamic nominalism' (1986) that looks into the history of how names constitute human beings and the acts they are labelling, Koggel (2002) has suggested that when we create figurations, such as 'the nomadic subject', we actively intervene in shaping the world we describe and the groups we name. Nancy Baker (2002) has further argued that exclusions in language games create scapegoats that ultimately define the groups or collectivities they are excluded from, be they real or symbolic.

In this sense the material, embodied and situated positions of migrant and refugee women crossing borders with too many [fake] passports or no passport at all, challenge the figuration of the nomadic subject of feminist theory. As Braidotti has pointed out, 'figurations are not figurative ways of thinking, but rather materialistic mappings of situated, i.e., embedded and embodied, social positions' (2011, 4). Moreover, Wittgenstein has called our attention to the effects of using language: What it is we actually do in coining concepts, using or refusing to use terms and notions, reading and rewriting documents, developing theories and unfolding textual practices. It is this sensibility to embodied and embedded figurations, as well as to the constitutive power of words, that I have considered throughout the book.

Following Wittgenstein's lyrical remark that 'to imagine a language is to imagine a new form of life' (1986, 8), in this chapter, I have problematized the nomad as a figuration, but also as a name, a word, and a descriptor. What I have argued is that the sociopolitical and material conditions of the current global *mobility assemblages* and particularly women's position within them have raised urgent questions that need to be addressed within the old project of re-imagining the subject of feminism. While pointing to its nominalist correlations with privileged mobility, I have nevertheless acknowledged the political imaginaries of radical and unregulated movement that the figuration of the nomadic subject has inspired in the field of critical feminisms. Drawing on Glissant's (2010) philosophical thought what I have argued is that there is a need for new modalities of nomadism to be charted, a move that I will further deploy in the following chapters of this book.

NOTES

1. See Weir 2016, Zavos 2017, Carastathis et al. 2018.
2. For more information about *Iliaktida,* see: https://iliaktida-amea.gr/en/about/
3. Tania's story, a flat in Mytilini Lesvos, narrated in Farsi, 12 April 2019.
4. Linda's story, a flat in Mytilini Lesvos, narrated in Greek, 9 April 2019.
5. Zahra's story, Kara Tepe refugee camp, Lesvos, narrated in Farsi, 10 April 2019.
6. I am writing this chapter in the aftermath of a series of refugee protests in Lesvos, against the inhumane conditions of their lives in the camps. See https://www.theguardian.com/global-development/2020/feb/04/greece-sends-more-riot-police-to-lesbos-after-migrant-clashes [Accessed, 7 February 2020].
7. See Boer 1996; Gedalof 1996, 2000; Kaplan 1987; Wuthnow 2002.
8. Hanna's story a café in Athens, narrated in English, 8 December 2018.
9. Nadia's story, a café in Athens, narrated in English, 25 July 2018.

Chapter 2

Who Are You?
The Art of Listening

Listening is a relational practice that enables us to live-in-the-world-with others, but it is also a complex political and agonistic process: While we focus on the speaker, we never listen in a void, but within a background that we have to map and understand. In the same way that we are situated speakers, we are also always, already situated listeners: We always listen from somewhere, no matter how open or willing we are to move from our position. In this chapter, I draw on my experiences of listening to migrant and refugee women's stories of displacement and explore questions around discourses and practices of listening across borders and languages. In doing so, I particularly focus on the materiality of listening, the force of corporeal voices, the rhythms of embodied listening and their effects on understanding and making connections within the web of human relations. This chapter unfolds in five parts: First, I look at a body of literature around sounds and voices in narrative analytics and feminist theory, and then, I consider the importance of *narrative rhythmanalysis* as a mode of understanding and as a method. In the third part, I explore dangerous liaisons between voices and texts, and then, I make a cartography of rhizomatic relations between listening, feeling and understanding in the archive of the stories that migrant and refugee women have generously shared with me. Finally, in the conclusion, I map diffractions and affinities in listening and writing.

SOUNDS AND THE POLITICS OF VOICES

Sounds and voices in life history interviews have become a burgeoning area of interest in narrative research, particularly around the emotional and cognitive impact that sounds and modalities of voice can have on both listeners and storytellers (see Mildford and Kinzel 2016). Human voices can both speak and sing amongst other sounds that they continuously create. Moreover, if we follow a long critical tradition accepting that meaning is not fixed in language, then 'the motion of its words, its medium, is like sound'. Ruth Salvaggio has suggested following the oral and literary traits of feminist theories (1999, 2). In the process of listening to the sounds of words and stories, voices emerge as corporeal and unique: 'the task of the voice is to be a pathway, or better a pivotal joint between body and speech', Adriana Cavarero has argued (2005, 15). 'We are living in a matrix of our own sounds, our words resonate, by our echoes we chart a new geography', Susan Griffin has influentially written (1978, 195). Within this matrix, changes in tone, pitch, timbre and tempo can create different effects in the emotions, affects and meanings of what we communicate. In this light, voices are inextricably interwoven in storytelling and listening practices, as 'the uniqueness of the human being [. . .] is manifested in the uniqueness of the voice' (Cavarero 2005, 2).

Drawing on the singularity of the corporeal voice, Cavarero has deconstructed the voice/logos binarism in the long durée of the western [male] philosophical tradition. Corporeal voice [*phone*] is no lesser than speech [*logos*], it actually intervenes, interrupts and subverts the rational hierarchy of logocentrism: 'the voice does not mask, but rather unmasks the speech that masks it' (2015, 24). Voice is thus inextricably relational, revelatory and communicative: 'it takes at least a duet, a calling and a responding – or better a reciprocal intention to listen, one that is already active in the vocal emission, and that reveals and communicates everyone to the other', Cavarero has noted (2005, 5). Moreover, voice implies 'a reciprocity of pleasure' (2005, 7), emerging from the musicality of its embodied emission: 'the voice flows and inundates, like a song, inaugurating the musicality of language' (2005, 140).

Cavarero's philosophical thought on 'the vocal ontology of uniqueness' (2005, 173) is also a pathway to understanding how voice is inextricably related to politics. Drawing on Arendt, Cavarero defines politics as 'the reciprocal performance of doing and saying', further linking it to the politics of voices, since 'vocal expression has in this kind of theatre a really important role, because it expresses the uniqueness and it also contains what in ancient Greek was called lexis, the tonality, the way the voice is set up, the rhetoric of communication'. (Cavarero in Farinati and Firth 2017, 65) Susan Bickford (1996) also draws on Arendt's performative politics to dig deeper into the political aspects of listening. Although Arendt did not write about listening per se, active listening is implied in the way she configures the importance of the public realm for political communication and the formation of opinions: 'So "common sense", a sense of oneself as not alone in perceiving is perhaps a model for both solitary thinking and actual listening interaction, for both individual and collective opinion formation', Bickford has commented (1996,

90). It is while listening to others that we think, speak and act and thus 'solidarity is the principle that guides listening action' (90)

Thinking about listening in Arendtian terms, Bickford dissects the vocality of political expression, but more importantly considers the way listening practices create exclusions and inclusions. As Gloria Anzaldúa has poetically put it, even 'when we do speak from the cracked spaces, it is *con voz del fondo del abismo,* a voice drowned out by white noise, distance and the distancing by others who don't want to hear' (1990, xxii). What Bickford, therefore, suggests is that the way we are heard (or not) by others charts our presence or absence in the political arena: 'I need to know that my voice matters' in Nick Couldry's words (2010, 1). Audibility then goes hand in hand with vocality in what Iris Marion Young has configured as 'deep democracy' (2002, 5), practices striving for inclusion within *assemblages* of social, political, economic and cultural differences. This is a domain wherein we are experiencing a contemporary crisis of voice, Couldry has observed (2010, 2). Moreover, 'political listening is not necessarily a caring or amicable practice and it does not necessarily evoke empathy' (1996, 2), Bickford argues, flagging up conflict as a necessary component of politics that is rather downplayed in Arendtian politics.

Migrant and refugee women's corporeal voices were at the heart of how I have made connections with their stories of travelling. My encounter with them was an instance of what Young has highlighted as 'the concrete encounter with others' (1990, 106), an event which created conditions of possibility for situated knowledges and understandings to arise. Attentive and affective listening has facilitated such concrete encounters, although it did not necessarily involve or generate empathy, neither did it always end up in agreement or in a harmony of viewpoints. Following Young, I am against erasing differences and the effects they make: 'when class, race, ethnicity, gender, sexuality, and age define different social locations, one subject cannot fully empathize with another in a different social location, adopt her point of view; if that were possible then the social locations would not be different' Young has wisely pointed out (1990, 105). And yet the acknowledgement of difference does not preclude the possibility of recognizing the needs, desires and perspectives of differently situated subjects. On the contrary, listening to the expression of the needs and desires of others is a precondition of being listened to in the dialogics of what Young has configured as 'communicative ethics' (1990, 106).

On a plane of communicative ethics and aesthetics, or what I have configured as 'the art of listening', there were times when the semantics of women's speech and the sounding of their vocal cords were entangled in my listening practices. Such were the cases when women were narrating their stories in English, Greek and French, languages that I could follow and understand.

But there were also cases when their stories were narrated in languages that felt like music to me and there were continuous gaps between the musicality of their voices and their discourse, which was mediated via the interpreter.[1] In many parts of the world, music is not an art, but a language, Trinh T. Minh-ha has argued: 'one finds music in listening [. . .] in moments of collective tuning, in the midst of a crowd, or while working for a communal issue' (2011, 55). In such moments of collective tuning, it was the sound of women's voices rhythmical movement that I have tried to follow, including moments when the narrators' and the interpreters' voices were intermingling in unexpected chords and dynamic duets: 'voice then, not in the words, but in their sounds, in the way it sounds and sculpts the space it traverses' (80). As I will further discuss in the next section of this chapter, what I think I have discerned in such stories were patterns of words, sounds and voices brought together only temporarily and provisionally as an effect of experimenting with music and rhythm. The sonics of women's stories, thus, gave rise to unexpected affinities, 'flows, forces and energies' (Mason 2018), which created connections within the narrative scene itself, but also beyond it, in the on-going process of listening again to the recorded voices.

NARRATIVE RHYTHMANALYSIS

A lot has been written about relations between language, narrative and music particularly drawing on the structuralist field of narratology: 'perhaps the structures that literary theorists have found in narrative resemble the structures that music theorists have found in musical compositions', Fred Everet Maus has pithily noted (1991, 1). Music is both patterned and communicative, but it also always eludes systematic meaning analysis. As Theodor Adorno has famously put it in his work on Mahler, 'music narrates without being a narrative' (1992, 76). But although music evades narrative tropes, it does inspire us to imagine and indeed create new narratives or analyse and interpret existing ones. Music evokes memory and triggers imagination, effortlessly bringing both faculties together in telling, writing or listening to stories.[2]

For Edward Said, music can also be taken as

> another way of telling [. . .] digressive, reiterative, slower in its effects because built up through a whole series of affirmations and associations that come with not getting through time but of being *in* time, experiencing it together, rather than in competition, with other musics, experiences, temporalities. (1992, 100)

Said's musical elaborations have implications on how life stories are told, listened and understood, not simply as narratives unfolding over time, but also as *rondos* and *refrains,* musical variations on a theme. There are two different ways of deploying musical tropes in listening practices on Said's plane of analysis: 'Looked at horizontally statement is melody, to be pronounced robustly, carefully developed, definitively ended' (101). This was definitely not the way migrant and refugee women's stories were told and or listened to, as I will further show in the last section of this chapter. 'Looked at non-narratively however, music is not just statement, but statement and infinitely possible variations' for Said (101). What I have repeatedly highlighted in my work with narratives, however, is that music's 'infinitely possible variations' are in fact components of *narrative assemblages*, within which stories are told, listened to and analysed (Tamboukou 2010). I have explicated the notion of the *assemblage* in Chapter 1, but what I want to highlight here is that *narrative assemblages* enlarge the plane of analysis to include diverse narrative forms, across genres, media and sources, both oral and written. *Narrative assemblages* also include fierce power relations and strong forces of desire that have to be considered in the analysis of how meaning is being constituted as an on-going process, a becoming. On this plane of narrative analytics, musical analogies in travelling stories and beyond, unveil themes, characters and events that are continuously affirmed and reaffirmed through rhythmical repetitions.

Rhythm is of course one of the most important musical and linguistic concepts: As an unfolding of sounds and silences, it creates patterns through which music and language move and flow. We all know and feel how important rhythm is not just in music, but also in storytelling, not to mention art and everyday life. 'Rhythm, like language is a form of meaningful differentiality; a beat becomes itself by its relation to the other beats, in the same way that the I of reflection is dependent upon the not-I, the signifier on the other signifiers' Andrew Bowie has written (1990, 79). 'All method is rhythm' (Novalis in Bowie 1990, 79) after all, in the context of the early nineteenth century philosophy tradition. For Deleuze and Guattari, rhythms orchestrate otherwise chaotic instances that elude measure and can be found in the passages between milieus or environments: 'meter is dogmatic, but rhythm is critical; it ties together critical moments, or it ties itself together in passing from one milieu to another' (1988, 313). In this plane of analysis, rhythms are important in discerning repetitions or what they configure as 'the refrain' [ritournelle] (312).

Moving beyond philosophy into the wider realm of human sciences, Henri Lefebvre's *rythmanalysis* becomes particularly pertinent here. 'What we live are rhythms, rhythms experienced subjectively', Lefebvre wrote in his major work, *The Production of Space* (1991, 206). But it was only at the end of his academic life, when perhaps he had more time to indulge his love for music (being a pianist as well as an intellectual and activist) that he wrote a small book on *rhythmanalysis*. The book was published in French after his death in 1992. However, it took twelve years to be translated in English, being published in 2004, which explains perhaps why this approach has yet to be taken up more fully in methodological discussions in the social sciences. The fact that Lefebvre's three-volume *Critique of Everyday Life* – wherein *Rhythmanalysis* appears in context – was only published in its full form in 2014, throws further light on the neglect of this approach. For Lefebvre then, rhythms are of the world and in the world, they are cyclical repetitions entangled with linear processes, and they are never identical – there is 'always something new and unforeseen emerging from their repetition' (2004, 15). Lefebvre also warns against confusing rhythms with movement or sequence of movements, speed or machines. Moreover, the meaning of rhythm is obscure and so we need to learn to listen to the rhythms of a house, a street, a neighbourhood, an archive or a story in the case of this chapter.

But what does it mean to think and live rhythm? 'Rhythmanalysis could change our *perspective* on surroundings', Lefebvre notes; it makes us aware that there is 'nothing inert in the world, *no things*: very diverse rhythms' (2004, 17). In this light, rhythmanalysis could also change our perspective on embodied and embedded narrative contexts I would add, being reconfigured as *narrative rhythmanalysis*. Following Lefebvre, this is an approach, which is entangled in the here and now of listening to the rhythms of movement and activities including the vocal expression and embodied sonority of storytelling. *Narrative rhythmanalysis* eventuates in recognizing the existence of repetitious patterns in the semantics of storytelling, as well as in the modalities of voices and sounds. Attention to sonic repetitions and their affective entanglements with meaning is downplayed in narrative analytics revolving around Paul Ricoeur's (1984) notion of 'emplotment' – the process that brings heterogeneous components, actions and characters of a narrated situation into an imaginative order, thus rendering them meaningful as part of a larger context.[3] *Narrative rhythmanalysis* thus brings to the fore the catalytic role of the story space/time/matter not just on the level of context, but also and perhaps more importantly on the level of vocal expression and embodied listening, thus opening up new analytical paths and insights.

As it repeatedly engages with a mechanical restaging of storytelling however, *narrative rhythmanalysis* can never be conclusive: It is rather a process, constantly unearthing new signs and meanings. Audio technologies in their capacity to store and reproduce are fundamental in the creation of archives of stories in a variety of disciplines, but they also become co-constructors of meaning. Alessandro Portelli (1998) has influentially discussed how the story's imagined future repetitions will shape both its form and content at the moment of telling. The presence of a recorder in the narrative scene is indeed a constant reminder that 'these words will be repeated elsewhere to an absent undetermined audience' (32). Following Portelli's important reflection on how machines intervene in storytelling practices, as well as in shaping the genre of oral history, what interests me more in the context of this chapter, is how the recorded voice is entangled in future listenings, as well as in shaping the meanings that will derive from them. There is an organic 'orality of voice and sound' founded on an 'ideal immediacy based on the body and its expressive rendering through speech', Katherine Hayles has argued (1997, 98). But when this corporeal immediacy is interrupted by the passing of time and yet is restaged through audio technologies, epistemological questions arise about what it is that we do when we listen again to voices that persist through time, outside the bodies that have created them: 'a present without presence. A voice (re)recorded' (Trinh 2011, 80).

Although the recorder destroys the aura of the voice's presence, in time and space, 'its unique existence at the place where it happens to be' (Benjamin1973, 214), it is through its ability to inscribe and retain sounds emitted on the occasion that it recreates a disembodied voice, which makes connections with the still embodied presence of the listener/researcher. A new narrative scene of affinities is created here, wherein understanding arises, even when 'body and voice no longer imply each other' (Hayles 1997, 85). But when space/time/matter interfere in the process of repeated listenings, then different meanings, understandings and interpretations also arise. Although the recorded voice with all its sonic traits has somehow been preserved, its sounding keeps changing as the listener and the soundscapes also change. In the context of this fluidity, an important question arises: How can the dynamics of *narrative rhythmanalysis* be transferred to the text?

VOICES AND TEXTS

As most oral narratives, the stories that I have heard were never told in grammatical, fully structured and comprehensive sentences, even when women were speaking in their mother tongue. In transcribing the stories, I thus decided to create two modes of written texts: proses and poems. Catherine Riessman's scholarship was influential in my experiments with different modes of textualizing oral narratives. Transcripts are constructed narratives for Riessman: 'by our interviewing and transcription practices, we play a major part in constituting the narrative data that we then analyse', she has argued (2008, 50). In looking back at her work with South Indian women's stories of infertility, Riessman has given an example of constructing two different transcripts: (1) a written record of the conversation and (2) a version where the interviewer's intervention is 'omitted' so that the voice of the narrator can be highlighted (29). The construction of the second version was informed by James Gee's ethnopoetics, whose method requires that the transcription follows the oral features of narratives: 'how a narrative is actually spoken with pauses and "pitch glides" (subtle falls in the pitch of the voice)' (33). These two modes of transcription align with different perspectives around language, communication and the self, Riessman notes, adding that there are more ways that her interviews could be represented (29). There is indeed a great variety of approaches within the ethnopoetics tradition, which can further be applied to a variety of settings in which narratives are produced cross-culturally, as was indeed the case with all the stories of my research (see Blackledge et al., 2016; Blommaert 2006, Maryns 2006).

In the field of oral history, however, where the transcript/voice debate has been raging for years, Raphael Samuel has been less sympathetic with the violence of the transcript: 'the spoken word can very easily be mutilated when it is taken down in writing and transferred to the printed page', (1972, 2) he has written, pointing in particular to the perils of the written prose:

> A much more serious distortion arises when the spoken word is boxed into the categories of written prose. The imposition of grammatical forms, when it is attempted, creates its own rhythms and cadences, and they have little in common with those of the human tongue. People do not usually speak in paragraphs, and what they have to say does not usually follow an ordered sequence of comma, semi-colon, and full stop; yet very often this is the way in which their speech is reproduced (2).

Keeping Samuel's 'perils of the transcript' (1972) in mind, but also taking the multi-modality of transcriptions as a mode of experimenting with the voice/text dangerous liaisons, stories transposed to proses chart the Ricoeurian 'emplotment' of the narrative. In creating these proses, I followed the storyline, taking out all the hesitations, repetitions, sounds, pauses, twists and turns, in short, all signs of orality. The spoken story was, thus, flattened out into the monotone of the text to allow for its plot and characters to take the front stage. In constructing the 'poem' version on the other hand, I attempted to trace the dynamics of the listening process, following the sounds, rhythms and alliterative patterns of the narrative voice in the way I sensed them while listening. As Gee (1991) has noted, poetry takes its inspiration from the rhythms of our everyday speech. Despite this analogy however, 'the nuances of the performed narrative are completely lost no matter how many *stage directions* are inserted into the transcript', Sherna Berger Gluck has argued (2014, 139–40). In creating the poem version, I was inspired by Dennis Tedlock's work of creating free verses in an attempt to seize moments in the life of oral history narratives (1991). His attempt to enliven the printed version of the narratives reverberates with my experiment in tracing the aural signs of the narrative scene in the form of a poem.

In the margins and shadows of the ethnopoetics tradition then, my construction of the 'poem version' of women's narratives attends closely to how I feel the sounds of stories in terms of tone, pitch, rhythm and pause. Each aural change is signalled by a new line in the stanzas I have created. Apart from this simple line change, the poems do not follow any notation, as is usually the case with ethnopoetics: They are rather free verses that chart lines of feeling the narrative and thus unveiling moments of meaning making that were enacted by this feeling. As I have written elsewhere drawing on Alfred Whitehead's process philosophy, feeling in my analytics is a process through which both the analyst and his/her findings or understanding emerge in their interrelation and mutual constitution (see Tamboukou 2016a). Migrant and refugee women's stories as entanglements of prose and poetry, further create new storyscapes for the reader to be constituted in the process of feeling the text. Gloria Anzaldúa's *Borderlands/La Frontera* (1987), a book written half in prose and half in poetry, has been an inspiration in the adventure of mingling literary genres in the textual transposition of the narrating voice.

While composing proses and free verses, as an experimental mode of transcribing the sounds of narratives however, I am aware of Michel de Certeau's critique of the violence of the Western 'scriptural economy' (1984) and his deconstruction of the oral/scriptural dichotomy. In this light, it is only the remaining signs of narrativization and aurality that I have marked in the texts that I have composed. Outside these texts, women's voices keep on turning and returning, as in Marguerite Duras' films: 'from a nocturnal elevated space, from a balcony overhanging the void, the totality. They are linked by desire. They desire. They were wandering for a very long time' (1973, 105). And it is not only the transcribed texts and the voices outside them that are entangled, but also the reading practices that keep crossing the oral/written boundaries by transposing the proses or the verses that I have created into something more fluid and volatile: the reader's plane of seeing, listening to textual voices, desiring and understanding. As Jonathan Boyarin has aptly put it: 'orality and textuality, far from being opposite poles, interact in complex, multidirectional ways' (1993, 3–4).

In thus taking the decision to create transcripts in two experimental forms, I have effectively argued that transcription is always, already an interpretation, but also an act in and of itself that eventually transposes the audio document into a text with important epistemological consequences. Narratives are being created within specific space/time/matter *assemblages* in a distinctive voice, captured in the mechanics of the recorder. Through transcription the researcher and his/her assistants refigure this voice through writing. In doing so, they actually tame and effectively silence the vibrating voice; they transpose it into an unmoving text, and it is for the reader to search for voices in-between its words. And yet, Portelli seems to interrogate the voice/text relation, presenting the aporias of a search for either of them:

> This is what the impossible reciprocal search of voice and text is about. At the most naive level, orality stands for the desire of all that is 'authentic,' for lived experience, for the people; it stands for the body, the breath, the spirit [but] all this disappears when we reach out to touch it, and the only thing left is the 'difference' of writing. On the other hand, the textual, rational, documentary, and material certainties of writing slip through our fingers when we begin to listen for the voices inside and underneath the written page. (1994, xxi)

Like Portelli, I have always been sceptical about what authenticity might mean or involve, either in audio files or in written texts. In the context of my ambivalence, I have, thus, decided to take a detour: My analysis of women's stories has not drawn on the written transcripts I have created – experimental as they are – but rather on repeated and intense listenings. Riessman has noted that 'Gee's ethnopoetics requires close attention to the audio recording' (2008, 93), but in my case it was the audio recording that drove the analysis and indeed the writing, which is infused with the resonances of women's voices. Analysis became a process, where the researcher's discourse tried to move alongside the complex performance of storytelling with its inflections, pitch, pace and rhythm. By turning my sensory antennae to what is audible rather than merely visible in the transcript, I got immersed in an *assemblage* of sounds, silences, pauses, laughters and cries, soundscapes that enacted the process of understanding and meaning making and were later imbued in the writing. Women's voices, thus, became the sirens that have kept disrupting and destabilizing thought, releasing multiple significations around analytical tropes and themes. In Trinh's poetics: 'one goes on hearing, eyes shut. Loses one's breath, as time seems to come to a standstill. Here, where air is rarefied . . . A swoon. All lights become dimmers. Insight, intuition and other sensorial faculties let go of their ingenuity, leaving room for an overfocused in-. Intensity' (2011, 80).

Transcriptions were constructed after the analysis, for the needs of publications in the form of printed books and articles. Transcripts were also dictated by a narrative ethics of care, put simply the need to protect my participants who have often narrated their story within vulnerable situations. Here it is striking to note that out of the twenty-two stories that women shared with me, there was one case where the storyteller refused to be recorded and it is only the interpreter's voice that has been preserved. This stance made me much more sceptical and cautious about my responsibility to protect the storytellers, irrespective of the fact that they had given consent for the recording. What is about voices preserved and often archived in digital forms that makes them different in the way we have traditionally dealt with ethics in research? Quite simply it is the uniqueness of the voice that also renders it recognizable and, therefore, vulnerable and fragile that creates new conditions and considerations for the archives of the future. The text that flattens out the voice, also shields it against intruders and manipulations. Of course, texts can also be manipulated, there is no question about that, and yet voices are much more than texts, pouring into the senses of the hearers/readers, as I will further discuss in the following section.

LISTENING, FEELING, UNDERSTANDING

Taking up the salience of stories not only in recounting experiences, but also in forming an experiential basis for changing the subject and its world, I have interviewed twenty-two migrant and refugee women about their experiences of being on the move. As already highlighted in the introduction, I have encouraged these women to tell stories about their decision to leave, as well as about their experiences of travelling without feeling obliged to limit themselves within discourses of victimization and vulnerability. This research started as a way of challenging nomadism and eventually unfolded as a process of seeing, listening and understanding. As already noted above, Riessman's work was particularly influential in the way I deployed listening practices while conducting interviews in 'other' languages and diverse cultural contexts (Riessman 2005), as well as while reflecting on the sensuality and viscerality of the interview encounter (Riessman 2012). In this section, I focus on my affective entanglement with storylines and words through voice, music and rhythm. Following Riessman, I take 'the research interview as an embodied interaction that taps into emotions and the desires of both participants' (2012, 553).

In looking back and dissecting my listening practices, I will then go back to 'the beginning'. When conducting the interviews, I would ask the storytellers to recount their experience of travelling to Greece by starting and finishing wherever they wanted. But where does a story start and/or end? Well, the short answer is that it starts from any point and ends at any other. Or rather, the story, its happenings and its affective overflows emerge in the middle of a thought, a sentence or even a word. What is of interest, Deleuze wrote is what happens in the intermezzo, the middle of things:

> It is in the middle that one finds the becoming, the movement, the velocity, the vortex. The middle is not the mean, but on the contrary, an excess. It is by the middle that things push. That was Virginia Woolf's idea. Now the middle does

not imply to be in one's time, to be of one's time, to be historical – on the contrary. It is that by which the most diverse times communicate. It is neither the historical, nor the eternal, but the untimely (1997, 208).

Meaning is not simply localisable in the plot, or even the discourse of the narrative. Any line, word, hesitation, sound or bodily movement is entangled in the meaning of the whole, in the linguistic gesture alone; any point is always, already, overfilled with meaning; every part of a story is a knot of different potential meanings, affects, and expressions. So many lines of thought potentially passing through words, in the interstices of language in the stammering of speech, in-between linguistic codes and translations. The story is less a prose than an *assemblage* of language forces, a vectorial gestural nexus, wherein each starting point holds potential passages within its moment. The milieu, the middle, the intermezzo holds an infinity of meanings, thoughts and ambivalences, not all of which will be expressed in the unfolding of the story. In Christina's story below, meaning is entangled in an *assemblage* of love and camaraderie amongst women friends and across borders:

> I got sick and tired of going around, begging my friends for 2–3 leva to buy some bread. So, it was at such a moment when a very good friend of mine told me, 'let's phone your friend in Athens', who I knew since we were at school together. You know how friends from school, are friends for life. So, we went to the post office to call her and we only had 5 leva. My friend was checking the phone meter and I was talking on the phone. And I told my friend, 'can you please help me to come and work in Greece? I can't stand it here anymore'. And my friend told me, 'Christina I can deeply feel your anxiety. Hang up and I will call you from home to talk at ease.' And then she called me, and she said, 'do not worry, I will arrange everything, and I will send you money for your ticket to come here.'
>
> This is how I decided to come to Greece. But to do that I had the support of my women friends in Silistra. They gave me strength and they told me not to be afraid. I was also thinking that my best friend would be waiting for me in Greece, whatever happens, she would be waiting for me. So, when I first came to Greece, the only thing I knew was that my friend would wait for me. That was all, nothing else.[4]

Christina is a Bulgarian woman in her early sixties. She went to Greece to work as a carer to evade the post-socialism poverty trap in the early years of the new millennium. Her story revolves around her experiences in a chain of households and situations she has worked in the last fourteen years. But what runs as a red thread throughout her story is a network of women friends who have helped and supported her, both in Greece and in Bulgaria. At the time of the interview, she was contemplating going back to her country for a long break as she felt tired, albeit proud that she had managed to support her three daughters to study, get married and enjoy a comfortable life in the way she had never been able to manage for herself. Although I have known Christina for a long time through family networks, I had never realized the importance of her women friends in her life. Drawing on Deleuze's notion of difference, Bronwyn Davies (2016) has developed the notion of 'emergent listening' as distinctive from 'listening-as-usual'. If our listening is driven by what we already [think] we know, then we cannot immerse in 'a multi-sensual encounter with the world' (2016, 73), a process that can reveal more than, and at times against what we know. Emergent listening is a becoming, unfolding in the middle of stories, in the intermezzo of narratives and foregrounds the possibility of 'affective openness to the other' (74).

The trope of friendship and its significance in a migrant woman's life was something that erupted unexpectedly from the intermezzo of Christina's narrative and all of a sudden, her story was illuminated: It became meaningful from my situated listening perspective and created a new analytical theme that I had not anticipated or included in my initial question of what it means 'to travel alone'. As a matter of fact, the romantic notion of 'loneliness' sounded as a Western discourse that does not reverberate with migrant and refugee women's experiences of moving countries and crossing borders and has become a component of the overall project of challenging nomadism, as I have already discussed in Chapter 1. We can never really grasp the complexity of human experience and expression and thus the unpredictability of stories and the new meanings that can burst forth are often surprising. Oral history after all 'is less about events than about meaning', Alessandro Portelli has influentially argued (1991, 50).

Women friends have indeed appeared in stories of displacement in different roles: as confidantes, co-travellers, financial supporters, as well as conspirators in secret and dangerous escapes. Awat is a Kurdish woman in her mid-thirties. She grew up in Iran but after her marriage she settled in Iraq with her husband. I met her through the Centre for Research on Women's Issues (CRWI) Diotima, a non-profit, non-governmental women's organization, which addresses issues of gender discrimination with a particular focus on violence against women.[5] In her story, Awat talked about despair and hope, particularly stressing how she relied on a woman friend to survive her husband's ferocious violence:

I have tried to kill myself
many times
I have thrown oil over me
to burn myself

I have taken pills
to end my life
I had been in hospital for two days
because of this
I have tried to commit suicide
many times
and yet
I still had to find a job
to support myself
and I was working with a friend
who was a hairdresser
and had a salon[6]

It was the same friend who hid Awat in her house and helped her escape:

> I was therefore in despair, not knowing what to do. But my friend who had the salon, advised me to take all my things to her, together with my passport, so that I could find a way to run away. So, I took all my papers to my friend and waited patiently.

Awat trusted her friend and relied on her help to grasp the first opportunity to escape.

Friendship often exceeded kinship relations in my research. Erika is a young Ethiopian woman who escaped her country after her husband was killed by the militia. I met her through Iliaktida and I was rather struck by the casual way she referred to her sister, who she had met in Turkey, while they were waiting to be smuggled to Greece:

> When I went to Turkey I found my sister, half-sister from my mother, who was there already and we came to Greece together. I am not very close to my sister because we did not grow up together, but still we managed to come to Greece together. My sister has now got asylum and she is in Athens, I am still waiting.[7]

Although the two women crossed the sea together, they soon separated again and, in her story, Erika admitted that even after their sea crossing their emotional distance did not change. She seemed to be more interested in her new friends in Lesvos: 'While waiting I take lessons in Greek and English in Mosaik and in Bashira[8] and I have made friends with other women here'.

Friends more than family have, thus, created a matrix within which migrant and refugee women emerge as relational subjects: Although they have been labelled as 'women travelling alone', they were never lonely. Telling stories of friendship and camaraderie has thrown fresh light in their existential 'whoness', the unique and unrepeatable 'who' of Arendt's and Cavarero's philosophies:

it was night when we arrived
but my friend was waiting for me at the airport
when I saw her
it was like meeting my mum
this is how safe I felt
everything else was irrelevant
the only thing that mattered was that
my friend was there
waiting for me
I held her hand
and I am still holding it today
I never do anything
without consulting her
she is not just my friend,
she is my sister
and mother
she is the world for me
she is the best person on earth
she is my goddess
how can I tell you
she is my angel
I will never forget
what she has done for me

The passionate way that Christina told the story of meeting her friend at the airport, revealed an unknown and hidden part of her persona. I thought I knew Christina, but did I? Well, I knew her as a 'what', a migrant domestic worker, a wife, a mother and a grandmother; I had even met her family when they had visited Greece and I had hosted them in my Athens flat. But it was only through listening to the story of her love and attachment to her friend that I made connections with her existential 'who'. As Hanna, a migrant woman from Sierra Leone, has forcefully put it:

> We know you, but you don't know us. You just see us like immigrants. But we know you, we've been in your house, we worked in your house, we know how you live [. . .] some people they just stay there, and they say "the immigrants". You don't know the immigrants! Try to know them.[9]

If a story is evasive, creating an analytical grid of 'units of meaning' is not enough, no matter how well designed, organized and theorized this can be.

What the narrative researcher can do instead, is to move in-between listening positions, since a situated position can become a gateway to meaning and understanding, or rather to their dynamic movement, which keeps jumping and shifting. Understanding, or rather feeling a story is not simply about taking up situated positions, but rather about following the motion of meaning, its leaps, interferences and diffractions, in short, the activation of a story in becoming. But what exactly do we see of the process of a story in becoming? Simply put, it is lines of narratives and designs of figures, never whole plots or characters as such. A word, a sigh, a silence, a hesitation erupts, but this is just a trace of a narrative field that will never be fully discernible or accessible, not even to the narrator who inhabits it, let alone the listener, no matter how attentive or sensitive he or she is. As Trinh has poetically expressed it: 'when the non-representable finds its place in the relation of word, sound, silence and image, or of timbre, tone, dynamics and duration, meaning can only circulate at the limit of sense and non-sense' (2011, 80). The task of the researcher is, therefore, to make visible what can only be felt in the unfolding of the narrative.

In this sense, meaning is always in transit, in-between what is expressed, what is felt, what is registered and rewritten. Meaning circles around the rhythm of language. Anna's story was such a moment of a circular narrative that emerged from a phrase that she kept repeating during her story: 'there is deception everywhere' [c'est toujours la déception]. Anna is a woman from Congo in her early twenties. She had to leave her country towards the beginning of 2018 after she fell victim of a gang rape in the household where she was working as a domestic. 'The lady' of the house gave her the money to go, thus covering up her husband's violent crime, but while Anna was in transit in Turkey, she realized that she was pregnant. I met Anna through Iliaktida and interviewed her in a flat in Mytilini Lesvos, where she was living with her baby daughter. In its poem version, Anna's story unfolded in two 'stanzas'. The first stanza mostly revolved around her experience of living in Mytilini, Lesvos, in 'solitude' and 'tranquillity', avoiding people, who she could no longer trust; it was short and gave no details of her traumatic experience, which only appeared as the 'coda' of the Labovian model: it was the exit, not the recounted 'event'.[10]

I will tell my story of travelling to Greece
I had never travelled in my life before
I knew it would be very difficult
I want to be here without people
in tranquillity
people have always treated me badly
I want to be in solitude

I don't trust anybody
every time I have tried to confess my troubles to a friend
there is always deception
always deception
I have no choice but to live alone
like that
you see I have found a friend
I trust her like my sister
I tell her my story
everything about me
about my relations with people
but the experience I have is
better stay alone
yes
in tranquillity
lonely
only with my baby
without problems
I am from Congo
I have been here in Greece since April 14 last year [2018]
It's been one and a half year since I left my country
I came here through Turkey
I left Congo after I was raped[11]

Anna seemed to have concluded her story at that point. There was a long silence, as we were looking at each other and at the baby who was playing around. I wasn't sure whether I should ask her the second and last question about how she was imagining her life in five, or ten years' time, a question that I have asked all women as a way of opening up their stories to some sort of radical futurity, an urge for 'movement thinking', which according to Michel Agier 'helps people imagine the possibility of going forward in a completely hostile context' (2016, 62). And suddenly the silence broke with Anna's rape story, narrated again – a reiteration built up through the emotional experience of the first stanza, as well as her repositioning vis-a-vis her listener. It seems that at that moment, at the end of the first stanza of her story, she somehow felt that the fear of deception had momentarily receded. Or maybe Anna needed more time to narrate her experience. As Trinh has written in reflecting on the form of non-Western narratives: 'never does one open the discussion by coming right to the heart of matter. For the heart of the matter is always somewhere else than where it is supposed to be' (1989, 1). As in Trinh's analysis, the horrific experience of being raped was postponed in Anna's story, until it was 'ready to come' (1). When 'the heart of the matter' matured with 'no catching, no pushing, no directing, no breaking through' (1), Anna narrated not only the rape event, but also the fear and despair of her forced displacement:

That was a very difficult time
a matter of life or death for me
it was not easy
when I went to Turkey
I didn't know I was pregnant
I had never imagined that this would ever happen to me
I thought my life would be like any other women
being pregnant was not at all easy
I was telling myself
I must die
being pregnant
what could I do?
I couldn't work
there were not many jobs in Turkey anyway
what could I do?
being a woman
alone
I was always tired
I was feeling ill
I was crying all the time
I was crying
I was crying
and I was telling myself
I cannot go on like that
I felt alone
isolated and abandoned
deceived
it was not easy at all[12]

'Movement only comes from movement' in Spinoza's philosophy, Erin Manning and Brian Massumi have noted (2014, 41), creating an analogy between the sui generis of movement and the sui generis of language: 'words only come from other words, in recurring waves' (41). In the same way, events, plots and figures come from previous myths and storylines and insert themselves in the rhythmic composition of narrative worlds. It was through the narration of the first condensed and concealed part of her story that Anna's second stanza emerged. It is in the ebb and flow of words and storylines that temporary openings are activated, moments and events are illuminated in the dark and silenced fields of experience. Most strikingly for 'the consequence' or rather 'non-consequence' of her narrative, Anna talked about her disillusion of living alone in a flat and expressed the desire to do something with her life: 'My life here in Greece is not easy. I don't want to stay here, but there is no other choice at the moment [. . .] Obviously, I want to go to school [. . .] I need information about what I can do with my life.'

In Whitehead's *Process Philosophy*, 'consciousness flickers; and even at its brightest there is a small focal region of clear illumination and a large penumbral region of experience in dim apprehension'. (1985, 267) Anna's story forcefully expressed this moment of consciousness flickering, in letting out her desire to be in the world with others. As I will further discuss in Chapter 6, this desire of re-inserting themselves in the web of human relations runs like a red thread through all the stories, with education as its pathway. It goes without saying that Anna's desire of having a life is nothing but a trace of the complexities of her existential quest. In the same way that 'the simplicity of clear consciousness is no measure of the complexity of complete experience' for Whitehead (267), the clarity of a story is no measure of the complex field of experiences it has partially illuminated.

While immersing myself in narrative intermezzos, stanzas and postscripts, it was the feeling of what Édouard Glissant has discussed as 'the right to opacity' (2010) that has repeatedly struck me. For Glissant, the injunction of transparency in Western processes of understanding always involves a reductionism of complexities and multiplicities within the boundaries of conceptual norms:

> If we examine the process of 'understanding' people and ideas from the perspective of Western thought, we discover that its basis is this requirement for transparency. In order to understand and thus accept you, I have to measure your solidity with the idea scale providing me with grounds to make comparisons and, perhaps, judgement. I have to reduce. (189–190)

Mariam's story was short and opaque, although she was amongst the first women in Iliaktida, who volunteered to participate in my research. Mariam is a young woman from Congo. She had to leave her town, fearing for her own life after her father was killed, but she gave no details of what exactly had happened. The fear of political persecution is interrupted by the burden of poverty and the lack of opportunities in education and employment, while gender-based violence is almost always a component of the *mobility assemblages* within which migrant and refugee women's stories are entangled, as I have already discussed in Chapter 1.

my story is very difficult
I left Congo
life was very difficult there
I left
I was afraid they would kill me
as they killed my father
because I was in the streets
speaking freely
our life was very
very difficult there
going to school was very difficult
eating was very difficult
you don't have the right to talk freely in Congo.
if you talk,
then they kill you
so I decided to leave
I travelled to Brazaville
to find a job
but when I got there
a man who had promised to help me
and give me a place to live
raped me repeatedly
in the end
I left Congo
and went to Turkey
I stayed there for two weeks
I was repeatedly raped there
then I came here
I have been here for two years
I am ill
I have no money
I can't eat properly
I don't know what will happen to me
in the end[13]

In the past, I have written with colleagues about narrative analysis beyond the imperative of coherence as the ultimate guarantor of the quality of narratives and as a restrictive norm for good life stories and narrative identities. (Hyvärinen et al., 2010) Amongst other issues that we have traced in the narratological obsession with coherence, we have also raised the question: 'what happens to the desire for textual coherence when place and location as material coherences par excellence, melt into fluid spatialities, forced displacement and diasporic subjectivities?' (6). Mariam's story is such a fragmented narrative that carries traumatic experiences of rape, sexual abuse and the pain of forced displacement. Glissant's argument 'for the right to opacity' however, goes beyond the imperative for narrative coherence, highlighting the importance of 'relation without understanding' as a ground for freedom. 'Opacities can coexist and converge, weaving fabrics' he writes, further adding that 'to understand these truly one must focus on the texture of the weave and not the nature of its components' (Glissant 2010, 190). There were two levels where I encountered this moving experience of relating in opacity.

First, it was while listening to stories in a language I could not understand, in the short interval before translation, while I was looking the storyteller in the eye. During these fleeting moments, I felt that it was the rhythm of words, the musicality of the voice and the facial movements that wove the fabric of relation, leaving traces of embodied knowledge, the familiar feeling of *sapore* in Cavarero's conceptual vocabulary (2000, 40). It was in the interval between the opacity of unrecognizable speech and the clarity of translation, in the interstices of languages that I could feel 'the texture of the weave', 'the sound of narratives'. Sounding does not create meaning, neither is it about conveying emotions; it is more about being exposed to the opacity of feeling the world and the other. For Arendt, the state of sounding can only be found in love and in poetry and it never lasts, it always flees, Cecilia Sjöholm has commented (2015, 96–97). In Whitehead's philosophy (1985), life emerges from spatial and temporal interstices: the in-between zones of every living cell, as well as the intervals, between contrasting moments, notes, acts or events. Rhythm is what brings both the temporal and the spatial dimensions together, Didier Debaise (2017, 103) has eloquently noted: 'rhythm of the living, rhythm of the creative process, rhythm of events', and the rhythm of spoken words, I would add. Zahra's story of escaping an abusive husband in Iran and fleeting to Greece via Turkey walking in the wilderness, was such a moment.

In the beginning of the interview, Zahra was coughing and she apologized for her cold and her croaky voice. But as her story was unfolding, her voice was becoming more and more intense and high pitched. When she reached the point where she was recounting the experience of crossing the Iranian–Turkish borders on foot, walking in the cold and with barely any food, her voice also reached high levels of clarity and tone. Moreover, her excitement was manifested in her body language and gestures; she was literally becoming a tragic opera performer, an alto soprano in front of my eyes. In contrast, the translator's voice was flat and monotonous, somehow creating a minimalist sound context, allowing the storyteller's voice to vibrate:

> We were walking in the cold
> for three days and three nights
> there were many people
> we were walking
> and walking
> we were hungry
> there was nothing to eat
> there was no water to drink
> I only had a packet of biscuits
> and I was giving it to my mum and my nephew
> it was horrible
> I hope nobody ever has such an experience
> but I was trying to keep up my spirits
> so that my mother would not be afraid
> at the borders of Iran and Turkey
> there was one road only
> there was shooting from the Iranian police
> many people were shot down
> but we kept walking
> I was holding my mum in one hand
> and my nephew in the other
> some people crossed the borders
> others stayed behind
> and were arrested by the police

So intense was my experience of listening to Zahra's story that the first thing that I did upon returning to the silence of my hotel room was to listen to the recording over and over again, while taking notes not of what had been narrated, but rather of the how of narration, its music and its rhythm. Song is the element that never stops resonating in women's speech, Helen Cixous has written. It is the element, 'which, once we've been permeated by it, profoundly and imperceptibly touched by it, retains the power of moving us' (1981, 881). Having been profoundly touched by Zahra's singing voice, the idea of immersing myself into the sound of the storytelling first dawn on me. It was at this point that I decided not to have the stories transcribed, but rather let myself dive in the diverse wavelengths of their sounding – the idea of experimenting with multi-modes of transcription came later.

Apart from driving the analytical process in the way I have already noted above, the sound of women's voices has triggered intense memories and has evoked 'affinities' of being in the field: I could see their eyes and faces again, I would remember the spatial context of the storytelling, the rare occasions that they laughed and the many moments that they cried or held their tears back. Affinities, as flows of energy manifested in the realm of sensations are 'personal connections that have *potency*' Jennifer Mason has argued (2018, 1, emphasis in the text), further suggesting that 'taking them seriously and exploring them opens up new and exciting possibilities for conceptualising living in the world' (1). Voices and texts are, thus, always entangled in my analysis, in the way de Certeau has pondered upon their aporetic relation in his critique of the Western *scriptural economy*: 'we can distinguish between writing's effort to master the "voice" that it cannot be but without which it nevertheless cannot exist, on the one hand, and the illegible returns of voice cutting across statements and moving like strangers through the house of language, like imagination' (1984, 159).

But there was also a second level of opacity, far more resistant to 'transparency' than the non-yet translated language. As Clevis Headley has argued, Glissant's opacity functions as 'a form of ontological self-defence' (2015, 77). It is entangled with practices of resistance against the colonization of the Western culture and expresses what has been absorbed or distorted in the histories of the transatlantic slave trade and conquest. Opacity is a practice underpinning post-colonial rhizomatic subjectivities, creating conditions of possibility 'to develop everywhere, in defiance of a universalizing and reductive humanism', Glissant has argued (1996, 133). In this light, opacity is a mode of accepting, recognizing and sustaining 'the irreducible density of the other' (133). In the case of the travelling stories that comprise the archive of this book, 'opacity' was deployed as a practice that I have reconfigured as 'the will not to tell a story', or the art of listening to the language of silence. In doing so, I have joined the club of narrative theorists that have interrogated the thesis that 'human beings are inherently storytellers' (Fisher 1989). 'Life tells us that we cannot tell it while we live it, or live it while we tell it' Dorrit Cohn has written (1999, 96), creating a temporal tension between experience and narrative that a lot of narratological literature has revolved around. Galen Strawson has been more provocative in his anti-narrativist thesis that 'the more you recall, retell, narrate yourself, the further you risk moving away from accurate self-understanding, from the truth of your being' (2004, 447).

The opacity that I encountered, however, in 'the will not to tell a story' was more agential, 'silence not as opposed to language, but as a choice not to verbalize' (Trinh 2013, 12), grounded on a deep ambivalence around the power effects of storytelling. The stories of my archive are full of such moments; some of them were even marked by the teller: 'Just out of revolt I did certain things, but I don't want to talk about them and that's how I decided to leave the Islamic democracy', Zahra said while recounting her story of escape. Her will not to say emerges here 'as a necessary interval in an interaction – in brief, as a means of communication of its own' (Trinh 2013, 12).

Thus, while I see the desire to tell a story as a deeply existential force, a Spinozist expression of the self, 'the will not to tell a story' is a political gesture of non-disclosure, what paraphrasing Foucault I have felt as the idea that 'the self must be defended'.[14] It is this glimpse of a woman striving to defend herself against the pragmatic dangers of narration that the will not to tell a story has unveiled. Although I have written about narratives as 'technologies of power' (Tamboukou 2013), I do not want to move towards any hermeneutics of opacity. Here, I agree with Glissant that 'the thought of opacity distracts me from absolute truths [. . .] making me sensible to the limits of every method [. . .] saves me from unequivocal courses and irreversible choices' (2010, 192). The rhythm and patterns of the narrative structure helped me trace this modality of agential opacity as manifested in Sima's story, below.

I met Sima at the Athens Solidarity Centre, a central hub for civil society organizations in Greece.[15] The interview was facilitated by the Refugee Legal Support-Athens – a legal clinic providing free legal support to refugees – and was held on their premises in the centre of Athens.[16] Sima is an Afghan woman in her mid-forties. She left her country when she was four years old at the time when the Russians attacked Afghanistan. Her family lived in Pakistan for four years, but they eventually moved to Iran where she grew up. Sima got married when she was seventeen years old and had four children. Her story was brief, condensing many important events together and mentioning none of the details of her actual journey to Greece. One could say that Sima was not 'an inherent storyteller' as William Fisher (1989) would have liked her to be. Most probably, she was tired of telling her travelling story over and over again to different authorities in the long process of asylum seeking. There is already a significant body of literature on how stories addressed to institutions are being crafted to fit legal grounds and needs of recognition.[17] And yet there was a significant 'irregularity' in the density of her narration. While overpassing the little details of how she travelled from Afghanistan to Greece, including her failed attempt to cross the Serbian borders, when she was violently separated from her teenage daughter, her story revolved around an apparently important event in her life – defending her migrant children against the bullying of their neighbours:

so the kids were growing up
but we couldn't stay any more in Iran
my husband had some kind of a construction job
he was building
tiling
doing all kind of building jobs
and I was working at home
with my kids

but there was a time
when I was pregnant
my kids were in the street
and there was a fight
I went outside
and I was trying to find a solution
because they were beating my kids to death
but the neighbours came out
 and they started pulling me
they hit me in my stomach,
and after two months
my baby was born
but three months later my baby died
because of that beating[18]

Sima's story was not about the traumas she experienced as a child and later as a woman, caught in lethal wars and territorial conflicts, but rather the cruelty of her neighbours towards her children and herself as a migrant pregnant woman in Iran. Listening to her otherwise condensed and brief story, I was struck by the detailed way she remembered and recounted this incident. Oral narratives are entangled with mnemonic practices: they don't follow linear plots but rather erupt from the storyteller's memory in dialogue with specific listeners: Sima talking to a university woman about her children, who had been deprived of their right to education. And it was not just the detailed semantics of the narrated event that surprised me, but also the vocal aspects of her episodic narrative. While she was mostly speaking in a low and subdued voice, her tone and tempo changed at the phonic moment of the beating event. What counts as an event and how do we know when it is narrated? Sima's detailed narration and the dramatic changes in her voice were the signs of 'the event' that left its traces in the sounds of her story: 'the pure event is tale and novella, never an actuality', Deleuze has written (2001, 73). It was after listening to Sima's story over and over again that I started discerning the *rondos* and *refrains* of her narrative: Her story was not about her experiences of travelling; she was simply not interested in my research topic and she dismissed it altogether. Her story was a variation on a painful theme: seeing her children grow up being deprived of their rights to have an education:

My father was working in Iran until I grew up and became seventeen years old. After that I just married, but my husband didn't have any identification and so my kids were not able to study. When my husband finally registered and was able to get some identification, my kids had grown up and they were too old to go to school My elder kid couldn't study, my other one, was only able to study for five years. My other two kids went to school when they were six and seven; but then we changed city and so in the end they didn't finish school, they were not able to continue their study.

As I have written elsewhere, narratives do not represent the real, but rather respond to it (Tamboukou 2010, 26). Sima's story was such a response to the injustice of her children and maybe herself, not having access to education. Her story revealed the theme that she wanted to protest against but hid everything else. In Glissant's analytics, opacity is an existential affirmation of difference, against the imperative of sameness and mimesis: 'that which protects the Diverse we call opacity' (2010, 62). While Sima's journey to Greece remained opaque, what her story forcefully unveiled was the pain of living a life as a serial migrant and eventually a refugee. Her discourse also revealed in no uncertain terms the absurdity of creating legalistic and nominal separations between these two conditions of forced displacement. Moreover, her story is an exemplar of Said's musical elaborations, as discussed above: 'another way of telling [. . .] built up through a whole series of affirmations and associations that come with not getting through time but of being in time' (1992, 100). For Sima, it was the time of her children's exclusion from their right to education, which she felt the urge and need to narrate, as an inscription of her pain and protest.

While declaring and indeed demanding 'the right to opacity' (2010, 189), Glissant nevertheless weaves this need into his poetics of relation. As opposed to the reductionism and violations of transparency, opacity is a force 'considerate of all the threatened and delicious things joining one another (without conjoining, that is, without merging) in the expanse of Relation' (62). Migrant and refugee women's 'unruly stories' that resisted the transparency of their travelling experiences – the 'object' of my research – opened up a new analytical pathway: quite simply, considering the effects of decolonial thinking in unsettling processes of knowledge production within critical feminist theories. While the underpinning research of this book was triggered by a critique of nomadic thinking, the opaqueness of some stories through which women have escaped the researchers' problematics have made me sensitive to other ways of living and thinking relations, of other becomings. I will come back to the effects of decolonial thinking in the last chapter of the book.

DIFFRACTIONS, AFFINITIES, INTERLUDES

In this chapter, I have drawn on entanglements between narrative, music, sounds and rhythm to consider the salience of feeling and understanding women's stories of forced displacement. In doing so, I have drawn on a rich body of literature around voices and their dangerous liaisons with texts. Following tracks and traces of this literature, I have turned my attention to aurality, listening practices that we deploy to make sense of orally delivered stories. Listening has been at the core of my analysis, although experimental transcripts have also been created for the purpose of publications, but also as an effect of my entanglement in narrative ethics of care – the importance of protecting storytellers in particularly sensitive and vulnerable situations. When transforming women's voices into texts, I have experimented with two literary genres, prose and poetry, as a way of 'practicing, reworking, critically negotiating our way through the language we have, the texts we read, and the language we use to reread those texts' (Salvaggio 1999, 121). In problematizing the ways I have engaged with the archive of women's stories of travelling, I have, thus, deployed diffractive ways of reading and writing, pointing to the limitations of reflexivity in narrative research. It is with some thoughts on diffractions and affinities that I want to conclude this chapter.

There is a strong tendency in narrative research for reflexivity: We are expected to reflect on our approaches and situate ourselves in the narrative scene by thinking about the effects of our encounter with the storytellers upon the form and content of the stories we hear. While positing the epistemological project of 'situated knowledges', Donna Haraway has criticized reflexivity: 'my suspicion is that reflexivity, like reflection, only displaces the same elsewhere, setting up worries about copy and original and the search for the authentic and really real' (1997, 16). Haraway's critique of the imperative to reflect runs in parallel with Glissant's interrogation of transparency as discussed in the previous section. 'Transparency no longer seems like the bottom of the mirror in which Western humanity reflected the world in its own image', Glissant has written (2010, 111). But while for Glissant there is opacity now at the bottom of the mirror, 'indistinct and unexplored even today and with an insistent presence that we are incapable of not experiencing' (11), Haraway has put forward 'diffraction' as an alternative way of looking at the mirror.

As an optical phenomenon in classical physics diffraction follows the bending of waves as they move through passages or encounter small obstacles: think of how a rainbow of different colours is being formed when white light enters a prism. What happens when two or more waves arrive at the same point is also interesting, since unlike particles, waves can overlap at the same point in space creating *superposition* effects. Consider the all too familiar moment when we throw pebbles in a lake: the waves that appear as an effect of this disturbance interfere with each other in different ways, depending on their properties and corresponding forces – they can create a more intense wave together, producing constructive interferences or they can cancel each other out in the mode of destructive interferences. The superposition of most waves, however, produces a combination of constructive and destructive interferences, which vary from place to place and time to time. In Haraway's analysis, then diffraction becomes a metaphor for the effort to see difference and its effects at the bottom of the mirror or on the surface of a pond: 'diffraction patterns record the history of interaction, interference, reinforcement, difference. Diffraction is about heterogeneous history, not about originals' (1997, 16).

Following a vibrant body of feminist literature that have deployed diffractive methodologies in research,[19] I have taken diffraction as an approach 'of reading insights through one another in attending to and responding to the details and specificities of relations of difference. Put simply, diffractive ways of thinking and doing are not only about how I understand the structure of reality as a continuous becoming on the ontological level – migrant and refugee women's experiences of travelling in the case of this book. It is also about how I get to know 'the real' on the epistemological level through listening to, understanding and analysing their stories. In the light of wave phenomena, the meanings that are enacted by my listening practices keep creating a variety of superimposition effects, producing constructive and destructive interferences. Finally, diffraction changes not only the way I see difference and trace its effects, but also how I mark and change my position vis-a-vis the phenomena I am studying.

'Can the subaltern speak?' Gayatri Spivak (1988) has provocatively asked in a question around which a lot of feminist ink has been spilt over the years. Even if 'the subaltern can speak', 'can the coloniser listen?' Emma Jones (2020) has wondered proposing 'ontological deafness' as a component of Western listening practices within feminism and beyond. This is the point where I return to the politics of listening, through the lenses of Young's (1990, 106) notion of 'communicative ethics' that I briefly discussed in the first section of the chapter. In doing so, I consider the effects that difference makes in listening to women's stories of forced displacement. Here, my situated position as a nomadic and yet white and privileged academic feminist interferes with the radical activism of my youth creating *superposition* patterns in between construction and destruction, always in the middle, the intermezzo.

It is not only through nostalgia that I consider my years of feminist activism in Greece, when I was still a university student. Apart from the joy of being in the newly emerging feminist movement of post-dictatorship Greece, those years have also forged life-long friendships with women who are now in the fore front of a wide range of non-governmental and civic organization for women's rights in Greece. In the past twenty years, migrant and refugee women have been at the heart of feminist activism in Greece and it was mainly through these networks that I was introduced to the women, who shared with me their stories of forced displacement.[20] My entry in the field was, thus, marked by trust and feminist solidarity, and therefore, the feminist activism of my past created the conditions of possibility for this research. Having mapped my situated position in the narrative field of my inquiries, I now want to follow affinities as 'flows of energies' (Mason 2018) that have permeated and shaped the plane of 'communicative ethics' (Young 1990), within which it is still possible to speak and to listen. In doing so, I will go back to a significant event in my research: my talk in the Kara Tepe refugee camp that I briefly referred to while introducing Zahra's story in the previous section.

When making contacts with civic organizations in Mytilini, Lesvos, I got in touch with Caritas Hellas Lesvos, amongst other groups. After talking to the organizers about my research, they invited me to give a talk to a group of women who were participating in the programme 'Transition: Co-operation, Empowerment and Social Integration for migrants and refugees in Greece'.[21] Their idea was that once women had met me and listened to my talk, they could decide whether they wanted to participate. I accepted of course, but I was both excited and deeply problematized. Being aware of the huge debates amongst feminists around the discourses and practices of empowerment,[22] I was wondering about how I could talk to these women being true to them and to myself. My situated position as a feminist narrative researcher took me out of this impasse: 'I have always believed that no matter how abstract our theories may sound or how consistent our arguments appear, there are incidents and stories behind them which, at least for ourselves, contain as in a nutshell the full meaning of whatever we have to say' Arendt has written (2018, 201–2). Stories, in Arendt's thought, ground abstractions, flesh out ideas and, thus, create a milieu where thought can emerge from the actuality of the recounted event. Within the narrative sensibility of my research, I thus decided to share Nadia's story with the women of the Kara-Tempe camp, as a narrative of perseverance and hope.[23] In doing so, I was honouring Nadia's desire for her story to be shared with other refugee women, as an Arendtian way of inserting herself in the web of human relations through narratives. 'With word and deed we insert ourselves into the human world, and this insertion is like a second birth' Arendt has written (1998, 176), highlighting the importance of others to inspire, albeit not to condition or determine this second birth, which is existential and political: 'its impulse springs from the beginning which came into the world when we were born and to which we respond by beginning something new on our own initiative' (177).

My talk at the Kara Tepe refugee camp was arranged for April 10, 2019. Unlike the notorious Moria camp, which was a hot spot, a Registration and Identification Centre,[24] Kara Tepe was a refugee camp run by an organization linked to the Municipality of Lesvos.[25] This medium size camp could only accept a restricted number of refugees – 800 at the time of my visit – usually those who were in particularly vulnerable conditions. Each family lived in a container, while several civic organizations had their offices and facilities there, including a women's friendly space, where my talk was hosted.[26] I had already visited the Kara Tepe camp in March, when I gave a seminar in 'the force of life histories' to a group of service providers, including teachers, advisers, psychologists and health carers working in different state and civic organizations in Lesvos, so I was familiar with the premises and procedures.[27] This time was different, however.

It was a rainy afternoon and I could see that the organizers were apprehensive and worried about women's participation: 'We don't expect many women' they told me straight away 'and because of the rain we expect even less'. There were two groups of women when I entered the container, no more than eight altogether, and two to three prams. 'Well, if we have twelve attendees, that would be excellent' the organizers told me. I mingled with the women and with the help of the interpreter I started chatting with them. There were some younger women, who could also speak English, so we were laughing our mutual embarrassment away. But as it was getting closer to 3 p.m., more and more women started coming in the container. We were initially sitting in a kind of circle, but I had to stand up to give space for more chairs and prams to be accommodated. By 3.10 p.m., the container was literally packed, and the door was open for a large group of women who were standing outside to be able to listen, as the rain had fortunately stopped. The desired number of twelve had blown up to sixty plus, when I started narrating Nadia's story. As the story was unfolding, I could see it in the women's shining eyes that they were listening. As they were gradually drawn into the space/time of the narrative, they were becoming part of its process and practice: They were nodding their heads; they were smiling and when the talk was over, a young Afghan woman with a beautiful pink scarf stood up and said: 'Let's clap for Nadia'. When the applause was over, she stood up again and said: 'and now, one for Maria'. 'A story told is a story bound to circulate', Trinh has beautifully written (1989, 134).

I was terribly moved by this warm response, and after surpassing my initial fascination, wondering and puzzlement, I encouraged these women to ask questions. And they did: There were all sorts of questions, mostly about getting access to educational opportunities, but also more personal ones, around my project. They wanted to know about my website and about my research more generally. Some of these women were very well educated: There were lawyers and doctors and nurses and teachers amongst them. There were several young mothers and some older women as well. The organizers advised me to ask them whether they wanted to take a group photo for the Caritas archives, but beyond the formal photo there were many women gathering around me, taking selfies. What was mostly moving at these moments of group selfies was the touching. They would touch my shoulders and hold mine and each other's hands in an embodied cadence. As Tim Huzar (2021) has suggested, touching becomes a modality of knowing beyond representation – an apprehension that brings together the body and the flesh in an entanglement of opening and closing, vulnerability and care:

> who it is that is in the flesh is not represented but apprehended, and in this apprehension, in this inclined touching an ineluctable reciprocal relation is made apparent, where the one apprehending is also apprehended, made apparent as a unique existent who lives in the flesh' (Huzar 2021, 3).

The moment of touching was indeed one of the most forceful moments in my experience as a feminist activist, and I will never forget it. 'We have never seen such a thing before' the organizers told me.

Narratives have the power to involve us in the dynamics of thinking differently and as Salvaggio has pointed out, feminist theorists have used stories to unsettle theoretical abstractions and move into 'a place where truth and narrative intermingle in the endless telling of stories' (1999, 39). In looking back at the affinities that were manifested in the Kara Tepe event, what I wanted to highlight is Young's idea of the possibility of communicating in difference within concrete encounters and situations (1990, 106). In doing so, I have tried to move beyond binarisms and dichotomies of 'the subaltern' and 'the coloniser' that create unbridgeable gaps in our capacity to connect and communicate. This is not to say that relations of power and domination are discarded in this approach. Rather my point is that a homogenization of refugee women under the label of 'the subaltern' unavoidably erases their agential moves and cuts. The refugee women that I met at the women's friendly container of the Kara Tepe refugee camp had marked their own situated position. When they decided to come to the talk, they brought their own experiences, educational and cultural backgrounds, interests and dreams. They decided to listen and what they made of Nadia's story was different for each of them. As Salvaggio has pointed out: 'by telling our specific stories, by allowing a multiplicity of stories to be told, we can articulate our specific historical and cultural positions and use them to negotiate both our differences and connections' (1999, 53). In this context, there were two women in the Kara Tepe group, who after listening to Nadia's story offered to share their own, as a reciprocal narrative act. Their desire to tell their story erupted from affective listening to another woman's story, in Cavarero's intertwined I/you scene of relational narratives:

> At once exposable and narratable, the existent always constitutes herself in relation to an other. With all the inimitable wisdom of a familiar feeling [*sapore*], she knows that she is an unrepeatable uniqueness, but does not know *who* she is, or *who* is exposed. She knows she is a narratable identity, but also knows that only another can correct the fallacy of the autobiographical impulse. The unity of the desire – namely the unity entrusted to the tale that everyone desires – is not, in fact, an aspect of unconsciousness or a problem of introspection. It is rather the irreflexive object of the desire *for* the unity of the self in the form of a story. (Cavarero 2000, 40)

In the light of diffractive practices that I have discussed in the beginning of this section, this irreflexive move of telling one's story is one of the patterns of difference, interferences and superimpositions in the wave phenomena of listening that I have tried to sketch in this chapter. Like water, light and sound waves, women's stories have circulated 'like a gift; an empty gift, which anybody can lay claim to, by filling it to taste, yet can never truly possess. A gift built on multiplicity. One that stays inexhaustible within its own limits. Its departures and arrivals. Its quietness.' (Trinh 1989, 2) In receiving the free gift of migrant and refugee women's stories, what I have argued is that perhaps we should move beyond the imperatives of clarity and transparency in an attempt to be in the world with others. Here, the sound of narratives could become a trope that can take us down the path of decolonizing our ways of knowing and understanding.

NOTES

1. As already shown in the list of interviews in the introduction, out of the twenty-two life history interviews, six were conducted in Farsi, five in English, four in Arabic, three in French, two in Greek and two in Pashto. The Arabic, Farsi and Pashto interviews were conducted with the presence of an interpreter.
2. The field of music and narrative is vast and cannot be reviewed in the limited space of this chapter. For an important overview see Klein and Reyland 2012.
3. See Dowling 2011 for an illuminating discussion of Ricoeur's concepts in *Time and Narrative*, particularly Chapter 1 in *Mimesis*.
4. Christina's story, a flat in Athens, narrated in Greek, 13 April 2019.
5. https://diotima.org.gr/en/about-us/#1528727001873-55b07841-b1f7
6. Awat's story, Diotima centre, narrated in Farsi, Athens, 22 April 2019.
7. Erika's story, a flat in Mytilini, narrated in Arabic, 10 April 2019.
8. Mosaik and Bashira are two important NGOs in Lesvos, operating a range of educational, cultural and support courses. See https://lesvosmosaik.org and https://www.sao-english.ngo/bashira for more details, [Accessed 27 July 2020].

9. Hanna's story, a café in Athens, narrated in English, 8 December 2018. I have already introduced Hanna in the introduction and I am going to return to her story in Chapter 4. Her full story is narrated in interlude 3.

10. In the Labovian structural model, stories revolve aroumd six elements: abstract, orientation, complicated action, resolution, evaluation and coda. For a critical discussion of this approach to narrative analysis, see Patterson 2013.

11. Anna's story, a flat in Lesvos, narrated in French, 8 April 2019.

12. I have decided to omit the rape details in the light of an ethics of narrative care.

13. Mariam's story, Iliaktida premises, narrated in French, Lesvos, 8 April 2019.

14. I refer here of course to Foucault's 1975–1976 lectures at the College de France: 'Society must be defended' (Foucault 2003).

15. See https://www.solidaritynow.org/en/kentro-allileggiis-athinas/

16. See, https://www.refugeelegalsupport.org/athens

17. See amongst others, Burrell 2017; Boswell et al., 2011; Eastmond 2007, Daniel and Knusden 1995.

18. Sima's story, Athens Solidarity Centre, narrated in Pashto, 13 December 2018.

19. See Taguchi 2012; Bozalek & Zembylas, 2017, Uden 2018; van der Tuin 2019; Goodman 2019.

20. See https://mariatamboukou.org/revisiting-the-nomadic-subject-2/reflections-and-diffractions/august-2019/ for a full list of the feminist organizations and friends that supported this research.

21. For more details of this organization, see https://www.caritas.eu/19828-2/

22. See amongst others, Kabeer 1994, 1999, 2005; Rowlands 1997; Jones 2020.

23. I have already referred to Nadia's story in the introduction and Chapter 1, but I will also return to it in Chapters 4, 6 and 7. See also her full story in the first interlude.

24. Moria was burnt down to the ground in September 2020. During this time, it had become the largest refugee camp in Europe. See https://www.bbc.co.uk/news/world-europe-54082201

25. Soon after the Moria fire, a new temporary camp was established in a military zone next to the municipal accommodation facility of Kara Tepe, whose operation was decided to be terminated, alongside PIKPA, another alternative refugee camp for vulnerable asylum seekers. I was amongst the academics and more than 160 Greek and international organizatios, as well as other Eutopean actors, who undersigned an appeal to the Greek authorities to revoke their decision. The appeal was unsuccessful and both camps have now closed. See https://www.hrw.org/news/2020/09/30/save-dignity-save-pikpa-and-kara-tepe [Accessed 15 November 2020].

26. For more details of refugee reception sites in Lesvos, see http://urmi.fi/wp-content/uploads/2017/05/Asylum-seekers-in-Lesvos.pdf

27. See https://mariatamboukou.org/revisiting-the-nomadic-subject-2/entanglements/seminars-and-workshops/ for details of these talks.

Chapter 3

Crossing Borders and Inhabiting Borderlands

it was daytime
a sunny day
it was like a normal journey
but of course
I was all white
and very anxious
excitement
nervousness
I felt like
I would faint
something like that
it was like a two hours journey
and throughout
I was trembling

but at some point
the captain said
now we are within the borders of Greece
it was one of the best moments of my life
I felt free after two years
I really felt free

ok
the captain said
now there is no problem
now we are not in the borders of Turkey
you crossed the borders
it was wonderful

freedom is so important
I have understood
more important than money
you can live anywhere
you can eat anything
it is ok
but if you don't have freedom
you have nothing

I cannot tell you how I felt
at that moment
when I heard the captain
I can still hear his voice
we are safe now
we are within the borders of Greece[1]

In this cinematic part of her story, which sounded like a freedom song in my ears, Derya revives the moment of crossing the borders. Since hers was a maritime escape, it was the sonics of the captain's voice that marked her passage and filled her with joy. Derya is a well-educated Turkish woman in her mid-thirties, who was caught in the persecution of the Gülen movement in the aftermath of its conflict with the Turkish government and particularly after the July 2016 coup attempt.[2] As one of the most powerful religious organizations in Turkey and worldwide, this movement encourages its followers to master the sciences as a way of engaging with secular modernity. The movement's focus on the importance of education has made it widely popular among young women, who see their organizational involvement as an opportunity to enhance their knowledge and change their lives.[3]

I met Derya in April 2019 through the Research Legal Support Group (RLS-Athens) and I interviewed her in a café in Athens. At the time of the interview, she was waiting to reunify with her husband and two children in Belgium, after two years of persecution, imprisonment and failed attempts to escape. Her story encompasses many elements of the experience of thousands of Gülenist women imprisoned in Turkey because of their connections with the movement (see Gergerlioğlu 2021). As Derya told me in the very beginning of the interview: 'Thank you for listening to me, because I need to tell this story; this is not only my story, this is the story of many women and children and many families in Turkey now.'

Taking Derya's narrative moment of defying territorial restrictions as my starting point, in this chapter, I look into different discourses, practices and lived experiences revolving around borders and border crossings. The chapter unfolds in three parts: first, I look at borders as components of *mobility assemblages*, particularly focussing on what they do as political, cultural and material practices and discourses in constituting 'the real'. Then, I consider border situations within symbolic and imaginary spaces inspired by feminist critical poetics. Finally, I turn to the stories of my archive, which were not so much about understanding borders and their contested politics, but rather about the risks and joys of crossing them at any cost, as well as about surviving the borderlands. As Michel Agier has put it: 'a whole life is organized in these border places, marked by the uncertainty of the moment and the immediate future, as well as the uncertainty of the gaze directed at them' (2016, 3). Women's stories revolved a lot about their struggles of inhabiting borderlands, whether as workers, students, volunteers or through their kinship roles and relations: widows, run-away wives and daughters, mothers or just single women.

WHAT DO BORDERS DO?

In addressing the question of 'what is a border?' Étienne Balibar (2002) points to the complexity of the notion and proposes three ways of understanding it: overdetermination, polysemy and heterogeneity. In their long history, borders have always been overdetermined, he argues: 'no political border is ever the mere boundary between two states, but is always overdetermined, and in that sense sanctioned, reduplicated and relativized by other geopolitical divisions' (79). Their poysemic nature means that borders are never experienced in the same way by subjects with different, social, cultural, ethnic, political or gender identifications: 'they do not have the same meaning for everyone' (81). Finally, borders are heterogeneous and ubiquitous and *some borders are no longer situated at the borders at all* in the geographico-politico administrative sense of the term' (84, emphasis in the text). The Berlin Wall is one of the most well-known cases in the Cold War era: It illustrates Balibar's configuration, particularly in highlighting the politically relativized character of borders and the way they are differently experienced by its 'insiders' and 'outsiders', which are also unstable and volatile subject positions. As Trinh T. Min-ha has poetically put it: 'Call it a fence "to make good neighbors", but it is still a wall and remember what the Berlin wall was called on the other side; it was an Anti-Fascist Protection Barrier' (2011, 1). Moreover, despite the jubilations of the western world on the aftermath of the fall of the Berlin Wall, we have now entered a new era of wall politics, or what Wendy Brown calls a 'desire for walls', which is manifested in four popular phantasies: the fear of the alien, the need to be protected, the demand for insulation and the will for purity (2010).

What Balibar (2002) highlights in his political analysis of the impossibility of grasping the notion of the border is that borders have different histories and geographies, and they are always both real and imaginary, as well as visible and invisible. André Green's pithy observation that 'you can be a citizen or you can be stateless, but it is difficult to imagine being a border' (1990, 107) brings the complexity of the multiple and split migrant and refugee subject positions in the *assemblage* of border discourses and practices that I want to unravel in this chapter. But instead of raising the aporetic ontological question of 'what is a border', I rather turn my interest in what borders do. In doing so, I follow the Spinozist route of getting to the knowledge of a thing (border),[4] by tracing its expressions – what it does – as well as its conditions of possibility, how it has come to be constructed and conceptualized in the way we perceive it today. The question of what borders do in expressing the conditions of their existence seems to reverberate with Deborah Dixon's question of 'what can a feminist geopolitics do' (2015, 1). Her configuration of feminist geopolitics as a critical field that illuminates people's lives across the globe, with the aim to understand, but more importantly change the sociopolitical, economic and cultural conditions of their existence, becomes the plane on which I want to explore gendered experiences of crossing borders and inhabiting borderlands:

> Imagine you are standing on the shore of a sea staring across at a landmass opposite, which forms your horizon. You know, although they are not visible to you, that beneath the surface of this sea are the corpses of thousands of people who tried to cross it in order to arrive where you are now standing. Your horizon, then, is a border. This sea has long been viewed as a threshold, and yours is not the first epoch during which it has been crossed by masses of people in a rising tide of desperation, propelled by unspeakable violence. But crossing it has, in your epoch, become a crime. (Tsilimpounidi and Carastathis 2017, 405)

What the authors highlight in the above extract from a dialogic art/theory essay mingling photography with theoretical analysis is not only the invisible liquid borders of the Aegean Sea, but also and perhaps more importantly the histories of previous crossings. What has dramatically changed, however, in the Aegean 'refugee crisis' is that 'the solid ground on which you are standing' (405), the island of Lesvos in the case of the above essay, is also the entrance gate to Europe and has thus become a 'hot spot' in the European policy of migration management. Remember that borders are overdetermined, polysemic and heterogeneous in Balibar's analysis (2002), so they need to be mapped within situated histories and geographies.

The formation of 'hot spots' has become a crucial aspect of the European migration policy. According to the 'European Agenda of Migration'[5] hot spots were conceived as registration and identification centres that would administer and facilitate the relocation of refugees, in all EU member states according to their admission quotas and needs. By dividing those eligible to seek asylum status from those deemed ineligible, the hot spot's main function was initially conceived as a way to manage the waves of refugees at the point of their emergence in the EU borders. In this way, Lesvos along four other Greek islands in the Aegean borders with Turkey – Chios, Leros, Samos and Kos – were eventually separated from their Greek/European context and were transformed into gateways to the Fortress Europe. The border 'is both a threshold and an act of institution', Agier has argued and its action is both internal and external (2016, 18). But what happened in the actual enactment of 'hot spot' policies is that these islands became sites of indefinite detention: The promise of relocation was only partially realized and thousands of refugees found themselves stranded in Greece, either on the islands or in the mainland, particularly after March 2016, when Balkan countries sealed their borders.[6] As Myrto Tsilimpounidi and Anna Carastathis have commented on the function of the hot spots on the Aegean Greek islands: 'the national border is moved inward, separating the islands from the mainland, creating a liminal zone of questionable legal status, but also multiplying the border through so-called "mobile hot spots," which follow people on the move who have circumvented the security regime' (2017, 406).

Well before the Aegean 'crisis', in an essay that was presented in the conference 'L'idée de l'Europe and la philosophie' back in 1993, Balibar had highlighted the instability, porousness and vacillation of European borders. This state of vacillation according to Balibar, not only destabilizes any static notion of what a border is and how it functions within and beyond Europe, but it also interrogates, and even shatters given and accepted conceptions of what a European identity might be (2002, 88). Moreover, this fluid border condition transforms questions of border policy and policing into philosophical issues and speculations about 'the meaning of defining an "interior" and an "exterior", a "here" and a "there"' (2002, 88). In Balibar's analysis then, the vacillation of borders is an important aspect of 'being a border', despite the aporias that Green (1990) had identified in this condition, as already noted above.

I have already shown how European borders are still vacillating within the hot spot approaches to the migration and refugee issue. As a matter of fact, this vacillation has eventually exploded to an unprecedented crisis of human mobility management. At the time that I was writing this chapter, thousands of migrants and refugees had been trapped in a no-man's land, in between borders, after Turkey's decision to suspend the bilateral EU–Turkey agreement of March 2016, which gave the right to European border authorities to return to Turkey those refugees who had been deemed ineligible to seek asylum in Europe.⁷ The decision of the Turkish government to 'open the doors' and no longer prevent migrants from crossing into Europe came as a result of the European Union's failure to intervene in the 2020 military crisis of Northern Syria.⁸ But while borders are done and undone as the unfolding of war tactics and diplomatic negotiations within local and global geopolitical crises, they create unforeseen effects in the *mobility assemblages* within which border lines are drawn, erased and redrawn: There are some people out there who are caught in the interstices of failed political actions and whose lives are at the point of annihilation. What Balibar's analysis of borders within 'the real' highlights is that far from being mere geographical limits between territorial entities, borders are complex social, political and cultural battlefields, historically marked by intense power relations at play between practices of border enforcement and border crossing.

But beyond geopolitical contexts, impositions and limitations, borders always raise philosophical questions and issues at the level of the symbolic and the imaginary for Balibar. They are dynamic and mobile, and their heterogeneous manifestations include cultural, linguistic, political and existential boundaries that need to be charted and analysed. In Balibar's analysis then, the border has ceased to be a marginal phenomenon (according to its conceptual and cartographic representation as an edge and as a limit) and has been transported into the very centre of the public space, into the middle of our experience' Mezzadra has argued (2019, 2). In this context, the role of 'internal borders' in the construction of 'foreign bodies' is a useful tool in feminist geopolitical analytics, as I will further discuss, drawing on feminist spatial poetics in-between and across borderlands and borderlines.

ON BEING A BORDER WOMAN

Cuando vives en la frontera
    people walk through you, the wind steals your voice
    [. . .]
To survive the Borderlands,
    you must live *sin fronteras*
    be a crossroads

                                       (Anzaldúa 1987, 194–5)

Published in 1987, Anzaldúa's *Borderlands/La Frontera* has become an influential intervention in configuring social, political and existential entanglements of living and moving in between countries, cultures, languages, identifications and subject positions, a critical celebration of radical difference par excellence. In her preface, Anzaldúa draws the geographical lines of her 'actual physical borderland' as 'the Texas-US Southwest/Mexican border', but she is quick to observe that the psychological, sexual and spiritual borderlands she is dealing with are not specific to her geographically situated position. (i) What is also significant in the poetics of being 'a border woman' (i) is that difficulties, pains, traumas, pleasures and joys are entangled in the mestiza experience: 'It is not a comfortable territory to live in, this place of contradictions. Hatred, anger and exploitation are the prominent features of this landscape. However, there have been compensations for this *mestiza* and certain joys.' (I, emphasis in the text)

Anzaldúa's ambivalence vis-à-vis the existential condition of being 'a border woman' runs like a red thread not only through her *Borderlands* book, but actually throughout her whole corpus. 'Caminante, no hay puentes, se hace puentes al andar (Traveller, there are no bridges, one builds them as one walks), she wrote in the last sentence of the preface to the second edition of *This Bridge Called my Back,* a collection of writings by women of colour (Moraga and Anzaldúa 1983). With this poetic ending, she reconfigures the Spanish poet Antonio Machado's famous verse: 'Caminante no hay camino, Se hace camino al andar' (Traveller, there is no path you make your own path as you walk). As Norma Elia Cantú has commented, in choosing the trope of the bridge [el puente] to replace that of the path [el camino] in Machado's verse, Anzaldúa's traveller does not just open a path for himself or herself, but actually builds bridges that connect.

Among the many insights and ideas that emerge from Anzaldúa's border theory, I have been particularly interested in the concept of *nepantla*, as a liminal transitional space. As Cantú explains, the concept's roots are in Náhua thought: 'to be in *nepantla* meant to be in a space – theoretical and abstract – where two seemingly opposed views must be negotiated and synthesized' (2013, 182). Anzaldúa interprets the Náhuatl notion somehow differently however, highlighting transition rather than synthesis: 'an in-between state, that uncertain terrain one crosses when moving from one place to another, when changing from one class, race or sexual position to another, when travelling from a present identity into a new identity' (2009a, 180) Thus, in Anzaldúa's conceptual vocabulary, *nepantla* is a space in the intermezzo, wherein ruptures and shifts happen: 'nepantla is the space in-between, the locus and sign of transformation' (2009b, 310), which she also calls 'a transitional nepantla space' (310) This transition is not always internal and it is always harsh and risky, as for example, the moment when the immigrant crosses the barbed wire fence (180). In Anzaldúan spatial analytic then, 'one does not remain in nepantla, but rather one lives that moment of in-betweenness and moves on' (Cantú 2013, 182). It is in the *nepantla* that cultural identifications and subject positions are created and negotiated. Put in Foucauldian terms, the *nepantla* becomes a spatial component of 'technologies of the self' (1988), practices and discourses that Anzaldúa deploys in becoming a subject. If the border 'is a place, a situation or a moment that ritualizes the relationship to the other' in Agier's thought (2016, 6), it is also an instance that crystallizes the relationship to the self, I would add: 'I had to leave home so I could find myself' wrote Anzaldúa (1987, 16).

The poetics of 'the border woman' fleshes out Balibar's 'internal border' as an analytical tool of dissecting gender and race relations within feminist geopolitical analytics: 'The woman of color does not feel safe within the inner life of her Self. Petrified, she can't respond, her face caught between *los intersticios,* the spaces between the different worlds she inhabits' (20, emphasis in the text). More importantly for Anzaldúa, the border experience is corporeal and visceral: 'The body is smart. It does not discern between external stimuli and stimuli from the imagination. It reacts equally viscerally to events from the imagination as it does to "real events"' (38) The body as a plane of internal borders then, can either become 'foreign' as in Balibar and/or a site of resistance. Pain itself transposes itself into a tactic of resistance: 'pain makes us acutely anxious to avoid more of it, so we hone that radar. It's a kind of survival tactic that people caught between the worlds unknowingly cultivate. It is latent in all of us' (39).

Writing from the heart, Anzaldúa's poetics beautifully express the contradictions and aporias of what Agier (2016, 17) calls 'border situations', that is time/space conditions within which borders are lived and experienced. And whilst she does not idealize the nomadic condition of life as an incessant wandering in between the striated spaces of nations, empires, capitalism and patriarchy, she does choose resistance as the coda of her stanza:

In the Borderlands
you are the battleground
where enemies are kin to each other;
you are at home, a stranger,
the border disputes have been settled
the volley of shots have shattered the truce
you are wounded, lost in action
dead, fighting back;

(Anzaldúa 1987, 194)

Anzaldúa's poetic figuration of fighting back reverberates here with Trinh's observation that despite its immanent sadness, exile 'can be worked through as an experience of crossing boundaries and charting new ground in defiance of newly authorized or old canonical enclosures' (2011, 35). In her work, Trinh also takes up the question of 'the foreigner' and 'the other' in relation to migration and forced displacement, but instead of bridges, she has turned her attention to walls, the stories that have revolved around them, as well as their peculiar seductions: 'whoever is tempted to climb up the wall to look at what lies on the other side, ends up happily jumping over it, never to look back again' (2011, 1). The wall then is a border that incorporates the desire to cross it. It is there not to restrict and confine, but to be circumvented, a material trace of resistance, or what Agier calls 'the paradox of the wall, which is at the same time an imitation and a negation of the border' (2016. viii). Kapka Kassabova has expressed this double function of the border in a most forceful way: 'Once near a border, it is impossible not to be involved, not to want to exorcise or transgress something. Just by being there, the border is an invitation. Come on, it whispers, step across this line.' (2017, ii) In this state of ambivalence, 'outside' and 'inside' are always labile spaces, particularly so for those living in border situations: *the high wall that keeps out is the same wall that keeps in*' (Trinh 2011, 3, emphasis in the text). It is through travelling that borders are crossed, but also redrawn: 'every voyage can be said to involve a resitting of boundaries' Trinh has written (27). In her critical poetics, then the internal border takes a centre stage:

> The traveling self is here both the self that moves physically from one place to another, following 'public routes and beaten tracks' within a mapped movement; and, the self that embarks on an undetermined journeying practice, having constantly to negotiate between home and abroad, native culture and adopted culture, or more creatively speaking, between a here, a there, and an elsewhere. (27)

Trinh is very sceptical about the wandering self however, and her analysis exposes what she articulates as the doubleness of being a stranger: 'as a foreigner on foreign land and as a stranger at home' (55). The experience of forced displacement has made her uncomfortable with what used to be her home country: 'their country is my country' (55). The feeling of being a border, a split self is disorienting and painful. Having left her country behind, she cannot escape the condition of being a stranger: 'if it is problematic to be a stranger, it is even more so to stop being one' (55). Within this incessant process of being or rather perpetually becoming a stranger, 'every voyage is the unfolding of a poetic' for Trinh (39) as it follows the rhythms of movement: 'the departure, the crossover, the fall, the transformation' (39–40). The power relations that enforce displacement are also entangled with forces of desire for detours and wanderings.

Trinh's take of travellers' tales and the entanglements of sadness and joy that they entail make connections with Maria Lugones' (1990, 390) articulation of 'world'-travelling, as the outsider's experience of playfully moving among different modalities of life, albeit in the ruins of failed love. Lugones' argument is that it is through loving each other that we can travel to each other's worlds. Here, it is important to clarify Lugones' conceptual vocabulary and particularly her materialist approach to a what 'a world' can be or become: never a fixed entity, but rather an *assemblage* of real and imaginary bodies and/in places (395). In the same materialist vein, travelling is a modality of existential transformation: 'the shift from being one person to being a different person' (396).

Lugones' philosophical reflections on the connecting powers of love, as well as her quest of how a traveller can be 'at ease in a world' (397) remind me of what Arendt has configured as 'amor mundi', love of/for the world. Having emerged from the experience of being a refugee, a paperless and stateless person for more than twenty years, this is what she wrote to her Ph.D. supervisor and life-long friend Karl Jaspers in August 1955 from the country of her exile: 'I've begun so late, really only in recent years, to truly love the world that I shall be able to do that now. Out of gratitude, I want to call my book on political theory *amor mundi*'.[9] Being at the heart of Arendt's philosophical thought, love is intertwined with the crucial concept of plurality in her unique take on politics: 'In this realm of plurality, which is the political realm, one has to ask the old questions – what is love, what is friendship, what is solitude, what is acting, thinking, etc., but not the one question of philosophy: Who is Man' Arendt wrote in an entry in the *Denktagebuch*, her philosophical diary.[10]

In the same way that love is for Lugones a force that facilitates 'world travelling', love for Arendt creates conditions of possibility for our immersion in the web of human relations, the necessary condition for the constitution of the political. Lugones' quest for 'being at ease in a world' reverberates with Arendt's dream of being 'at home in this world' in the aftermath of her own and a whole people's forced displacement, as pithily expressed in her influential essay 'We Refugees', first published in January 1943, while she was still in the thick of the displaced experience:

> We lost our home, which means the familiarity of daily life. We lost our occupation, which means the confidence that we are of some use in this world. We lost our language, which means the naturalness of reactions, the simplicity of gestures, the unaffected expression of feelings. (Arendt 1943, 69)

Feeling at home in this world does not mean a return to any kind of motherland or fatherland. As a matter of fact, Arendt never returned to Germany, although she frequently travelled to Europe and Israel when her 'sans papier' condition ended. Home is, thus, configured as a map of cultural, political and affective relations beyond geographical borders and spatial limitations, an *assemblage* of 'here', 'there' and 'elsewhere' in Trinh's analysis above, an Anzaldúan *nepantla,* a place where Lugones can feel playful in saying: 'that's me in there' (1990, 396). In this context, home is mapped as 'a smooth space', entangled with the striated spaces of barbed wire fences, walls and treacherous sea crossings (Deleuze and Guattari 1988).

Thinking about borderlands through Deleuze and Guattari's spatial analytics, I have, thus, drawn on the Leibnizian concept of the fold. Deleuze (1993) has used this concept to trace connections between spaces and bodies: The world folds into the self in different speeds and on a variety of levels and intensities affecting the ways we live, relate to other bodies and make sense of our worldliness. At the same time, however, we keep folding out into the world, Foucault (1988) in his later work argued, acting upon received knowledge, discourses and practices and, thus, moulding ourselves as subjects through the deployment of *technologies of the self.* In this light, the different spaces and places that we live in fold into our bodily activities as a series of movements, practices, thoughts and affects. As we fold out into the world, the spaces that we move through keep changing with us rather than staying lifeless, static or monolithic. We are, thus, continuously surrounded by what Deleuze and Guattari (1988) have theorized as *striated and smooth spaces.* In their analysis, striated spaces are hierarchical, rule-intensive, strictly bounded and confining. 'But there are always forces of deterritorialization, lines of flight', Deleuze and Guattari (1988, 474) argue, 'that shatter segmentarities and open up smooth spaces that are unmarked, dynamic and create conditions of possibility for transformations to occur' (474). Moreover, there is no dualistic opposition in this configuration; as a matter of fact, the world is being experienced as a continuum of striated and smooth spaces: 'smooth space is constantly being translated, transversed into a striated space; striated space is constantly being reversed, returned to a smooth space' (413). It is such unfoldings of smooth and striated spaces that I want to consider next, drawing on migrant and refugee women's lived experiences of inhabiting borderlands.

BORDERLANDS AS LIVED SPACES

Living at the borders means that one constantly treads the fine line between positioning and de-positioning, Trinh has thoughtfully commented (2011, 54). Derya's joy of crossing the sea borders soon turned into the nightmare of a detention centre in Athens, when her subsequent attempt to cross the borders at the airport failed, and she was arrested. The monotonic narrative of her incarceration would only be textually transposed in prose. The freedom song that initiated this chapter had been crushed in my ears:

I tried to cross the borders and fly to the US, but they arrested us. They kept us for three weeks in some kind of detention centre. The conditions were really very bad there. I want to say it: I am very grateful to Greece, because they accepted us; I really feel free here, I am grateful to the Greek people, but the conditions at the detention centre were horrible. There were bugs everywhere and it was very crowded. There was not enough water, enough food. . . Let's forget the food, but these bugs everywhere. We had a lawyer, he tried very hard, but he didn't manage to let me go. But after three weeks, I got very sick. It was a kind of allergic reaction, I don't know, maybe because of the bacteria, or the dirt, or maybe because of the food, I really don't know. There was redness and wounds all over my body and they took me to emergency. They gave me some medicine, but the next night I fainted two times, I lost my consciousness. So, after all these things happened, they let me go.

Crossing borders cannot, thus, be idealized, not even within the limits of a single narrative, as in Derya's story. For people who have been forcefully displaced and turned into wanderers with uncertain futures and destinies, borders become marks of shifts and traumatic events in their lives, but also zones of indeterminacy and endless waiting, spatial traces of their desire to be accepted. 'I am grateful to Greece because they accepted us' said Derya while also giving an account of the horrible conditions of her detention. As Trinh has noted, being accepted is a fundamental problem of the refugee condition, a means 'to overcome the humiliation of bearing the too-may-too-needy status of the homeless-stateless alien' (2011, 29). What does it mean to inhabit such zones, where life is suspended while waiting to be accepted? Moreover, what if living in borderlands has been your life?

A usual starting point for travelling stories is the beginning of a journey: 'where do you want me to start?' most women asked me in the beginning of the interview. My answer was always the same, 'start wherever you want'. But while, most women would choose to start from an event that had radically disrupted their life-course as adults, Warda looked at me in a pensive way and after taking some time to think, she went back to her early childhood in what sounded like a poetic narration of five stanzas:

I will speak from the beginning
I was born in Somalia
in Mogadishu

when I was born
there were many troubles in my country
and when I was four
there were many problems with my family
because of the troubles

so my father and mother took the decision
that the whole family had to move to Yemen
we went to Yemen
and we stayed there for a year
at my aunt's
my father's sister house
I was very young at the time and
I did not understand
why my family had taken the decision to move

one day
my family sent me out
to play with the children of the neighbourhood
I was out all day
but well before the afternoon
I went back home
just before the sun set
when I went into our house
there was nobody there
it was empty
there was no furniture
nothing

I could not understand
how they had just gone
without a word
it was a very difficult time for me
this incident
became a traumatic experience
in my life
for ever[11]

Warda is a young Somalian woman in her early twenties. I met her through Iliaktida and the interview took place in their premises in Mytilini, Lesvos. At the time of the interview, she was learning Greek and she was enrolled in the local secondary school. Her dream was to go on with her studies and become an airhostess. She was also participating in the intercultural adult choir *CANTAlaloun* [CANTAλαλουν][12] and when I visited Lesvos in June again, I attended one of their beautiful performances in the opening ceremony of the University of the Aegean Social Sciences Conferences. Hers was one of the harshest stories of serial borders crossing and gender-based violence that I listened to in Lesvos. Warda has lived her whole life in borderlands, in-between zones as a 'sans papier' stateless person:

After some time, that is after 10 years without my family, and while I had grown up and had come to realize certain things, I learnt that my family had been in Saudi Arabia and I started communicating with them. In the beginning it was through mobiles and then when internet came, we would talk via skype and other platforms. When my mother went to Saudi Arabia, one of her two brothers invited her to Italy, where he had already migrated. But the invitation was just for my mother. So, my mother went there but she didn't stay for long. From Italy she went to Sweden and she applied for asylum there. She also asked to reunite with her children. When she started this process of reunification, she put down my name together with my other siblings. But I was still in Yemen. So, my mother got in touch with my aunt and told her that she had asked for me to join her in Sweden with her other children and so I had to leave within a month. So, I went to Saudi Arabia to prepare my papers for Sweden. But the Swedish Embassy in Saudi Arabia had taken the decision not to take any more refugees for Sweden. I thus stayed in Saudi Arabia for some time, as there was no other solution for me, and I had found myself in a limbo. I know Arabic very well, so while in Saudi Arabia, I would gather the neighbours' children and help them with their school study as a kind of job. I didn't have any other means, so I had to earn my living. I stayed there for 2 years and then my mother tried to take me to Sweden again, together with my siblings. But we had been staying in Saudi Arabia illegally and I had to pay a lot of money to Saudi Arabia, more than 40,000 riyals as a penalty for staying there without papers. My mother could not possibly gather this money, and we didn't have it either. So, my mother told us, don't go on with this process in Saudi Arabia, because there is no way I can collect so much money to send you. You should rather go to Ethiopia, where there is a Swedish Embassy and it will be easier, you can definitely go there. You see, there was no Swedish Embassy in Somalia. But first we should go back to Somalia as they would deport us from Saudi Arabia without paying any money for the transportation, via the process 'go home'. Since there was no other solution then, we decided to go back to Somalia first. But when travelling back to Somalia we decided to get off at a town that is very near the borders with Ethiopia, rather than go to Mogadishu. From this town it was easy to cross the borders to Ethiopia, illegally of course. We finally reached Ethiopia and when we got there, we applied for reunification at the Swedish Embassy, but we were rejected, so we finally had to go back to Somalia after all.

Warda's story sketches a subjective geography, which defies state borders, but becomes too dense and too heavy to be poetically expressed. Her trajectory unfolds as an Odyssey of forced displacement, an *assemblage* of countries with different legislations and administrative arrangements vis-a-vis, migration, illegal crossings and residencies, diverse spatial practices and tactics, adverse economic conditions, complicated family relations and obligations, as well as unpredicted effects. But her journey also differs from the real Odyssey in the sense that her Ithaka was not meant to be her native town, but rather her mother's settlement in Sweden. Warda had found herself in conditions of what Jennifer Hyndman calls, 'extended exile' (2019, 7) and her journey was meant to be without return.

In moving between countries, Warda had to adapt to a range of cultural practices and ways of thinking, communicate in different languages and succumb to different modalities of government. Her condition is that of what Alfred Schuetz (1944) calls the 'labyrinth of the stranger', a condition of disorientation in which she cannot find shelter in what is being offered to her and even worse, she cannot find her way out, despite her continuous 'zigzagging between prohibitions' (Agier 2016, 2). In a tragic way, the maze of her wanderings did bring her back to her birth city, but it was in the short period that she resided in her 'home country' that the most horrible events in her life happened: being brutally raped at her friend's house and being forced to stay silent and undergo abortion and infibulation by her father.[13]

While Warda's life has unfolded in the comings and goings, settled in the border situation, it was in the in-between spaces of movement and temporary residencies that 'agential cuts' (Barad 2017) emerged. As Trinh has noted, the middle ground in Chinese theories of art and knowledge 'is where extremes lose their power; where all directions are (still) possible and hence where one can assume with intensity one's freedom of movement' (2011, 70). Warda did not exactly become free to move, but she did manage to escape the striated spaces of violent patriarchy through her elder brother's help. The dark times she went through became too heavy for a poetic rendition of her narrative:

> I didn't know what to do, so I thought of a solution. I found my elder brother and talked to him, I told him the whole story from the beginning. My brother told me that he had felt that something bad had happened to me, but he hadn't found the strength or the courage to talk to me and ask me what I had gone through. He then told me that if father had taken the decision for an arranged marriage, then it would eventually happen, so there was no other solution than run away in secret. But I was wondering, how am I going to run away? My father knows everybody here. But my brother said, 'there is no way you will stay here, the best pace to go is Turkey, everybody is going there now. I know people who do fake papers and stuff, I will see to it.' And then I asked him, yes but I will need money, how can I go away like that, on such a long journey without money?' My brother was saving for his wedding, but he told me you can take this money and go. When you find another country and settle down and get a job, then you can send me back money for my wedding and my family. So, this is how I went to Turkey.

In seeking and accepting her brother's help, Warda made an agential cut in negotiating 'her own protection, but not under conditions of her own making', as Hyndman has aptly observed (2019, 6). Her narrative is underpinned by a reflective mode that emerges from the cosmopolitan experience of what Seloua Luste Boulbina configures as 'between-worlds' (2013). But Turkey was a different local world from the countries that Warda had previously lived in: It was very difficult to find a job and impossible to socialize. Warda's experiences had created a condition of what Agier calls 'banal or ordinary cosmopolitism' (2016, 9). His argument is that cosmopolitism should not be restricted to the practices of a globalized elite, but rather the consolidation of 'the experience of the roughness of the world by all those who, by taste, necessity or compulsion, by desire or by habit, are led to live in several places almost simultaneously and, in the absence of ubiquity, to live increasingly in mobility, even in an in-between' (viii). Agier's notion of 'banal cosmopolitism' as a condition enforced upon stateless subjects like Warda, makes connections with a body of feminist literature that has introduced gender analytics in the discussion of minoritarian cosmopolitanisms, including the experience of migrants, refugees and asylum seekers (see Vieten 2012). It was through this enforced mode of gendered banal cosmopolitism that Warda fell out of place in Turkey and sought alternative ways to emerge from the labyrinth:

> I thought Turkey would be perfect, the best country in the world, but it was quite the opposite. I had imagined Turkey being like Saudi Arabia, but I was with my family then. I thought that I could join a group of people, find a job, even offer some volunteering work, but nothing happened, I did try to do something, but in vain. I had no job, no home, there were some people who offered hospitality for one or two days, but then it was understood that you had to go out and find a job. So, I was again desperate and didn't know what to do and I didn't know the language either. When we were in Saudi Arabia, Somalian girls who didn't know Arabic could find a job. They would become cleaners, or work in restaurants, doing the washing-up, but in Turkey it wasn't like that at all. Then I talked with my mother; she didn't know why I had gone to Turkey in the first place. I just told her that I was in Turkey and that I wanted her to invite me to Sweden. She sent me some money and I found the smugglers who took me to Greece by boat.

Borders in Warda's condition are, thus, endlessly redrawn, negotiated and resisted: They become central in her lived experiences, thus fleshing out what Agier has identified as 'the centrality of the border' (2016, 8). Borderlands, however, are time/space blocks with multiple and diverse functions and manifestations, even when their geographical territories are the same. While Lesvos became for Warda a refuge from extreme regimes of gender-based violence, for other refugee women it would be experienced as a zone of settlement. Once arriving in Lesvos by boat, Linda took the decision not to move on to Europe, at a time when she could still do it, but instead find a job as an interpreter and experiment with a new beginning in her life:

> So when we reached there [Lesvos], they left the group with other people and they only took me to their offices. They prepared coffee, they called a doctor to examine me, they offered me cigarettes and they even called my family, to say that I had reached Greece and I was fine. They told me I was safe and that I shouldn't be afraid and then they asked me: 'What are you going to do now? Are you going to leave? I said 'I don't know' and then they told me 'since you know Greek, you should stay here and work as an interpreter'. I still said 'I don't know what I am going to do' and it is true: I had nothing in my mind. That was on February 6, 2016. So they told me, 'ok, think about it'. Because at the time, most people were leaving – going to Germany, France and other European countries. But I didn't have anything in my mind. I hadn't thought about anything. The only thing I knew was that I wanted to leave Turkey, just this.[14]

I have already introduced Linda in Chapter 1, in fleshing out entanglements of power relations and forces of desire within *mobility assemblages*. Linda recounted the process of her decision to settle in Lesvos in a cinematic narrative mode: scene after scene, line after line. The advice she got in her first encounter with the border authorities carry signs of what Kelly Oliver has configured as *carceral humanitarianism*: 'asylum seekers become targets of the new humanitarian military – in the case of Syrian refugees, navies and coast guards operating in the Mediterranean Sea. Their rescue at sea becomes a way of containing their unauthorized movement. Once rescued, migrants are sorted, contained within fences and checkpoints, and monitored' (2017, 185).

In reviving her dialogue with the border authorities in Lesvos, it was as if Linda was contemplating her decision once again. At the time of the interview, she had already worked three years in Lesvos as an interpreter, she had fallen in love and got married and she was living in a rented flat with her partner. She had settled, or had she? When I visited Lesvos again in June 2019 and we met, she was trying to get an official recognition of her sociology degree in Syria, while also thinking about moving to the mainland with a rough entrepreneurship project in mind. Linda had become 'a border woman', but not in Azaldúan terms, as she was never free to go back and forth the sea borders. Her condition cannot fit into Agier's three figures of the border dweller either – the wanderer, who seeks an entry to Europe, the *métèque* who works without documents and the pariah, who resides in camps. (2016, 58). Hers is rather a gendered banal cosmopolitism, 'a prolonged time and a border space, in which people learn the ways of the world and of other people [. . .] a place where a new cosmopolitan subject is emerging' according to Agier (9). Living in this in-between place, the borderland leaves open possibilities for future real and imagined journeys. The border becomes the space of the adventurer, as Agier has aptly observed (62).

But 'there are different degrees of foreignness depending on the border situation and the moment in the situation' Agier has argued (59). Linda's ambivalence around her decision to stay in Lesvos was very different from the majority of my interviewees, who expressed their frustration of being stranded in Lesvos without anything to do but wait, or just 'push time' (36). Their experience is a manifestation of spatiotemporal borders at work, since borders are simultaneously spatial (here and over there), temporal (before and after) and socially constructed (us and 'the other') Agier has maintained (23). It is precisely the experience of being in-between places and times that pushes border dwellers in the margins of the social: 'all I do here is sleep, wake up, go to the bathroom, do kitchen chores. I will go mad, if it goes on like that',[15] Anna told me in frustration at the end of her story, while expressed her desire to do something: 'my life cannot go on like that, seven days a week stuck inside this flat. It is not easy to live like that, day after day, this is my life. But how long can I live like that? How long?' As Jennifer Hyndman and Werona Giles have argued the material conditions and depictions of refugees waiting endlessly for some sort of legal recognition contributes to 'a feminization of asylum' (2011). Moreover, this endless waiting is a form of 'slow violence' (Hyndman 2019, 7).

The uncertainty of a life in suspension, the liminality of border situations is also, always, already political, depending on both local and global geopolitical situations. At the age of twenty-one, Somi found herself in an Iraqi refugee camp for Iranian dissidents fighting for the dream of a secular democracy. But when Iraq was invaded in 2003, everything changed and Somi found herself entangled in a war machine that was beyond her control and comprehension: 'I had never seen a war in my life, so I was only there for six months and then the US started attacking and bombarding Iraq. We were very scared'.[16]

Borders are bound up with lasting regimes of violence and states of war. But the atrocities and impasses of the Iraqi war in its multifarious entanglements with histories of colonialism and imperialism have created an extremely oppressive state of domination not just for the Iraqi people, but also for the various groups of its migrant and refugee population. Thus, global wars have transformed, shifted and multiplied borders, rendering them riskier and more uncertain. The transition to the US occupation seemed to be the end of violence, but was it? Somi's story vividly recounts the frustration of being enclosed 'in safety': 'this was a closed camp, you didn't have the permission to leave, to go outside, it wasn't like this'.

The proliferation of walls and of confinement technologies mark new border situations of a supposedly globalized world. By making the interns of the Iranian dissidents' camp invisible, the Iraqi occupying forces prolonged the time and space of the interns' border lives, while at the same time creating pools of human ammunition for future wars. Somi found herself caught in a border trap, unable to communicate with the outer world both physically and virtually. Moreover, there were internal borders within the camp itself and a harsh regime of gender segregation in place: 'men and women were separate from each other, they were not in the same area and they were not allowed to communicate; any communication between men and women would have been severely punished'. This regime of proliferating borders was finally blown up after 2006, when the US army handed over power to the Iraqi government, who took control of the camp, but this time under new relations with the Iranian regime: 'at one point the Iraqi government started attacking the camp through the Iranian Cat forces, as they called them'. The first time they attacked the camp they were only using clubs, sticks and whips'.

But there were more fierce attacks with machine guns, tanks and many victims. In the end, the United Nations Refugee Agency (UNHCR) had to intervene recognizing all the residents of the camp as persons of concern and that's how a long process of relocation started which eventually took Somi to Albania and through 'illegal' border crossing to Greece. Situated within the context of global wars, then, is cosmopolitanism a useful lens in understanding women's lived experiences of forced displacement? This is what I want to consider in the concluding section of this chapter.

MOVING BETWEEN WORLDS

The history of the concept of cosmopolitanism goes back to Diogenes the Cynic (412-323) and his claim to be a cosmopolitan [kosmopolitês] when asked about his place of origin. But as Nina Glick Schiller and Andrew Irving point out (2015, 1), when we consider the emergence of this concept, we should not forget that it was first articulated by a philosopher, who in the process of his life also inhabited the subject positions of a criminal, an exile, an outcast and a slave.[17] Whether as a philosophical idea, a political stance or a set of cultural practices, cosmopolitanism is not easy to pin down as a notion and there is a significant body of literature in the field of cosmopolitanism studies, populated by tensions, disagreements and debates.[18] 'Who can afford a cosmopolitan identity?' Zygmunt Bauman has asked linking cosmopolitanism to a globalized way of life, structured by the inequalities of those who float above the local world and those who are constrained and sometimes confined within it. In developing the idea of 'a cosmopolitan vision', Ulrich

Beck has argued that 'in the struggles over belonging, the actions of migrants and minorities provide examples of dialogic imaginative ways of life and everyday cosmopolitanism' (2002, 30). There is indeed today a strand in the relevant literature that have brought the figures of the migrant, the uprooted and the exile in the cosmopolitan condition. As Steven Vertovec has suggested migrants regardless of their wealth, bring 'a cosmopolitan competency' as a toolkit for their journey: 'we might understand cosmopolitanism as comprising a combination of attitudes, practices and abilities gathered from experiences of travel or displacement, transnational contact and diasporic identification' (2009, 5).

What is missing from all these studies according to Agier, is an engagement with the everyday lived experiences of sharing the world. It is from this gap that his notion of 'banal cosmopolitism' emerges to address the ordinary experience of crossing borders: 'Who better than "the uprooted" to give us the concrete and empirical trace of this new cosmopolitan condition and to reflect on the political perspective that it establishes on a common world scale?' Agier asks (2016, 76). As I have already shown in this chapter, there were several stories conveying experiences of banal cosmopolitanism, but my counterargument is that despite its porousness and flexibility, 'banal cosmopolitanism' cannot be stretched in the cases of displacement under conditions of war and destructive violence, wherein both 'cosmos' and 'polis', as its two main etymological parts, are simply annihilated. 'Can war be the vehicle of growing cosmopolitan consciousness of the world?' Galin Tihanov has succinctly asked (2015, 29) In response to this question, what I argue is that extreme circumstances of displacement might foreclose possibilities for being open to the world and can also disrupt dreams of mutual understanding and hopes for acting in concert. Here, I agree with Hyndman about the need 'for a larger project of *feminist political geography*' (2019, 6, emphasis in the text), since feminist geopolitics may have reached its limitations as a methodological and epistemological framework.

Rather than engaging with theories of any of the strands within cosmopolitan studies what women's travelling stories unravel is what Luste Boulbina (2013) has called 'between-worlds' emerging from 'the science of the concrete'. Migrant and refugee women's stories were about their experiences of tinkering with what they encounter as they passed through places and spaces; this is what Luste Boulbina means by 'the science of the concrete'. Their trajectories were never linear, but as we have seen above, always complicated and unpredictable. Women's stories did not so much focus on places of departure or arrival, but rather in the in-between, places they crossed and passed through. It is when relations with places and spaces are broken that one starts to think about them, Luste Boulbina argues: 'to migrate is to wander, to remove obstacles, to bounce' (2013, 21). In Luste Boulbina's configuration then, mobility under conditions of forced displacement is not just physical and geographical, taking you from one place to another, but also imaginary and symbolical, marking ruptures and 'shaking the ghosts of the past' (21). Migrant and refugee women's storyworlds were made up of mobilities, which were either chosen or compelled, of ruptures with roots, of absences of 'home', as well as of temporary and uncertain anchorages.

NOTES

1. Derya's story, a café in Athens, narrated in English, 17 April 2019.
2. For a critical discussion of these events, see Yavuz and Balci 2018 and Shiveley 2018.
3. For an extended analysis of the histories and politics of the Gülen movement, see Tee 2016.
4. In *Expressionism in Philosophy: Spinoza*, Deleuze (1992) contrasts Spinoza's and Descartes' methods by claiming that the former works under the assumption that the cause of a thing is known better than the thing itself, while the latter claims the exact opposite.
5. This agenda was presented in the European Commission in May 2015. See (EC, 2015).
"Explanatory Note on the 'Hotspot' Approach.", Statewatch, https://www.statewatch.org/news/2015/jul/eu-com-hotsposts.pdf [Accessed 1 March 2020].
6. See Amnesty International, 2016: 'Our Hope is Broken': European Paralysis Leaves Thousands of Refugees Stranded in Greece. https://www.amnesty.org/download/Documents/EUR2548432016ENGLISH.PDF [Accessed 1 March 2020].
7. For a full text of this agreement, see https://www.consilium.europa.eu/en/press/press-releases/2016/03/18/eu-turkey-statement/ [Accessed, 1 March 2020].
8. For details of this crisis, see, https://www.nytimes.com/2020/02/29/world/europe/turkey-migrants-eu.html
9. Hannah Arendt to Karl Jaspers, letter dated 6 August 1955 in Arendt and Jaspers 1992, 264.
10. Arendt, *Denktagebuch. Bd. 1: 1950–1973. Bd 2: 1973–1975* in Ludz and Nordmann 2002, XIII.2.295.
11. Warda's story, *Iliaktida* premises, narrated in Arabic, Mytilini Lesvos, 11 April 2019.
12. See https://www.facebook.com/CANTALALOUN/
13. Infibulation is the most severe type of female genital mutilation. See https://www.endfgm.eu/female-genital-mutilation/what-is-fgm [Accessed, 5 March 2020] .
14. Linda's story at her flat in Mytilini, Lesvos, narrated in Greek, 9 April 2019.
15. Anna's story, a flat in Mytilini Lesvos, narrated in French, 8 April 2019.
16. Somi's story, a café in Athens, narrated in Farsi, 7 December 2019.
17. For a critical overview of Diogenes life and philosophical ideas, see amongst others, Navia 2005.
18. See Vieten 2012 and Schiller and Irving 2014 for a comprehensive overview of this field.

Interlude I

NADIA'S STORY

I am Nadia and I am from Afghanistan. I was born on 24 October 1998 and when I was very young, we moved from Afghanistan and we travelled to many countries: We went to Iran, then to Syria and then the war started. Our life was very normal in Syria and we were happy. But when the war started there, it was unbelievable. My mother used to tell us about the Russian war with the Afghani Mujahidins. She was young then, but this war was very similar to the war in Syria. So that was the reason we travelled from Syria to Turkey. I was very young at the time, fifteen years old, or rather fourteen and a half, and I stayed a little more than three years in Turkey, alone.

When we went to Turkey, the circumstances were not good for Afghan refugees. Arab refugees were welcome, but not the Afghanis. So, these were very difficult days. This is when we decided to travel to a European country, because my mother could not go back to Iran or Afghanistan. There were other families, who moved from Syria to Turkey with us, we lived in the same area and we left together; we were about eight families. But these families didn't want to stay in Turkey, life was not easy. So, my mother decided to travel with them, for my future, for my younger sister's future.

But when we travelled to the border, the Turkish–Greece border, unfortunately that was the bad time when I got separated from my mother and my sister. We had never anticipated that, and I could never have imagined my life without my mother. I was young at that time. Somehow, the smuggler took us from the city to the border site. He kept us in different cars, because there were many check points on the way, and he wanted to show the guards that there was a family inside each car. There were three cars, and they asked my mother whether they could put me in a different car, with another family who didn't have a child. They said that we would all be together at the border point, where they would put us in a boat and help us cross the Turkish border to go to Greece. But when we reached the border point, the police arrived and only the first group with my mother and my sister managed to cross the river. We stayed behind and escaped, while the last car was arrested.

This was the sad night that I got separated from my mother and sister. But the river they crossed was not a Greek river; it was a small river between Greece, Bulgaria and Turkey. So, they found themselves in a forest in Bulgaria. My mother had a phone, but because I was very young, I didn't have one, so it was not possible to contact them and keep in touch with my mother. I was feeling lost, I was crying a lot and I started asking the smugglers, 'where is my mother and my sister?' And of course, my mother was worrying more than me, because she was an adult and she knew how to deal with the situation, but I was not with her. Later, when I found her, she told me that she almost died that night because I was not with her and she was on the other side of the border. And then my mother and sister spent three nights in a forest in Bulgaria. They stayed there to wait for me, but also because they didn't know where to go, which way to take; they had just crossed a river and they didn't even know that the country they were in was Bulgaria, not Greece. So, after I think two nights there were some robbers who came and stole their money, watches, mobiles, everything. And I am not sure, but my mother and my sister told me that it was the police, who robbed them that night. They recognized their faces the next day when they came to arrest them with their uniforms: They were clearly the same people. So, they took them to a camp and for one week they put them in an underground prison, and they didn't have anything, they had taken everything from them. My mother was so upset, and she was telling me that she was alive, but she was feeling like dead and I was feeling the same.

I was crying for many, many hours and I didn't eat anything for two days, I think. I didn't eat, because I was thinking, 'where will I go?' I didn't have any family in Turkey, or anywhere else. Just in Afghanistan I had some of my uncles, my father's brothers. But it was because of them that my mother had escaped from the country. So, I didn't know anybody and the people I was travelling with were also strangers to me, they were not my family, or even friends; we were just refugees and we had come together to cross the border.

And then the smugglers were trying to calm me down and they were telling me, 'we will get you through' and I kept asking 'where is my mother?' and they were telling me that my mother was in the only group that had crossed the border. And then I said 'ok, if she has crossed the border, I want to hear her voice'. But because my mother didn't have her cell phone with her, none of them had, it was not easy to contact them.

This is how I got separated from my mother and later in Turkey without my family and without any money I faced so many difficulties. At one point I wanted to die, I didn't want to live anymore, because I didn't have anyone, no family, nobody who knew me, and I was so young at that time. I didn't know what to do and the smugglers kept telling me, 'we will get you through', but after many days I realized that they would not.

I stayed some months with these people. They were not letting me go and I didn't have any place to go, so it was very difficult; one of the worst parts of my life is that time, when I was in Turkey alone and I didn't have anyone with me and I was very young. If I was mature and I was like an adult, I would know how to handle the situation, but I kept listening to them and they were lying to me and they were so bad to me as well.

And then, after some time I managed to move from that place to another, but that was not very easy. They were so powerful people, the smuggles; they were mafia and they had guns, they had power; in front of them I was nothing. During this time, I didn't know where my mother and my sister were, but then I was taken to another family. This family was nice, and I started working in their textile workshop.

I worked with them until I came to Greece and yes during the first months they didn't pay me anything; I was working twelve hours a day there, from morning until evening, for seven, eight and sometimes nine to twelve hours, doing over time; some of the work they had was urgent to finish and I was working with the other workers of the textile workshop, but in return I didn't get anything. It was, yes, it was I think for five to six months that they didn't pay me because I was staying with them for free. I didn't have any money and they were helping me with food and accommodation and after five or six months, I think it was six months, yes, they talked to me and said, 'we will give you 500 Turkish lira per month'. I was so happy, because I was, I was alive. I needed to survive, so I was happy for this, otherwise I was not happy in my life, because I was living with strangers.

I had very hard days there and life was very difficult for me; nobody understood my feelings and I didn't know where my family was. So yes, it was I think 500 lire, I started with a salary and I kept paying back for my accommodation and for my food; they gave me lunch, but for dinner and breakfast I had to manage with my own money. Everyone in the textile workshop used to have lunch for free, but for breakfast and dinner, we had to manage.

And then, yes, the days passed, and they were a big family. Somehow, they were nice, but in some ways, I was not their daughter or their sister, so I didn't have anyone. And again, when it comes to religion, I am a Muslim and they were Muslims too, so there are some instructions and rules in the Muslim religion and they kept talking about me, like 'she is alone and now she doesn't have anyone', so I became close to them. And they had one son who was mentally disabled, so after some time I found out that they were trying to marry him off to me. Their son was not very young, he was very old I think, yes, and he was working with his brothers in this workshop. He didn't speak a lot, and they were so cruel to him, they just exploited him. So, while we worked together, I was helping him a lot; I had seen how the other brothers tortured him because he didn't understand. So, they were asking him, 'bring the large size sleeves' and perhaps he would bring the small size, or he wouldn't understand the colours. When I started working, I had the same difficulties. I didn't know what they were asking me to do, as I didn't understand the language. I was not able to speak at all, but in the area we were living there were many refugee workers from Afghanistan, Pakistan and Iran. So, I could speak with the Afghanis in Farsi, and I had also learned Urdu when I was in Syria. Knowing Urdu helped me a lot in Turkey, while working in the garment industry. Some of the workers were from Pakistan and they would help me with the language, but I still used to make many mistakes, like the brother of the family. They used to shout at me and sometimes, they shouted a lot, but with their brother, they were really cruel: they tortured him, they used to beat and slap him. So, when I saw what they were doing to him, I could not keep calm, I was trying to move in fast and help him quickly. I stayed three years with them, and they started thinking that since I didn't have anyone and I was so kind to their brother, it would be a good idea to marry him off to me. I became so upset about this and I didn't know what to do.

There were some refugees, who used to come and stay for some months and then they would travel to Greece. I knew about these things, because many of the refugees when they came, they were hired, although they were paid less, and then they travelled. So our textile was like a family textile and most of the girls who were working there came from the same family, like the wife of our patron, our boss I mean. She was working with us and so was the sister of the patron, as well as his sister in law. Some of their cousins were also working there and the rest of us were refugees and strangers. So, I started talking with some of the girls and I was asking them about how they had come from Afghanistan, and they were telling me their story: 'we paid an agent' and these and these things. I wanted to know because when we came from Syria, I didn't know how my mother had managed the agent. I knew how we had left Syria, but I didn't know how she had paid, who she had paid, how much she had paid. I hadn't got the chance to talk about this with my mother, because in Syria it was not an easy situation, we had escaped the war and we were not even sure that we would survive. There were so many air strikes, it was not easy.

So, I started asking around, since there were many refugees in that area. There were mosques there and some people when they came to Turkey for the first time and they didn't have a house, they used to go to the mosques area. They used to hang around, take showers, sleep there and after some time if they had money, they would travel to Greece. If they didn't have any money, they started working in the same area, as there were many job opportunities.

You could easily find a job, because there were thousands of thousands of textiles, where people, refugee people used to work. And then the girls were saying 'we will go to Greece and our life in Afghanistan was in danger and this way we can go' and so I was always thinking of going, wondering whether my mother and sister were alive or not.

The patron's wife was a very nice woman; she was very kind, very different from her sister in law. She was always talking to me like her younger sister. Sometimes I cried with her, mostly I cried alone, because I didn't know anybody; these people were not my family, and nobody cared about how much I was suffering. I didn't know how to live this life and it was all very hard. And then in 2016, in December, the people I was talking with, told me: 'if you want, you can travel, but you will need this much money'. So, I started saving, as I was hoping to come to Greece to find my mother. I didn't know then that they had never come to Greece and that they had gone to Bulgaria, by mistake.

After some time, the situation became unbearable for me, as I felt that they really wanted me to marry their mentally disabled son and I didn't want it. The patron's wife, was telling me 'you shouldn't because their son is mentally disabled', and I was telling myself, 'I don't know what to do, I want to run away but where can I go? I don't have anyone'. So, I kept begging the patron's wife to help me somehow. People, when they are refugees in Turkey, they go and register at the UNHCR offices. But my bad luck was that in the city I was living, there were no UNHCR offices. There was actually one, but it was just for disabled people, pregnant women, or other refugees in very serious situations. I had to go to Ankara, which was six hours away, as I was living in Istanbul. So, yes, I kept asking the patron's wife to let me go and register. I needed to have a document with my name, my age and my nationality, so if something happened, I would have proof of my identity and nobody could force me to do anything. But in order to register, I needed to travel, so I started saving; I didn't spend money for anything other than my rent and my very basic needs. The rest I used to save with the patron's wife and the patron, so I was asking them to allow me to go to Ankara and get an ID or an asylum card, any identification document really. The patron's wife said, 'I will ask my husband and if he agrees, I will help you with this.'

As I told you, there were many refugees in the area, so there were two other families, who wanted to go to Ankara and I said, 'I can go with them'. I asked them to take me with them, because since the day I had entered the family of the textile workshop, I had never travelled anywhere. We had never separated, and I had never gone anywhere without the family. But the patron was reluctant to let me go and he was saying, 'no, you are alone, how can I give you this permission, tomorrow if something happens, people will blame us', and this and that. But I also kept telling them, 'look, if I get sick, what shall I do? I don't have anything, there are so many problems you should understand'. After asking them many, many times they let me travel to Ankara with one of the families going there. I went to Ankara, but it was not very helpful.

I travelled all night with the family and when we reached there, we went to find the UNHCR offices. It was early in the morning, 6 o'clock and there were many people queuing, waiting to register. We stood in the queue until 10 or 11, and when my turn came, they asked me many questions. They were asking for my guardian because I was underage, I was very young, but I said, 'I don't have anyone' and they said, 'how did you come here?' I told the truth, everything I knew. They were asking about Afghanistan, but I was very young when we left Afghanistan with my mother, so I remembered very little about Afghanistan and Iran, but I did remember everything from Syria. They kept asking questions and taking breaks for thirty minutes and then again, they would call me in a different room, asking questions and then they asked me to wait again. So, they made me wait until the evening, but in the end, they didn't give me any document, yes, they didn't give me anything. They asked to see somebody from the Istanbul family with their ID card and everything. I said 'these people are very busy, they will not come for me, they are not my relatives'. I kept asking them but they didn't listen to me and I was the last person there, when they closed the UNHCR office. There was the watchman, two officers and I was the last person. And there was also the family I needed to go back with, because my boss had bought a return ticket for me and I had to go back with them to Istanbul; otherwise they would think very badly of me and maybe they would not take me back again. So, I kept asking the family that we had travelled together to wait for me, and they were nice, they did wait for me, until the UNHCR office closed.

So, the UNHCR people in Turkey were not very helpful, they were not like here, in Greece. Here there are difficulties, but once you get a chance to go to the asylum service, they register you when you declare your nationality or your country. They do not interrogate you about your guardian, even if you are underage. I think this is right, because everybody is in a different situation, there is nowhere to escape, some other things might have happened. If people don't have any documents, and you don't help them, their life will be like an animal: without identity, you don't have any right, you are nothing. In Turkey, my life was like an animal, I was living an animal's life, I didn't have any family or friends, and I had no identity. But as I said, the UNHCR people closed their office in Ankara and they told me: 'if you want to stay tonight, you should stay here and then tomorrow we can talk again'. I said, 'tomorrow nothing will change, I will give you a phone number, you can talk to these people, the family I am living with, please'. But they didn't listen to me; they only asked me to stay for one night. But where could I stay? I could not stay there. There were some refugees, who were sleeping rough outside the office, but I could not stay with them, I was afraid.

So, I went back with the same family, but I was very sad, because I had gone to Ankara for nothing. When I went back, I kept one thing in my mind: I will not stay in this country, I don't have anything and they will force me to marry their brother, since the father of the family was very strict. Everybody obeyed and respected him: they watched and fulfilled his demands. I was feeling so scared, I was even afraid of myself, what would I say if he asked me to marry his son? I had heard from many of the family members that they were really planning to do this. And then they did come, and the father asked me about the marriage, but I said 'no, I cannot do this, it's better to kill me, I cannot do this.' And they said, 'you don't have anyone, what we have decided, is a good thing, and you should obey, you are a Muslim, so you cannot stay your whole life like this'. I said, 'yes, but I have my mother'. I was always hoping; sometimes I became disappointed, I was thinking that maybe my mother had died, but most of the time I was hoping that I could find them, or maybe they would find me.

While all this was going on, I kept talking with the patron's wife, who was compassionate and understanding. I told her that I wanted to go to Greece, but she was shocked to hear this. She said, 'you have just travelled to Ankara and now you think you can go to another country?', I said, 'no, I need to go, I have to go, otherwise I may kill myself here, I can't stay here anymore'. And then I asked her 'how much money do I have with you? I work here' and she said you have this much money. Then I kept asking the girls at the workshop about how much their brothers or fathers had paid the smugglers. The patron's wife told me 'it's not easy, what you are thinking, you know how difficult it was to come here from the other family'. She knew that when I was with the smugglers, they were not letting me go anywhere, it was very, very difficult to release myself from them. So, she was asking me: 'why do you want to do this to yourself? It's not easy; if any of them knows that you don't have any money, that you are alone and so young, they might kidnap you or take you somewhere else'. I said 'I know, but if your husband talks with one of the families that are going anyway, and they help me, I can go with them, I will pay of course. If there is not enough money, I will work more to raise it, I will pay for my way, I will not ask anything from you'. She said, 'no, the money you have worked, we have it with us, but the thing you are thinking, to travel to Greece from Turkey is illegal, I am sure they will not allow you'.

I was so disappointed, and I was not eating properly, I was so depressed and mostly I was crying. I remember when I was working in the textile, everyone was busy with the stitching and when I was walking around, so nobody could see me, my eyes were always full of tears, I was always crying, I was not happy at all. Finally the patron's wife said, 'Ok, I will talk to my husband' and there was a nice family, there was a mother with two sons, six children, yes, two elder sons and four daughters. Two of the daughters were very young, but the other two were working with us at the textile and the mother was also working there. And so, I came to Greece with them, they were an Arab family and we came the land way in one container, forty people; they allowed me to come with this family.

And then I managed to come to Greece and I still remember that when we arrived, they left us at Larissa station. There is a park and I slept there for two nights with some Afghani families. The Afghanis stayed for some hours and then they found accommodation, as they had some money. Later I learnt that they travelled to another country. I had very little money and I didn't want to spend it, so I decided to stay in the park. There was an Arab family there and as I could understand Arabic, I could hear them saying that they were trying to find somewhere they could stay for free. So, I was hoping to do the same, go to a place where I wouldn't have to pay. I stayed in the park for some days and now that I work here, I see this park every day on my way to work. It feels strange to see the same place that I first stayed when I came to Greece and I didn't have anything, maybe two shirts, one or two pants and no house, nothing: and now it's more than a year.

After two nights, the Arab family found a squat, which was in Aharnon Street and its name is Yasmin 2. It was a school, so they went there, and they took me with them. I went and stayed in this squat. It was a five-floor building and I was staying on the fourth floor, but again life was not easy. You have to fight with life, I learnt this, otherwise I could not have got out of all the situations I had to confront in my life. At some point I felt I would kill myself, because when you don't have a home, when you don't have anything, you think your life is useless.

I stayed in the same squat for one month and twenty days and from there I started talking with other Afghani families. There were many families in the same squat, Arabs, Kurdish, Afghanis and also two Turkish families. It was very crowded, and the conditions were very bad. There were just two toilets, one for men and one for women, and the door of the bathroom was broken. So, during the time I stayed there, I couldn't take a shower and you can imagine my situation. There was no one to watch the door for me, because when you take a shower, it doesn't take one or two minutes, it takes many minutes and that's why I couldn't shower, I was afraid. Some of the Afghani families, who were looking for a house said that rents were cheap in that area. I asked them 'how much?' and they said, 'you can pay five Euros per night'. I said, but in a month, it will still be 150 Euros. They said 'yes, but it's better and safer than this squat.' We didn't have any information about the squat before we went there, but some of the people used to take drugs. In the room they gave me, there was one mother, a single mother with her baby, and there were also two men. They had divided the room in four, with blankets as separators; there was no wall and it was not very safe. Those two men used to bring their friends in the room and the single mother always went to a friend's house and she wouldn't come back for two or three days. So, I was staying awake all night, because the men were smoking hashish, they played loud music and they didn't care if the other person wanted to sleep. We were in the same room; it was very exhausting, and it was not very good. So, that was the situation in that squat and after that I decided to rent a house with the Afghan family.

I went to the GCR, the Greek Council for Refugees for help, but they said, 'until you get the asylum card, the pre-registration card for asylum, we cannot help you'. So yes, I came here May 2, [2017] and after I think seventeen or eighteen days, on May 19, I got my asylum card. I was going regularly to the *Caritas* organization and I was calling from there to the asylum service and luckily one day, they answered my phone and they asked me to go there the following day. I went there on May 19 and I registered myself. I got my white card and then I went to many organizations, which provide free accommodation. But they said, 'yes, we have registered your name, but it's a long queue, you need to wait, it may take months, sometimes it can take eight months, the waiting list is very long. Your name is now registered, but we have many others, who registered before you.' I didn't see any hope, so I said it's better to find something by myself and I started looking. I was walking in the streets of Athens a lot, and in Victoria Square, there were many Afghanis. People were saying that it's not safe to go to these areas, but I thought, there were so many things that were not safe for me, but I had to do it. And then we tried to look for a house, with the Afghani family at the squat and in the end, we managed to find one. It was an underground flat, and it was not a good place, but at least it was better than the squat. It had a bathroom, where you could take a shower, you could sleep safely as there was no hashish or drugs. So, it was better than the squat and we moved there. And then I met another family, a woman, her daughter and her son; they were looking for a better place and they had money. So, I asked them if they could take me as well and they said 'yes, yes, why not?' And yeah, this is the flat I am staying now. We managed to rent it and now I am staying here.

After I came to Greece, I got my pre-registration ID card and I started taking some lessons in Greek. It was just after two weeks that I had started my lessons and there was another fortunate event for me. I saw there was a scholarship from the American College of Greece. When I saw that scholarship, an English learning programme for young refugees, I became very excited and I said, 'it's a good opportunity'. In the meantime, I had started going to the GCR, Greek Council for Refugees and I asked the social worker, who helped me to register to show me how to fill in the application because

I didn't have any degree or any certificate, nothing. She said, 'there are very few chances for you' but I said, 'it's OK, even if there are few chances, let's try'. I was waiting for some months for the answer and during that time I was looking for a job, because I didn't have any money. The GCR helped me register with the UNHCR Cash programme, which gives 150 Euros per month, but it is not enough. I had to pay my rent and house bills with it, but I also needed money for food and public transport. So, I registered myself in the UNHCR office and there was a very nice girl there and a Greek woman. They both approached me and told me: 'why don't you do some voluntary work? If you start with volunteering, it will be easier for you to find a job, and to start building you cv; it will somehow fill one space of your cv, your work experience.' So, I said, 'yes, I never thought of that, where can I do volunteer work?' They said, 'there are many organizations, you can go and search'.

So, I started searching; I was looking for a job, but because here in Greece, you know, there is a crisis, even for Greek people, it is even more difficult for us. I could not speak Greek at all, and I didn't even know how to get from one place to another, I was very new here. So yes, I was looking for something in several organizations and then the Red Cross, asked me to start volunteering there and I said yes. And then I went to Khora, which is a refugee community centre and they also said, 'yes' and I was very happy. I didn't find a job, this was a job without money, but I have worked with many organizations since then as a volunteer and I feel so relaxed, like serving humanity, it's something different. At some point, they started paying me, in some sections, although most of the time I am not paid, but still I am happy. I have worked with them, and I have also started working with the RLS-Refugees Legal Support in Khora. I have learnt a lot from the RLS. And in the meantime, I have been working at the Red Cross with women activities and health issues. I am also working at the children's space, children who are coming for tuition after school and I have been helping them, yes, so it has all been a very good experience.

And also, with the GCR help, I registered myself in the Red Cross tracing service: they trace refugees, families who lost relatives while travelling from one country to another. So, they registered me and after some time I received a phone call from my social worker at the Red Cross. On that day I was a little bit sick, so my phone, was in the kitchen or somewhere else. They called me many times while I was sleeping, but because I was very sick, I had not answered any calls. After two o'clock in the afternoon, I saw that there were many calls, but I didn't have credit to call them back. I never thought what they were going to tell me. I thought, maybe there was something, like I needed to go and see my social worker. Most of the times I see her by appointment, and sometimes she would call me to go. So, yes, at five I think, at five o'clock I received again a call and it was not the GCR, or the

Red Cross, but a different number. So, when I answered the phone, it was my social worker and she said, 'are you OK, where are you? We were calling you many, many times'. I said, 'I am sorry, I received all your calls, but later, I was sleeping, I am not well, I am sick'. She said, 'what happened?', I said, 'I am sick, I don't know'. So, she said, 'please come to meet me tomorrow, early in the morning'. I said 'OK', so I didn't go for my Greek lesson the next day. Instead, I went to the GCR and she said, 'look, we filled the form at the Red Cross tracing service, and I received some information from them, I wanted to talk to you about. I don't want to give you big hope but following the information you gave us about your mother, they found similar information, from another person, who is looking for a family member. And I said, 'can I see her photo? Because when I registered, they took my photo. It was a very bad photo because on that day I had been crying a lot. There is a woman in Red Cross, her name is Angelina, she is like an angel, she is very nice to me, she is like an angel, yes. She was so nice to me and she was asking questions, about how I separated from my mother and how my life was in Turkey and she was filling a form, a very large form. I kept telling her my story again, I had started my life from zero, and I was telling her everything up until my life in the squat, so, it was all about sad things and the many difficulties I had faced and I had cried a lot. And when she said, 'I need to take a photo, because without a photo, this information will just not work, and don't worry, nobody can take your photo, it's safe in our site', I said 'OK'. And then she took my photo, but I was very sad, and my eyes were very red from crying a lot.

So, that's how I asked my social worker, 'can I see the photo of the person?', because I remembered that Angelina had said that in all countries, when they fill the form, they give information and then they take photos. But my social worker said, 'I don't have it now, but we can have it later'. I said 'OK' and she asked me to go to Angelina, and I went to the Red Cross. There are different branches in the Red Cross, there is one for abducted people and they trace families; there is one for other facilities for refugees, and the way they work may be different. So, I went to the Red Cross, to Angelina, and she said, 'yes, with the information you have provided, we have found one woman' and I said, 'can I see her photo?' She said 'no, we will verify it first, before we give you any big hope. This is the rule, and the process is that we send our information to the country, they give it to the Red Cross, they contact the person and then, we will tell you'. And then I said, 'OK' and she asked me to go to my social worker the next day.

And then the next day, when I went to my social worker, she started showing me photos, and there were more than 2,500 women's photos from Afghanistan, same age with my mother. Some countries and cities were similar, but some of them were different. I looked at all the photos, but I couldn't see my mother, yes, because it was more than three years that we had got separated. In the same way that I had changed physically and mentally, they had also changed. So, I didn't recognize my mother and the social worker showed me more photos, again and again, like many photos. And then she would stop and talk with me, and then she would ask again: 'did you find someone, who looks like your mother?' and I would say, 'no'. And then she showed me again some of the photos and one of them, when I saw it, I felt like, 'yes, she is my mother'. But my mother's skin was so fair, and she didn't use to wear glasses and the woman in the photo was with glasses and her skin was very dark. I said, 'yes, she looks like my mother, but my mother was having fairer skin, and she was not wearing glasses'. And then she said, 'ok, look again carefully'. And then I looked at the photo again and I realized, 'yes, she is my mother'. I was thrilled at that time, I was shivering a lot, yes, I was, I was, I don't know. My feeling was like, something like you still cannot believe it.

And then the social worker said 'the information you gave is the same and we contacted the person, but they didn't respond. Just wait, and let's see, let's hope'. And then I asked her, 'please give the photo to me, it's my mother'. But she didn't give it to me. She said, 'I cannot take this photo, or I cannot print it out'. I said, 'I am not very lucky, but if, like I feel, she is my mother, if she is my mother, everything will change for me'. I went home, I was waiting for the information they would receive. I didn't sleep, I didn't sleep, I was very uncomfortable, I had very uncomfortable feelings. I wanted to sit but I could not, I was sitting for a while and then I would stand up, I would walk, and I didn't know what to do. I came to this place [Fokionos Negri, the place of the interview], I sat down there at this bench and I cried a lot, for two hours, more than that. I cried and then I went back home. There was no news. Then I went to Angelina, the office was closed, I went very late, I wanted to know. And then the next day, yes, first, second, third, fourth day, they called me. I went to Angelina and she said 'yes, she is your mother, and this lady has been looking for her daughter since 2014'.

And, yes, you know, when a baby is born, when it comes to the world, you are so happy and I felt more than that, happier for myself and the world. And Angelina said, 'yes, the Red Cross confirmed that your mother is there', but she was hospitalized for two days, because she was thinking the same, that maybe I was not alive anymore. And after that Angelina told me, 'we will call them, you can come, and we will let you talk'. I was waiting very impatiently and they yes, they called me to go and I went there, and they called my mother. They called the Red Cross, and my mother was also there. And when I heard my mother's voice, I was feeling very lucky, I was feeling so good. I was always talking to God, 'why did you do this to me? There are many, many millions of people in this world, why, this to me? I never did any wrong to anyone'. But at that moment, I said 'Thank You'! I found my mother, Yes!'

My mother was crying a lot, me too, we didn't talk a lot. She just kept asking me, where I had got lost. And yes, and then yes, I was not able to talk a lot, because she was very happy, and I was very happy. And my sister, didn't know about that; she just knew that there was some information and that The Red Cross had called my mother. But the day when I talked with my mother she was at school. And then my phone was a cell phone, I had a simple cell phone, not a smart phone to call them through the internet and The Red Cross told them to give me some cards to contact my family and they told me how I could make a call to them. And then I called them and yes, we talked. I don't know how many cards they gave me; I think four of five cards and each card is more than two hours. So, I think I finished all the cards in one day. And we kept talking, I called my sister and my mother, I talked a lot, I listened to them and they listened to me. And then they told me what had happened to them: how they had reached Bulgaria and how they were in the forest and how they had moved from Bulgaria to other countries. And my mother kept asking about myself: how I was in Turkey, with whom I was staying. Some of the things I explained, but not everything, because from the photo I had understood that my mother had become very weak and I did not want to hurt her. And my sister said, yes 'we eat food, we cook very delicious food, we have many good friends, German friends, we go to them, but still your place is empty. We cannot fill that place with any other thing.' So, we had some good times, but it was not good time for us, we had good food, but we didn't enjoy it, it didn't taste good to us.'

And then my mother came, my mother and my sister came, they came to meet me, yes. And you know, the day they came, it was 11 October, and on that day, I learnt that I had got the scholarship! It was on the same day, I will never forget this date: it was the same day that my mother came to Greece and it was the scholarship day. So, we celebrated the scholarship together. Now, I have my family, and since October 2017 I have finished three semesters, yes! I am very happy, and I have a job. I am working with the Solidarity Now organization and at the same time with the Refugee Legal Support-Athens, RLS. I am so happy for everything I have in my life. And yes, I am in Greece, Greece is a very nice country. People are so nice here, yes, but I haven't learnt the language yet. Still people are so helpful.

As for my studies, I completed the course of English for academic purposes, and in September, this coming September, the College may offer the refugee students who are in this programme, a scholarship for further studies. Yes, I have filled my form, but they are going to decide in September. I selected 'International Tourism and Management Hospitality'. Let's see, let's hope, yes. But again, more than everything I want to reunite with my family.

And I will be very happy, because the College says, that I can transfer my studies to Germany. There is an American College in Berlin and they can transfer me there. It's not the same city where my mother lives, but it's the same country, so let's hope, yes. Now I am talking with my mother every day, in the morning, afternoon, or evening. And yes, they came here, we had a good time. My sister has grown up, and yes, and she has become totally changed. She is more liberal now, she is more open-minded, she is very smart now, yes. And I am happy for her, because this year is her first year at college; she has passed with very good grades and she speaks German very fluently. She will study economics, business and economics.

Now that I have everything that I want and need in my life, like my family, I have work now, and I am studying. I have goals in life, and I will try to achieve all of them. I want to be an educated person, yes I want to educate myself and later when I have completed my education I want to work and I want to spend the rest of my life with my mother and sister happily, as a successful person, yes.

PS. Nadia reunited with her family in Germany in October 2018 and she is now living and studying there.

Chapter 4

Feminist Genealogies of Labour under Conditions of Forced Displacement

I was working with the other workers of the textile workshop
but in return
I didn't get anything
[. . .]
and after five or six months
I think it was six months
yes
they talked to me
and said
we will give you 500 Turkish lira per month
I was so happy
because I was alive
I needed to survive
I was happy for that
otherwise
I was not happy in my life
I was living with strangers
I had very hard days there
life was very difficult for me
nobody understood my feelings
I didn't know where my family was[1]

I was introduced to Nadia in the summer of 2018 through the Refugee Legal Support-Athens and we met in a café at the heart of a very well-known green area in the centre of Athens. Her story, which is narrated in full in the preceding first *interlude*, emerges from the dark times of being a child textile worker in the Istanbul garment industry, but unfolds as a cartography of *lines of flight*. What emerges from her narrative is a whirl of existential forces that deterritorialize her from the black holes of patriarchal segmentarities, harsh border practices, labour exploitation and the pain of separation on a plane of remaking her present and re-imagining her future. Her story throws light on her emergence from dark times and leaves traces of her *conatus*, her perseverance of living in-the-world-with-others. While writing this chapter, I feel I hear the music of her voice, creating a rhythm for our long walk from the doorsteps of her Athenian flat where we met to an open café at the heart of a green little island in the heart of a busy urban environment. The itinerary of her journey that the reader followed in the prose of the previous *interlude* will now sound differently through the verses of her poem story.

Taking Nadia's poetics of displacement as my rondo, in this chapter, I look into the work experiences of migrant and refugee women by tracing a long genealogy of gendered memories of work in the garment industry under conditions of forced displacement. The chapter unfolds in three sections: First, I look at current phenomena of labour exploitation in the Turkish garment industry, then I revisit feminist genealogies of agonistic politics in the long run of the twentieth century and finally, I reflect on the insights that genealogical explorations in feminist labour histories under conditions of forced displacement have brought to the fore.

WOMEN WORKERS ON THE MOVE IN THE TURKISH GARMENT INDUSTRY

Turkey is today amongst the world's largest suppliers of clothing and the industry has been growing rapidly in the past thirty years (Sheng Lu 2019). However, informal economic structures and sweatshop working conditions have been recorded and exposed from the very beginning. As Saniye Dedeoglu (2008) has shown, global industrial production and trade channels have drawn on the labour force of women workers in family-based workshops and ateliers. Women's work in these garment workshops has often been hidden in the shadows of their domestic identities as mothers, wives and sisters within the family networks that support and sustain such production units: it has remained unrecognized, poorly paid, if at all, and under-recorded. Dedeoglu has further pointed to the fact that there are different types of industrial production in this sector targeting both local and global markets and using different categories of female labour: factory women, atelier girls and pieceworker housewives (2008, 85). Istanbul is also a city continuously attracting waves of migrants and refugee workers, mostly inhabiting the *gecekondu* neighbourhoods (86). It is in these neighbourhoods that most ateliers and workshops of the subcontracting system are based. This is because employers can easily draw on the pool of cheap and unregistered labour of the inhabitants, but also because rents are very low in these areas and having more space makes it easier to avoid inspection. Dedeoglu's field research is illuminating:

> In each atelier I visited a new story about how tax inspection was avoided, was told. The most interesting one was in a two-floor atelier with one floor in the basement and the other on the ground floor. During inspections all unregistered workers were kept in the basement, which was locked and hidden from public view. The owner only showed his ground floor as the shop floor. Keeping away from the scrutiny of bureaucratic institutions was the reason why ateliers are operated in the basement of newly built apartment buildings, where windows – if there are any windows – are covered with thick paper or painted to hide the business and its workers from public view and bureaucratic inspection. (2008, 71)

Alongside agriculture, domestic care work and construction, the textile and garment industries are characterized by a high degree of labour intensity, a history of informality, flexible labour conditions, as well as very low expectations in terms of language and technical skills. It is precisely because of these traits that migrants and refugees have been mostly employed in these sectors of the Turkish economy. As Nadia recounted in her story:

I was working twelve hours a day there
from morning
until evening
for seven
eight
and sometimes
nine to twelve hours
doing overtime
some of the work they had
was urgent to finish

What is then important to acknowledge here is that the mass movement of refugees into Turkey has not created new conditions in the Turkish garment industry: It has just made its already existing illegal, irregular and informal structures more complex (see Korkmaz 2019, 51). While in need of some sort of work to survive and usually without work permits, refugees and migrants have sought employment in the informal workshops within the sector. Nadia's story was simple and straightforward about the condition that underpinned refugees' willingness to undergo oppressive labour conditions:

There were mosques there
and some people
when they came to Turkey
for the first time
and they didn't have a house
they used to go to the mosques area
they used to hang around
take showers
sleep there
and after some time
if they had money
they would travel to Greece
if they didn't have any money
they started working in the same area
there were many job opportunities
you could easily find a job
there were thousands of thousands of textiles
where people
refugee people
used to work

Refugees, thus, comprise the largest part of the invisible workers in the Istanbul garment industry since restrictions in the work permit, employers' unwillingness to apply for them, as well as the paperless status of many refugees are all conditions that have been pushing them in the margins and shadows of the informal economy (see Korkmaz 2019, 44). According to the Social Security Institution data, published in 2015, workers employed in the textile and garment industries were about 8 per cent of the total labour force in Turkey. This percentage corresponds to around 903,743 people, but if the informal labour force was taken into account, the estimate is that two and a half million people work in this sector (Pinar et al., 2019, 31).

What is also interesting is that the Turkish garment industry relies on a combination of formal and informal economic structures. As Emre Eren Korkmaz has noted, 'the comparative advantage of the Turkish garment industry and its magical solution to provide good quality products with low cost rely on a collaboration of formal and informal economy within the supply chain of global corporations' (2019, 44). What this means is that in responding to the needs of global trade channels, the Turkish garment industry uses a limited range of registered factories alongside a huge network of undeclared subcontracting informal work arrangements. This combination creates an environment of harsh exploitation for workers in all kinds of vulnerable situations. In this light, informal labour can take many forms: a workshop or a factory can be completely unregistered, or workers can be unregistered. The latter is the usual form in the Turkish garment industry, where registered and unregistered employees work together in 'legal' and registered workplaces (44). The labour force of the textile workshop where Nadia was working is illustrative of this mixture of formal and informal labour:

there were some refugees
who used to come
and stay for some months
and then they would travel to Greece
I knew about these things
because many of the refugees
when they came
they were hired
although they were paid less
and then they travelled
so our textile was like a family textile
and most of the girls who were working there
came from the same family
like the wife of our patron
our boss I mean
she was working with us
and so was the sister of the patron
as well as his sister-in-law
some of their cousins
were also working there
and the rest of us
were refugees and strangers

Apart from the employers however, state authorities are also keen to tolerate such conditions in the labour market because in this way they avoid both the costs of subsistence support for the refugees, as well as incentives for employers to hire refugees. According to Christoph Scherrer, this is a process of 'integration by super exploitation' (2019, xi). Indeed in recent years and particularly from 2016 onwards, there were several reports about the harsh exploitation of refugees, many of them women and children: 'child refugees in Turkey making clothes for UK shops'[2] was on the BBC news in October 2016, followed by many journalistic, institutional, trade unions and NGOs reports across the globe around issues of labour exploitation. 'Women make up the majority of the textile workforce and are therefore particularly at risk, as are children who are also being used in large numbers',[3] a report from the Business & Human Rights Resource Centre highlighted, in developing an action directed to international leading brands in terms of their responsibility vis-à-vis phenomena of modern slavery.[4]

In negotiating low purchasing prices, global brands have indeed played a crucial role in creating and reproducing high levels of unfairness, oppression and injustice in the Turkish garment industry: 'if brands want Turkish suppliers to employ refugees and pay the living wage to all employees, brands should take this into account in their purchasing prices. If suppliers don't earn their living wage, how can they pay the living wage to their employees?', employers have argued (Korkmaz 2019, 45). Nadia's story about her failed attempt to register herself as an asylum seeker during the three years that she resided in Turkey is illuminating of the multifarious entanglements that have pushed and retained many migrant and refugee workers in the margins of the labour market in Turkey:

people
when they are refugees in Turkey
they go and register at the UNHCR offices
but my bad luck was
that in the city I was living
there were no UNHCR offices
there was actually one
but it was just for disabled people
pregnant women
or other refugees in very serious situations
I had to go to Ankara
which was six hours away
as I was living in Istanbul
so yes
I kept asking the patron's wife
to let me go and register

Nadia remembered how difficult it was to persuade her employer to let her go. She had never been separated from them before, and she never went out without the family. Every time she would ask her patron to let her go to Ankara, 'he was saying, "no, you are alone, how can I give you this permission, tomorrow if something happens, people will blame us", and this and that'. Nadia was, thus, effectively living and working under conditions of modern slavery in terms of its definition in the Global slavery index,[5] notwithstanding the controversies around discourses and practices of modern slavery and unfree labour, as I have already noted above. But it is also clear that the difficulties in registering herself as an asylum seeker was a combination of her employers' reluctance with stiff bureaucratic administration procedures that the state had put in place to make it difficult for refugees to register themselves and claim their rights. Even when she did manage to persuade her employers to let her travel to Ankara with another family, her attempt to register was both frustrating and unsuccessful. The temporal rhythm of her story becomes an echo of the agonizing waiting, the endless questioning and then the bitter disappointment:

I travelled all night with the family
and when we reached there
we went to find the UNHCR offices
it was early in the morning
six o'clock
[. . .]
we stood in the queue
until ten or eleven
and when my turn came
they asked me many questions
they were asking for my guardian
because I was underage
[. . .]
they kept asking questions
and taking breaks

[. . .]
and then again
they would call me in a different room
asking questions again
and then they asked me to wait again
so, they made me wait until the evening
but in the end
they didn't give me any document
yes
they didn't give me anything

Nadia was caught in the paradox of the inclusion/exclusion position that Michel Agier has delineated: 'inclusion through work, exclusion by almost everything else' (2016, 66–67). Moreover, Sandro Mezzarda and Brett Nelson (2013, 244) have shown that the worker–citizen relationship is dissolved within *mobility assemblages*, labour rights and precarious work with new figurations, patterns and relations emerging within manual labour. In their study of the relations between borders and labour histories and politics, Mezzarda and Nelson (2013, 244–46) have pointed to the need to rethink exploitation, beyond the wage relation and particularly so in relation to migration, and I would add forced displacement. In this context, what Nadia's story highlights is that there is a link between labour exploitation and forced displacement, since the lack of a place to call home, includes accommodation concerns and costs in the exploitation equation. It is no wonder that refugees are so keen to work for the home-based ateliers and workshops of the Istanbul garment industry, despite their miserable conditions and low wages (see also Yilmaz et al., 2019, 30). Nadia had to work without any wages for five to six months 'because I was staying with them for free. I didn't have any money and they were helping me with food and accommodation.' Her experience reverberates with many migrant women's experiences who go through long periods of time without payment, Agier has noted (2016, 66).

Despite its oppressive conditions, the Istanbul garment industry has offered refugees meagre and yet actual possibilities of collecting money to pay the smugglers for their passage to Europe. In this function, it has become a component of *mobility assemblages*, as already discussed in chapter 1. Kaya & Kıraç (2016) have particularly noted the informal labour networks that are deployed between local employers and refugees seeking jobs. When refugees move to Istanbul, they often come with crucial and concrete information about employment availabilities in its urban industry (see also Korkmaz 2019, 44). Moreover, when refugees' attempts to cross the borders were 'unsuccessful', their labour force would also return to the sweatshops of the garment industry as it was the case with Nadia: a vicious circle of exploitation, entrapment and escape.

Affective forces are also intertwined in this *assemblage*. As a defenceless child worker at the heart of this oppressive regime, Nadia was appreciative of the fact that the family who run the textile workshop were 'nice' to her. In her story, she tenderly remembers how the patron's wife became her confidante:

she was very kind
[...]
she was always talking to me
like her younger sister
sometimes
I cried with her
mostly
I cried alone

In her longitudinal study of the Istanbul garment industry, Dedeoglu has noted that within the family networks, which is the noticeable feature of many garment workshops ateliers, the mothers or wives of the workshop owners are 'the invisible heart' (Folbre 2002) of the ateliers' workforce, with diverse roles, ranging from sewing clothes, finding occasional extra labour resources, cooking for the garment workers, as well as cleaning the workplace (2008, 169–70). In her story, Nadia has mentioned that part of her salary would go back to the family to pay for accommodation and two meals, breakfast and dinner, as lunch was provided for free to all workers:

everyone in the textile had lunch for free
but for breakfast
and my dinner
I had to manage with my money

What we also hear in Nadia's story is the diversity of the emotional labour these women were doing, ranging from comforting family members to advising young migrant and refugee workers. As a young girl, a child worker in effect, Nadia thus found herself entangled in uncanny 'family relations', under conditions of what I have called 'home-based work without home' (Tamboukou 2019), a new component in the long history of industrial homework that reaches our days in unexpected formations. Moreover, in trying to make sense of the riddle of how Nadia got emotionally attached to the patron's wife, the question of how relations are being formed, becomes particularly pertinent. Here, Barad's notion of 'intra-actions' (2007), as already discussed in chapter 1, help us attend to the plurality and diverse nature of gender and labour relations through which entities – like Nadia's friendship to the patron's wife – emerge, within the current geopolitical context of 'the refugee crisis in the Aegean'.

Being a network of workshops, usually run by extended family networks, the Istanbul textile industry is very diverse, however. Speaking to Amnesty International about her experiences, Abigail, a young woman from Cameroon, who had fled her country to escape gender-based violence, talked about how she was sexually abused by her employer in an Istanbul sweatshop, where she had found temporary work.[6] Labour relations are, thus, entangled with gendered experiences, including sexual abuse. Nadia told me how helpless and desperate she felt, when she understood that the family who run the textile workshop wanted to marry her off to their son, who was much older than her and had a mental disability. According to Nadia, this idea came from the fact that the family had seen how much she cared for their vulnerable son, while working with him side by side:

they were so cruel to their brother
[. . .]
so during working hours

I was helping him a lot
because I had seen him
how the other brothers tortured him
because he didn't understand

Interestingly enough, it was the patron's wife who first alerted Nadia to the family's secret plan and advised her against it. Gender, disability, family cruelty, care work, women's solidarity and labour exploitation are entangled in Nadia's story, leaving their own traces in the long genealogies of gendered migrant labour under conditions of forced displacement. What such genealogies bring to the fore is the understanding that 'crises' do not erupt from nowhere, nor can they be considered as random geopolitical contingencies. On the contrary, such 'crises' are structural and systemic, very much part of what Guttiérez Rodríguez (2018) has configured as 'the coloniality of migration', looking into socioeconomic and political connections between asylum and migration in the process of their mutual constitution. In this context, a historical understanding of current issues and 'crises' can throw light on their complex nuances, particularly so since the current flows of labour mobility from the south to the north is an important component of what Agier has identified as 'the second great wave of migration in the world in the modern era, following that of the late nineteenth and early twentieth century, which was essentially marked by major movements from Europe to America' (2016, 46). It is, thus, genealogies of gendered labour under conditions of forced displacement of the first great wave of migration that I want to consider next, particularly within the context of agonistic politics within the labour movement and beyond. As histories of the present, genealogies keep challenging existing concepts, discourses, practices and figurations and open up new ways of conceptualizing and understanding 'the real' (see Tamboukou 2013).

MIGRATION AND THE LABOUR MOVEMENT IN THE GARMENT INDUSTRY

> When fire singes the hairs on the skin of the women workers, they will rise up like tigers.[7]

In June 1982, more than 20,000 Chinese migrant women garment workers took to the streets of New York, in demand of better wages and better working conditions. Within hours the workers and the International Ladies Garment Workers' Union (ILGWU) had won the largest strike in the history of New York's Chinatown. By the late 1970s, immigration had revitalized the New York garment industry, which had experienced a steep down curve in the 1960s when manufacturers moved their production to the south of United States and Puerto Rico first and then to Latin America and Asia in search of low wages. Chinese women workers were at the heart of this rebirth of the New York garment industry. They had started migrating to New York from Southern China and Hong-Kong *en masse*, after the 1965 Immigration Act, which changed discrimination against Asians. By 1980, there were 25,000 Chinese garment workers in New York working in 430 workshops and ateliers and women made up over 80 per cent of the workforce (Chan 2019). Women were excited at the opportunity of being able to leave their home and earn a living:

> Before there were garment factories, women didn't have that much work. They had to sit in the apartment and look out the window all day because their husbands won't allow them to go outside. So when the factories opened, they were so happy. Since the workplace was all women, some of the husbands said 'okay, you can go out and earn a little money.'[8]

But despite the excitement of a public life, Chinese migrant workers soon found the conditions in the garment factories backbreaking and appalling. They were also terrified by the demands of the trade: 'The work was really hard for me; like so many other women, I didn't have any experience sewing clothes.'[9] And yet they had to work and it was in the factories that they learnt the tricks of the trade: 'The garment shops were in such a high demand for workers that they gave us the opportunity to learn. So even if your hands shook and you were scared, you had to do it.'[10] But while learning to labour, these migrant women also learnt to fight, following the political activism of earlier waves of women migrant workers from Europe, the Caribbean and Latin America, who were at the fore front of the labour movement in the garment industry, as I will further discuss.

There is today a rich body of literature revolving around labour activism in the New York garment industry.[11] Gender and migration are central analytical categories in this strand of labour history, whose protagonists were Jewish and Italian migrant women workers. They were flocking in New York in the beginning of the twentieth century escaping either the Russian pogroms or the Italian repressive campaign against all socialist and anarchist groups. It goes without saying that beyond political persecution, poverty and lack of job opportunities in Southern Europe and particularly Italy was one of the main reasons triggering mass migration forces at the turn of the twentieth century and beyond. But garment workers, the majority of whom were women, were brutally exploited. In her autobiography *Days of Our Lives*, Rose Pesotta (1958) has given some vivid scenes of the labour conditions in the New York garment industry at the dawn of the twentieth century. Pesotta was an important figure in the U.S. labour movement in the first half of the twentieth century. Elsewhere, I have written extensively about Pesotta's politics, particularly highlighting her agonistic involvement in the U.S. anarchist movement, her struggles within the sexist structures of the U.S. labour movement, as well as her contribution to the cultural histories of modernity (Tamboukou 2016). What I want to do in this section of the chapter, however, is to consider hierarchies and internal and external exclusions and inclusions within mobile labour histories. In doing so, I want to highlight how relations within 'the coloniality of migration' (Guttiérez 2018) developed racist and gendered taxonomies and hierarchies even within the ranks of the labour movement in the U.S. garment industry, which was ironically dominated by migrant workers.

In looking at trade unions interventions in the Turkish garment industry, Korkmaz has underlined the fact that there are not any refugee union members in the sector. This is because 'unionized companies do not employ refugees [and] unions cannot recruit informal workers' (2019, 50). Although unions defend and support refugees' rights, they also operate in the discourse of 'our workers and them', (50) and they have expressed concerns about the effects of cheap refugee labour in the overall industrial relations in the sector. It seems that things in union politics have hardly moved from their position in different times and geographies, as I will show below, by focusing on two ethnic groups of migrant workers that are still prominent in the United States, as well as the global garment industry today: the Chinese and the Mexicans.

The 'Unbound Feet' Agonistic Politics

As I showed in the previous section, Chinese garment workers took on the struggle against sweatshop conditions well through the twentieth century and in doing so they crossed geographical boundaries and migration generations within the United States by reviving the agonistic politics of the New York garment industry. Their migration histories, however, can be traced back at the turn of the twentieth century when Chinese immigrants, mostly from the Pearl River Delta in Southeast China, arrived in the United States looking for a better future in the wake of the Californian Gold Rush. Very few women were amongst them, usually following their husbands, who had migrated first.[12] Women's lives in nineteenth-century San Francisco were doubly oppressed by patriarchal control within their community, and by racism outside the Chinatown borderlines.[13] As Judy Young has commented, 'whereas most European women found immigration to America a liberating experience, Chinese women, except in certain situations, found it inhibiting' (1995, 16).

Confined within their home however, many migrant Chinese women took on sewing jobs that although dreadfully paid, they were still the source of some extra money for the family: 'I worked in my room [. . .] my friend [sic] who know me well bring me work to do to [sic] my room', Low How See, one of the earliest Chinese women in San Francisco told the Collector of Customs on 26 March 1896 (in Ling 1998, 70). There were some women who worked in family-run workshops, but many women would also find employment in a garment shop. But because of care responsibilities women workers would opt for the piece-rate system, which gave them the flexibility of arranging their working days according to their family needs: 'Most of the women drift into the factory from ten to eleven in the morning. They return home when the children are due, around luncheon and at three in the afternoon before they go to the Chinese school.'[14]

Low as it was, women's contribution to the family income was important. Moreover, the possibility of getting out of the confines of the house was a nice break in women's homebound routine. As Yung (1995, 92) has noted, the garment workshops became social spaces, where women could find friends, talk and socialize. Having some money of their own also gave them a fleeting feeling of independence. Despite the positive aspects of escaping domestic drudgeries, Chinese women were harshly exploited and to make things worse, they were working without the benefits and support of labour organization, since only men were allowed to join the Chinese guilds that regulated working hours and conditions (329–30). Thus, unlike Jewish women workers in the garment industry, who had some chances for upward mobility, Chinese women were stuck in the sweatshop conditions 'lacking the same language skills, and political consciousness and further hindered by racism', as Yung has commented (89).

Working conditions did not change much in the interwar period; however, Chinese garment workers themselves did change. As Yung has noted, second-generation Chinese women took the first steps in challenging gender and race discrimination: 'compared to their mothers they were better educated, more economically mobile, socially active, politically aware and equally partners in marriages' (177). But when the stock market crashed in 1929, Chinese women's position in the garment industry became dire. During the 1930s, San Francisco had become the largest employer in the garment industry and there were over 300 women employed in the Chinatown sweatshops. Pesotta's political autobiography paints a grim picture of the Chinatown garment district even after the worst years of the Depression had passed: 'On Grant Avenue we entered a fashionable store, walked down steps that were little more than rungs of a ladder into a cellar and then descended to a second cellar. On both levels, men, women and children were working silently' (Pesotta 1987, 70).

It was in this context that when Pesotta arrived in San Francisco as an ILGWU organizer, she soon realized that this was going to be 'a tough job' (68). Moreover, when she tried to intervene in the dire condition of the sweatshops in Chinatown, she was appalled to realize that 'the Chinese did not have many friends amongst the San Francisco labor groups, and that all Asiatics were barred from union membership there except in our own ranks' (76). She was even more abhorred to understand that 'this was not only a San Francisco dressmaker' problem. It was closely bound up with federal government policy, the Chinese Exclusion Act, the attitude of the general labour movement towards Asiatics, the susceptibility of resistance of the young Chinese workers to union education' (76).

Pesotta's intervention in the Chinatown misery was to write an article with all her observations of the appalling conditions in Chinatown and send it to Justice, the ILGWU's newspaper. However, the Chinese women workers went far beyond reading or writing articles, although they did this as well: 'women in this community are keeping pace with the quick changes of the modern world. The sly Chinese maidens in bound feet are forever gone, making place for active and intelligent young women' Jane Kwong Lee wrote in the Chinese Digest in June 1938.[15]

Lee's optimism did not emerge out of the blue. She wrote this article on the aftermath of the longest strike in the San Francisco Chinatown garment industry, at the Joe Shoong's National Dollar Stores sewing factory (see Fong 1975). The strike lasted for fifteen weeks and although the agreement was rather disappointing in terms of the workers' initial demands, its effects were long lasting and turned a new page in the history book of Chinese American women. As Yung has commented, the strike 'proved that that Chinese women could stand up for themselves and work across generational, racial, gender and political lines to gain better working conditions in Chinatown' (1999, 209). Through their involvement in the strike Chinese women crossed the boundaries of their domestic sphere and got entangled in the ranks of the labour movement. The era of the bound feet was over and it seems that the strings of 'the unbound feet' have now become red threads that run through the agonistic politics of the garment industry in the United States, as well as in China's garment factories that have attracted many internal migrant women workers.

Indeed, most of the young women who work in the garment factories of Shenzhen and Guangdong provinces today are from the poor, rural areas of China. They migrate to southern coastal provinces, so that they can support their families. Their life is harsh since low wages make it very difficult for these young girls to survive. And yet there are increasingly reports that more and more women garment workers have been mobilized in asserting their labour rights. The Chinese Working Women Network, which is the first non-governmental labour organization in mainland China runs a series of projects that aims 'to promote better lives for Chinese migrant women workers by developing feminist awareness and workers' empowerment'.[16] Chinese and other Asian women workers, alongside the Mexicans and other Latin American migrant workers are also alive and kicking in the Los Angeles garment industry, which is now the U.S. fashion capital. It is to the intense agonistic politics of the Californian and Texan garment industries that I will now turn.

La Costurera: Mexican Garment Workers Inhabiting the Borderlands

The condition of the Mexican garment workers in the first decades of the twentieth century was an effect of wider geopolitical turmoil. More specifically in the period between 1830 and 1930, Mexico was hit by a series of political, social and economic crises, that made one and a half million Mexicans to be forcefully displaced and turn to the U.S. Southwestern states in search of a better future.[17] As a cosmopolitan city, which was also geographically very near to the Mexican borders, Los Angeles became a popular destination for migrant workers. It goes without saying that Mexican migrant workers came to the United States with their patriarchal luggage and women's role in the new country was very much restricted within the family. While Mexican women needed to work, the majority of them joined the garment industry as homeworkers, accepting meagre wages that allowed them to look after their husbands and young children.[18]

Although ethic, gender and cultural differences are important in understanding women workers' labour lives and attitudes, it is hugely problematic not to recognize differences amongst them. Chandra Talpade Mohanty (1988) has long ago criticized the universal and monolithic images of 'the third world woman' and the figure of the Chicana as powerless and submissive is part of such discursive constructions. George Sanchez has written that Mexican immigrant families were far from homogeneous. There were differences in terms of provenance, migration patterns and settlement destinations. Some came from rural villages, others from cities. Some chose to join Mexican communities in the borderlands, while others opted for areas mostly inhabited by Anglo-Americans (Sanchez 1993, 130). Many came as families, either at the same time or in waves, while others arrived as single migrants, although for women these were exceptional cases, usually after some rupture in their personal or family life (136).

There were finally generational differences, particularly within families whose children were born on both sides of the border. In this context, the image of 'the good Mexican woman' was an antithesis of 'the barrio girls': these were young women who were born and bred in the United States and they seemed to relate more to the American media images of womanhood than to their cultural heritage and traditions. Dress and appearance were very important for these young women who 'adopted fashionable short dresses and hair styles, smoked publicly and used cosmetics' (McCaffery 1999, 61). But these young assertive women also needed to work, both to support themselves and their families, as well as to satisfy their fashion and life-style needs. Working in one of the many garment workshops in LA was clearly a work path, but the working conditions were terrible.

In her political autobiography *Bread Upon the Waters*, Pesotta has painted a vivid picture of the state of the garment industry in California in the spring of 1933, where she arrived as an ILGWU organizer with the task of unionizing the Mexicans. Pesotta entered the field enthusiastically, but she immediately bumped into pessimistic reports to the ILGWU General Executive Board: 'Latinas were difficult to approach and still more difficult to retain in the organization'.[19] Proving them wrong became her biggest challenge as she was struggling on two fronts: the wider undermining of unionism and patriarchy at work. Hopeless as it seemed in the beginning, Pesotta's grass root campaign soon flourished and in October 1933, everything was ready for a strike. The 1933 dressmakers' strike in Los Angeles lasted four weeks; it became violent at times, with arrests and conflicts with the police, but the Mexican women's perseverance and the leading roles they took in the organization of the strike destroyed all the myths around their ignorance, weakness and submission to the patriarchal constraints of 'their culture' (de Soldatenko 2002).

The results of the strike were rather disappointing, however: It ended with an unsatisfactory arbitration and the ILGWU leadership was bitterly criticized about this 'sell out' of the strike. Despite the compromise of the strike, however, a dressmakers' union was eventually established and the ILGWU membership increased from thirty-five members in 1930 to 2,460 in 1935. But although Mexican dressmakers comprised three quarters of the ILGWU membership, these rank-and-file women never climbed the union's leadership. Out of the nineteen positions of the first executive board of the ILGWU local, only six were held by Mexican women and none of them was strategic (Duron 1984, 158). Overall, the ILGWU records are very poor vis-à-vis Mexican women's participation. As María Gutierrez de Soldatenko has noted, 'we do not have a documented history focusing fully on the participation of women of colour in the union' (2002, 46). The ILGWU leadership was very keen in organising the LA labour force, 'while refusing to acknowledge the contributions, talents, and potential of Latina and Chicana leaders working for them' de Soldatenko has argued, further adding that the situation had not really changed much even in the 1990s, when she conducted her research in the Los Angeles garment industry (46).

Writing about efforts to unionize migrant women workers in Los Angeles, Richard Sullivan and Kimi Lee (2008) have written that it is community-based organizations like the Garment Worker Center[20] and not the unions that work for migrant workers' rights. In their view, this is because unions are still 'highly gendered institutions' (2008, 527). Not only do they still focus on men workers but are often 'unable or unwilling to organize low wage workers' (527), the majority of whom are undocumented migrant and refugee women workers.[21] In contrast to the rigidity of traditional union activism, the Garment Workers Center has supported Chinese and Latino garment workers to claim back unpaid wages and employers' penalties, but it has also been offering weekly educational, cultural and political activities (530). Mezzarda and Nelson (2013, 246) have indeed interrogated the political effectiveness of labour institutions and practices either nationally based or international in scope, like the International Labour Organization (ILO). What they argue is that it is their form and structure embedded within nationalized systems and terms of reference that obstruct meaningful alliances with grass root organizations and movements, mobilized by migrant, noncitizen and irregular workers.

Beyond Los Angeles, Mexican and Chicana migrant women working in the garment industry have formed their own activist groups fighting against exploitation. La Mujer Obrera [The Woman Worker, LMO][22] is a Mexicana/Chicana women workers' organization that was founded by garment workers in El Paso in 1981. Over the years, it has organized thousands of workers and has fought against sweatshop conditions in the sector. Like the LA Garment Worker Center, the LMO has also been running educational and cultural activities opening up political, creative and communicative spaces in migrant women workers' lives.

Fuerza Unida [United Force][23] is another well-known workers' activist group, whose aim is to empower women workers through education, political and community organization and advocacy. It was founded in San Antonio in 1990, initially as a response to Levi's Strauss and Co. decision to close their production plants and move them to Mexico and other countries such as Costa Rica and the Dominican Republic in search of lower labour costs. The closure left 2,000 Mexican and Mexican-American women garment workers, who had worked there for over fourteen years, unemployed overnight (see Zugman 2003, 159). The group organized a series of protests demanding compensation through boycotts and hunger strikes that lasted for almost a decade.[24] Since then, the group has run a series of community and environmental activist projects, which today include amongst other, 'El Hilo de la Justicia' [Thread of Justice], a sewing project of alternative fashion production, which has provided support for workers who had been affected by the layoffs. Through its campaigns, the group has transformed not only labour conditions and relations, but also and perhaps more importantly women workers' consciousness of themselves and their position in the world.

What is particularly striking to note in the history of the Fuerza Unida activism is that when the women workers asked the U.S. garment unions for help, they were denied support. According to the Fuerza Unida activists, this was because back in the 1980s, the workers had refused to unionize when approached by the Amalgamated Clothing and Textile Workers Union (ACTWU). As Irene Reyna remembered: 'they tried to unionize us [...] and we said no [....] We were paid pretty good and thought it would make more problems for us with management to have a union'.[25] This refusal came back to haunt them or did it? It was from UNITE, which was a merger of the two biggest trade unions in the U.S. garment industry, ACTWU and ILGWU that they were denied support, an effect of the ethnic and racial divisions and hierarchies within the labour movement that I have explored throughout this chapter.

But despite racial, ethnic and gendered challenges, restrictions and hierarchies, even within trade unions, migrant and refugee women workers are mobilized against the oppressive conditions of their life and work around the globe. Their voices are loudly heard from Bangladesh, Cambodia, Egypt, India, Jordan, Malaysia, Mauritius, Poland, Singapore, Thailand, Taiwan, Turkey and Vietnam, amongst other countries with large flows of internal and external migrant women garment workers.[26] In following tracks and traces of formal and informal labour struggles in the garment industry, what I have tried to show is that women workers on the move have been a vital force of the international labour movement shattering all discourses and myths that have historically constructed them as vulnerable, oppressed and submissive subjects. Feminist genealogies in the labour movement are important in excavating women workers' agonistic politics under conditions of forced displacement, the theme of the concluding section of this chapter.

BECOMING ACTIVISTS

In this chapter, I have looked at contemporary issues in the Istanbul garment industry, which draws on the cheap labour of extended families and communities, as well as the waves of refugees and migrants, who pass through this cosmopolitan city in their attempt to cross the European borders. In further following stories of uprooted women workers, I have traced genealogical lines of gendered migrant labour in the garment industry. As histories of the present, genealogies have thrown light on the social, political and cultural conditions that underpin the state of the garment industry today, but they have also unveiled 'events' that have disrupted labour, gender and racial discrimination and oppression. It is in this genealogical context of analysis that I want to raise the question: How can migrant and refugee women workers help us rethink and redefine feminist labour analytics?

In deconstructing the myth of an 'Immigrant America', Bonnie Honig (2001) has looked closely at the problem of 'the undecidability of foreignness', the ambivalence of welcoming, hosting or persecuting foreigners. 'People cross borders all the time' she has noted, but it is 'the symbolic politics of immigration' that we need to understand and analyse: 'the struggle and counterstruggle to define the terms of foreignness' in relation to the always shifting terrain and values of national or democratic politics' (2001, 80). The flourishing of the Jewish-driven garment industry in New York at the dawn of the twentieth century is one of those success stories of 'capitalist immigrants', who relied on the exploitation of their own people. But the myth of their success was repeatedly challenged and deconstructed by a strong labour movement led by migrant workers, many women amongst them. Instead of staying away from politics, as the dominant discourse of America's model minorities would have them do, (81) the migrant activists in the garment industry fought against capitalist exploitation, as well as gender and race discrimination within their unions. In doing so, they responded to critical questions and issues of intersectional exploitation and grass roots democratic politics. Following Honig's line of thought around 'the undecidability and ambivalence towards foreignness', what my genealogical investigations have brought to the fore is that migrant labour struggles and politics is a crucial area in analysing feminist labour histories and understanding how political actors emerge from it.

When I interviewed Nadia in Athens at the end of summer 2018, she had been already living in Greece for almost two years. She was working as an interpreter in a range of NGOs and civic organizations, she had graduated from a course on English for academic purposes and she had applied for a scholarship to undertake a university degree in tourism and hospitality studies for which she was eventually successful. In her story, she talked about the happiness of doing work that was meaningful to her:

I have worked with many organizations
[. . .]
as a volunteer
I feel so relaxed
like serving humanity
it's something different
[. . .]
I am not paid
but still
I am happy

Nadia's experience of working in the garment industry did not continue after her escape from Turkey. She already spoke five languages when she came to Greece – Farsi, Urdu, Arabic, Turkish and English – and she had started learning Greek as well. Her future was going to be through educational pathways, but what is striking in her case is the way she transformed herself from a child labourer under conditions of modern slavery to a young, self-determined woman. I will come back to the importance of education in chapter 6, but here I want to follow Nadia's *'lines of flight'* from the capitalist and patriarchal regime of the Turkish garment industry as a way of understanding agential cuts and linear causalities within *assemblage* analytics that I have discussed in chapter 1.

As we have already seen, Nadia was trapped in the claws of the Istanbul garment industry as an unaccompanied child for three years and yet she did manage to make her crossing to Greece. Her escape does not mean that molar formations like wars or capitalism are downplayed as powerful institutions within *assemblage* analytics. As Anderson and his colleagues have noted, *assemblage* thinking offers 'a sustained account of the different ways in which orders endure across differences and amid transformations, in addition to a sensitivity to how orders change and are reworked'. But it was from the interstices of entangled oppressive regimes that Nadia's desire to escape, sprang and materialized, as a Baradian 'agential cut' par excellence (Barad 2007). My point here is that within a structuralist model of analysis, agency would emerge as a conscious realization of oppression and exploitation, linked to a determination to oppose it. Within *assemblage* thinking however, it is the components of exploitation that make relations of exteriority with components of other *assemblages*, imaginaries of escape and freedom in Nadia's case. It is through such relations of exteriority that agential cuts emerge. Remember Nadia's disappointment when her attempt to register in Ankara failed. At the time, she felt absolutely crushed and disillusioned, but she did not give up:

when I went back
I kept one thing in my mind
I will not stay in this country
I don't have anything
I need to go
I have to go
[...]
I can't stay here anymore

Nadia's resistance is discerned in her imagination of *'lines of flight'*. As her story unfolded, imagining a different future for herself became the vector that would ultimately take her to Greece, the first step to stand on her own, educate herself, work for the refugee communities in Athens and ultimately reunite with her mother and sister in Germany. Her desire to leave, cross the borders and look for her lost family ultimately became an existential force through which she emerged as a subject. This *passage* to the self, goes through the ruptures and gaps of dominant structures and institutions of power. It is such a plurality of relations within complex social formations that assemblage analytics have brought to the fore. *Assemblage* analytics do not attempt to downplay fierce regimes of domination that derive from powerful institutions, but they do trace and map agential moves and non-linear causalities: Nadia's failure to register created existential conditions of possibility for her ultimate escape. Her journey to Ankara was unsuccessful and yet it solidified her decision to go away and mobilized her desire to travel to Greece.

By focusing on processes rather than pre-existing entities, such as social and political bodies, institutions and structures, *assemblages* facilitate the analysis of multiple, diverse and complex relations at play and in effect interrogate the way we understand and analyse relations and their terms. As a consequence, *assemblages* further challenge linear conceptualizations of agency and causality and they offer a more nuanced understanding of change. It is in the context of *assemblage* thinking then that I have situated migrant and refugee women's political activism. Hanna's story, which can be read in full in the third *interlude* illuminates and beautifully captures the agential move of a woman who fled an oppressive political regime, became a domestic worker in Greece and is today an ardent political activist, labour organizer and performance artist:

for me
for African women
it is very difficult to speak in public
because in Africa
when I was there
everything you do
they tell you
shut up
you are a woman
what do you want to say?
[. . .]
when they asked me to get up and speak in public
I said
I cannot do that
I cannot do that
two times

but the second time
when I got home
because
whenever I have a problem
I talk to myself
I talk to myself
really
I said
look
what do you want now?
are you going to speak in public?
or are you going to leave
without a residence permit?
just think about that
I told myself
decide
here is not Africa
decide
what are you going to do?
and then
I *decided*
I said
no problem
I will speak[27]

Hanna's story reverberates with many of the migrant women workers' stories that we have followed in this chapter. These stories encompass moment of differentiation by staging a dialogue between two of the many sides of the self: 'to speak or not to speak, to act or not to act?' The dilemma is rooted in some essentialist perceptions and expressions of the migrant woman workers, who neither speaks, nor acts. However, the desire and need to protect themselves against annihilation have geared their *lines of flight*, have deterritorialized them from the dark holes of racial capitalism and patriarchy and have thrown them into the adventure of public speaking and labour activism. With words and deed displaced garment women workers emerge in the world as political actors in becoming.

NOTES

1. Nadia's story, a café in Athens, 25 July 2018.
2. https://www.bbc.co.uk/news/business-37716463 [Accessed 10 October 2018].

3. https://www.business-humanrights.org/en/modern-slavery/syrian-refugees-abuse-exploitation-in-turkish-garment-factories [Accessed 10 October 2018].

4. 'Modern slavery' is currently an umbrella term whose meaning and use has been fiercely debated. See Fudge 2018, for a critical overview of these debates.

5. The Global Slavery Index uses 'modern slavery' as an umbrella term to refer to situations of exploitation that a person cannot refuse or leave because of threats, violence, coercion, deception and/or abuse of power. (The Global Slavery Index, 2017 Global Estimates, p. 9, [Accessed February 12, 2019] https://www.ilo.org/wcmsp5/groups/public/---dgreports/---dcomm/documents/publication/wcms_575479.pdf

6. https://www.amnesty.org/en/documents/eur25/9071/2018/en/

7. Anonymous husband of a garment worker, cited in Quan 2009, 77.

8. May Chen, ILGWU labour activist interviewed by Huiying B. Chan (Chan 2019).

9. Connie, ILGWU labour activist interviewed by Huiying B. Chan (Chan 2019).

10. Alice, ILGWU labour activist interviewed by Huiying B. Chan (Chan 2019).

11. See Tamboukou 2016 for an overview of this literature.

12. See among others, Chan 1986, particularly chapter 1.

13. See Chan 1991; Yung 1995, 1999; Ling 1998; Lo 2008; Lee 2010.

14. Observations of the Industrial Welfare Commission Investigator in 1922, cited in Yung 1995, 88.

15. Jane Kwong Lee, "Chinese women in San Francisco", *Chinese Digest,* June 1938, vol. 4, no. 6, p. 9.

16. See The Chinese Working Women Network, http://www.cwwn.org/ [Accessed February 12 2020].

17. See Sanchez 1993, particularly chapter 1.

18. See Mirandé and Enríquez 1979; Ruíz, 1998.

19. Report and Proceedings of the ILGWU 19th Convention. Boston, 7–17 May 1928, p. 222–3. ILGWU Convention publications. 5780/193 PUBS. Kheel Center for Labor-Management Documentation and Archives, Martin P. Catherwood Library, Cornell University. Kheel Centre for Labor Management Documentation and Archives. Cornell University Library. (KCLMDA)

20. See more details about the Garment Worker Center at, https://garmentworker-center.org/ [Accessed 12 February 2020].

21. According to the Garment Worker Centre, 'Los Angeles is the nation's garment production capital and the city's largest manufacturing sector. Over 45,000 workers cut, sew and finish garments locally, a workforce comprised primarily of Latino/a and Asian immigrants', https://garmentworkercenter.org/ [Accessed 12 February., 2020].

22. See, http://www.mujerobrera.org/

23. http://www.fuerzaunida.org/

24. See Fuerza Unida announcement, for a Thanks Giving hunger strike, 13 November 1998, archived at the Library of Congress, http://webarchive.loc.gov/all/20011130173708/http://www.zmag.org/levihunger.htm [Accessed 12 February, 2020]. See also Martinez 2008.

25. Irene Reyna, interviewed by Kara Zugman in 1995, cited in Zugman 2003, 161.

26. It is not possible to follow migrant women garment workers' movement in all these countries within the restrictions of this chapter. For more studies, see amongst others, Ascoly and Finney 2005; Clean Clothes Campaign 2009; War on Want 2012; Theuw and ten Kate 2016; ILO 2017; Boudreau et al., 2018; GAATW 2019;

27. Hanna's story, a café in Athens, 8 December 2018.

Interlude II

SOMI'S STORY

First, I want to introduce myself: my name is Somi, I'm thirty-six years old, I've been in Greece for seven months now. I was born in 1982, my first brother was executed by the Iranian regime for political reasons, in 1981. When I turned five years old, my second brother, who was an activist and supporter of the movement against the dictatorship of Khomeini was also executed. I never met my first brother, as he was executed before I was born, but the second one, I remember him, because we used to go and see him while he was in prison, before his execution. After losing my second brother, there was sadness, the whole family was mourning, no one was happy anymore. After hearing the news of the execution of my brothers, my mother had two heart attacks. My father also suffered from a heart disease. One of my sisters was pregnant when she heard about the execution of my second brother; she was in so much discomfort and stress that she and the baby almost died. We all struggled, we had stress problems because of what had happened. My first brother was nineteen when he was executed and the second was twenty-three, so there was always this question in my mind, 'why were they executed?' they were so young.

My whole family were opposing the Iranian regime. At that time, Khomeini had come to power and it was a real dictatorship. Women were not allowed to go out without wearing the scarf, and men were not allowed to have short sleeves. My whole family was against this dictatorship, so they started to participate in demonstrations and protests. That's why, both of my brothers were arrested and executed. I used to ask my mother, my father and my sisters about the reason for all that, but I was so young, and they couldn't explain what the problem was. But the only reason my brothers were arrested was because they were selling newspapers for the movement that was against the dictatorship. They arrested them and they executed them, so that was what they kept telling me and I have been mourning since then.

I grew up in this kind of environment. My family, everyone, were all opposing the regime, so that's why they were always restricted and at the same time, they were telling me what the issues were, what it was like. So, I was watching everything at school: A lot of things were restricted, and I basically grew up in an environment where the whole family were always mourning and always restricted. At school as well, I was always restricted because the family was already known to the regime, so they were getting restricted more and more.

Especially, for girls and even younger girls, there were a lot of restrictions: To go to school, you had to wear what we call a 'chador', so we had a scarf on the head, we had to wear long things, and no parts of our bodies should be shown. Me and my friends didn't wear the chador, while walking to school; we just carried it in our bags and when we were at the front gate of the school, we put it on. Then, when we came out of school, we just took it off again, as they wouldn't even allow us to go to school if we didn't wear the chador.

But because my family was already known to the Iranian regime – they knew that we had two brothers, who had been executed – they were very focused on us, they were watching all our activities, they were spying on the telephone, everything, so we were always under surveillance.

Even at school, I was not able to fully participate, I couldn't go to the best schools in the city. I was only allowed to go to lower schools, the ones that were not in good areas, I was not allowed to go to better schools, with better teachers and everything. I was also banned from a lot of recreational staff, like even bicycle. As you know, women do not have the opportunity to enter sports stadiums in Iran. It's not possible to take part in outdoor activities freely, and this was always my question; why do these restrictions exist for women? Wherever I went and anything I wanted to do, there was an obstacle in my way. There were only specific places, where women could go. But I was always banned from everything in life, everything: I was always under restrictions.

When I graduated from high school and wanted to go to university, I sat exams for a state university because state universities have better lecturers, and overall better status. I signed up, sat the exams and passed with high grades, which are all available right now, too. But in the end, they didn't accept me in that state university because my family was a political dissent. Instead, they gave me a position in a university of a lower status in a different city. Although I wanted to go to a good university, with good lecturers and a high-status degree, I had to go to a lower class university with a lower certificate and worse lecturers; that was another restriction in relation to my university education. I was only allowed to go to a part-time university, which never had fully qualified professors.

I met a lot of friends at university and I realized that a lot of my friends, all the other girls, were like me: They didn't like the system, they were against the dictatorship, but no one had the courage to come and speak out. However, everywhere I felt this hatred of the dictatorial government. In the friendly conversations between my classmates and even among some university staff, this silent protest space always existed. At universities over there, there are dormitories where women students can sleep. So, we would write small letters against the regime and at night when everybody was asleep, we used to go door by door to dormitories and give the letters, telling students that 'you should start speaking out now, let's go to the demonstration, let's stand up against this criminal regime' and stuff like that. So, we did this political mobilization, as university students.

But in every university, there were also some students, who were supporting the Iranian regime; they were all, like sons and daughters of the higher council. So, they were reporting to the authorities what we were doing, stabbing us behind our back. These students also went to the university principal and gave him our names: What we were doing, what we were writing and all our political activities. At first, the university started restricting us more and more to stop us from what we were doing and then at one point they started expelling us. They hadn't expelled me yet, but I knew they were going to expel me soon because they had warned me a few times. So, there was a lot of pressure on me, inside the university, outside the university in our family, everywhere. I was not going to tolerate the situation anymore.

I had heard from my friends that there was a political group opposing the regime that began to work against this dictatorship after this government had come to power. My brothers too, were active for the same group, selling newsletters of the group. So, out of curiosity, I began to study more about this group. In those years (I mean, in early 2000), it wasn't simple using the Internet, and I did not know much about it. But through the radio, I was able to hear the website address of this group, so that I could find out more about it by searching the address of their website. They used to be in Iran, but they had moved to Iraq; they had a camp there for Iranian dissidents and I met them on the Internet: I wrote a letter to them and I said that I couldn't tolerate the situation and that I wanted to help. This is what I was thinking: I couldn't stay in Iran because they were going to expel me from University. I had restrictions on everything; I was not allowed to do anything, so I had to make a decision: I could either stay and continue my life like that or I could leave. If I decided to leave, I should go there, a camp in Iraq; it was like a refugee camp for Iranian dissidents.

But this wasn't easy, it wasn't an easy decision, because I had to leave my family and I couldn't tell my family 'I am going to leave you from now on'. My mother and father didn't want me to be there; they somehow wanted me to be free from this pressure; they wanted me to have a better life. But they didn't know what to do, they didn't have a solution. I knew I could have told them that I wanted to go to this Iraqi camp, but I also knew that if I had told them, emotionally they would not have allowed me to do it, because they didn't want me to leave them. I was the youngest kid of the family, so they didn't want to lose me. I was personally very frightened; I was very close to my mother and father. I didn't want to leave them, because I knew they had already lost two kids and if they lost me too, that would be very hard on them. And yet, I didn't really have a choice because I just couldn't continue my life there. I did a lot of study about this organization, finding out what they were doing. They had a lot of activities against the Iranian regime and what they were after, they wanted to free Iran from this dictatorship. They were against Khomeini, they were against the Mullah regime, they were against the Islamic Republic of Iran. So, I started studying more and more about this organization.

But I still had to make a decision: If I moved to that camp, I would be free from all the pressure in Iran, but at the same time I was giving up my life because I had to dedicate my life to having more activities just to help the Iranian people – this was a decision I had to make. It was also a very hard decision, because if I wanted to do this, I had to travel on my own. I had to leave Iran and go to Iraq and I was a young girl, I was only nineteen at the time. I wanted to just leave the city, but it was very difficult for me, because there was a lot of rape going on in Iran, sexual harassment; there were a lot of things going on and I was only nineteen. So, I had to do this all on my own, I had to decide whether I was going to take the risk or not. This was probably the most difficult decision I have ever made in my life because I had to leave my family, and if I didn't, I would have to just tolerate the situation in Iran, which was really unbearable. So that was the point I had to decide: am I going to do this or am I going to…

The thing that concerned me most, was the look on my father's and my mother's face, because I knew that they were very old at the time and they are now very, very old. I didn't want to see them concerned and I didn't want to see them worry about what was going to happen if I left, so I just had to make a decision. I knew I didn't have a future in Iran, so this is what I decided: I said, I am going to join the organization, even if it is only one per cent that we do something against the regime, so that the future generation, the other girls, won't have to go through what I went through in my life. So, at one point I decided to leave, I just wrote a letter to my mother and father, I didn't tell them I was leaving, I just left the letter in the house, I accepted the risks,

I took the fears and everything and I just travelled. I realized that if I told my family that I was going to leave the country, they would be emotionally disturbed, so the day when nobody was at home, I left without informing any of my family members, to seek an uncertain fate while I was very young and very afraid.

First, I went from Iran to Turkey, I was there for two weeks. When I went to Turkey I got in touch with the organization. They were not too active in Iran, because they were all suppressed, but in Turkey and in Iraq they were very active. So, I got in touch with them there. After two weeks, I was able to go to the refugee camp in Iraq. It was full of Iranian dissidents and they were all opposing the Iranian regime. The first year was very hard for me because I was always thinking about my family, the memories I had and everything. I was always concerned about my mother and father; it was very hard the first year. But then in the camp I realized that there were many other girls there and they were all just like me, escaping Iran for the same reasons. There were almost 1,000 girls in this camp, some of them were older than me, but the majority of them were almost my age and some were even younger than me. We were all there for the same reason. There were also other women there, they had to, they were forced to go there with their whole family. So, there was like a mother with her son, with her daughter, the whole family had escaped Iran and they had gone there. After a while, when I realized we were all there for the same reason, we were all suffering from the same thing in Iran, I started getting relaxed.

I was there for six months and in the first six months I was learning the background of this organization and stuff like that. After six months, that was the year 2003, the United States attacked Iraq. I had never seen a war in my life, so I was only there for six months and then the United States started attacking and bombarding Iraq in 2003. We were very scared, even though the United States were not directly attacking the camp, they were attacking Sadam's regime. But we could hear the noises of the war, everything was around us, so we were very scared. I was never injured or anything there, but there was a woman, who had moved there from another camp and she had lost both her legs in the bombardments. A lot of my friends however, particularly those travelling from one camp to another, were either injured, or got killed at that time. So, we were witnessing a very difficult situation, but we were stuck in this place.

After the war, the United States took over Iraq and they didn't have a problem with the organization. So, they took complete control of the camp, they brought the food, they did the security and there was no problem. However, this was a closed camp, you didn't have the permission to leave, to go outside, it wasn't like this. You weren't allowed to leave, because there wasn't anything outside; it was the Americans who were responsible for the provisions and everything, so we were all in this closed camp, with no Internet access or anything. We didn't even have mobiles; we didn't know that mobiles existed. We were completely disconnected from the outside world; we didn't know how technologies proceeded, we didn't know anything.

At this camp, the organizations were concentrating on things they had to do against the Iranian regime, that was the goal. They wanted to defeat Iran but at the same time they had a lot of rules and regulations inside the camp: Men and women were separated from each other; they were not in the same area and they were not allowed to communicate. Any communication between men and women would have been severely punished. On the other hand, it was almost impossible to communicate with my family because the organization did not allow contact. It was terrible because everyone needed to communicate with their families. They were worried about their children, especially after the war and bombing, but the organization refused permission.

After 2006, the U.S. government handed over power to the Iraqi government and the Iraqis took control of the camp. But as you know, the Iranian regime had very strong ties with the Iraqi government, so when the Iraqis took over, it was basically the Iranian regime that was controlling the camp and we were all Iranian dissidents in there. So, at one point, the Iraqi government started attacking the camp through the Iranian Cat forces, as they called them. The first time they attacked the camp, they were only using clubs, sticks and whips. During this first attack, they didn't kill a lot of people even though they killed some, as they were hitting them on their heads with clubs. Their main objective was to take some people hostages from the camp. But because they were hitting people on their head, there were a lot of incidents, we had a few people who died, a few people went to a comma or they had some kind of seizure, so we had a lot of problems and they finally took thirty-six people hostages. The camp was thirty-six square kilometres, it was pretty big, so the Iraqi government wanted to take control over everything, and they wanted to dismantle the camp. But because it was too big and there were a few thousand Iranian dissidents at the time there, who had started resisting, they were not successful in this first attack. Although the Iraqi government wanted to attack again, when the U.S. government was informed, the attack was stopped, after about forty-four hours.

But three years later, they attacked again, this time with machine guns, with tanks and everything. This time the objective was to kill as many as they could, so they started killing everybody. A lot of my friends were killed on that day: I was watching people just falling when they were getting shot and there was nothing we could do because we were all unarmed, we were just civilians with nothing to protect ourselves and they were just coming in, the tanks and everything, they were just shooting at everybody. This attack continued for two days; the camp was very big, they couldn't just come in at once but after two days the U.S. government interfered again, and they stopped the attack. At that point, everybody knew that from now on the Iraqi government was going to attack again and again, so everybody was scared about their lives and no one knew what was going to happen, but we knew it was going to happen again,

At the same time, the UNHCR, the United Nations recognized all the residents of the camp as persons of concern; they wanted to somehow stop the Iraqi government from attacking them, so we were all recognized as refugees and they were after a solution to get us out of the camp, out of Iraq. So, as a first step, the Iraqi government, the UNHCR and the U.S. government issued a remit to move us from this camp, which was further down near the border to somewhere in central Baghdad. Previously, there was an American camp and it was empty now, so they wanted to move us and relocate us there. Because our organization had a lot of political supporters everywhere across the world, they were people like John McCain or even higher people like the foreign Minister of France I forget his name, everyone was supporting the organization even John Kerry at the time was supporting, he was the Secretary of State, I think at the time, and they were all after a solution to stop the killing, they just wanted to relocate us somewhere else.

So, we were 3,000 people on the previous camp, which was very big. But then they relocated everyone, 3,000 people to a new site, which was previous an American camp. This camp was very small, so we were all crowded in one small area and we didn't have any kind of house or anything, we just had some wooden caravans with very small windows. If anything happened, but who cared. So, there was no kind of protection or anything. It was the United States that was doing the security there, so they couldn't directly attack us, but then they started attacking us in another way. We were in this camp for four years [2012–2016] and during this time, they attacked the camp five times with warders and some smaller rockets. Nearly sixty people were killed in the Iraqi attacks, even though the U.S. air forces were flying around, but there was no way they could stop everything because there were too many attacks. After four years, the UN and the U.S. reached a solution, because there was no way we could stay on that camp. The Iranian regime would not stop, and the Iraqi government were still attacking, so they reached an agreement that they had to move us to Europe; there was no way we could stay safe over there.

But this idea to relocate everyone from this camp to a European country got postponed for almost a year and a half. The reason was that the people in charge of the camp were afraid of this. If 3,000 Iranian dissidents went to Europe, nobody was going to stay with this organization, everybody was going to look after their own lives, because they would be in a free country. But at that point, the UN were twenty-four hours in the camp, so they were monitoring everything, and they started relocating some of the people who were from another country. We had people from different countries there, so they started taking them back to their own countries. Everyone who was there in the camp had come when they were very young and they had come there because they had problems with their government, we were all after some time of goal to achieve, to be able to free Iran someday.

At one point then, the UN started relocating all the residents of the camp, to Albania, because there was an agreement with the Albanian government. Germany took a hundred residents, the United States was supposed to take a hundred, but they only took forty residents, and every country had some. Norway, I think, they also took fifty, but Albania took the rest, so almost 2,000 something residents went to Albania and I was amongst them. When they were relocating everybody, they couldn't just put 2,000 people in one place, so it took like six months to relocate everybody, but I was among the first. So, after eight weeks they took us to Albania.

When we went there, I just wanted to go on with my own life. So basically, at that time, I had a lot of stress because I had lost my whole life, I was not allowed to go to university, I was not allowed to get a job, I had lost my family, I had lost everything, I was too old, I was thirty-four at that time and I couldn't go to school any more, I couldn't do anything. I was deeply depressed. At the same time at one point, I decided that I was going to start everything from scratch in Albania, I was going to go to school, I was going to start a new job. I wanted to make a new life there, but the Albanian government, were not supporting us: They wouldn't give us a legal status, they wouldn't give us asylum and they wouldn't give us medical insurance, work permission, nothing. After two years living there, I wasn't granted anything. They just gave us a blank piece of paper. On it, it just said that for humanitarian reasons we can live there, so if the police stopped you in the street, you could show them this paper. You couldn't even buy a sim card in a store with this. I wanted to get married, but they didn't even allow us to get legally married in Albania. So, me and my partner couldn't marry together there. At the same time the UN just kept telling us to wait, 'just wait and at one point everything is going to be better with the Albanian government; they are going to start working with you'. So, we stayed there for two years and after two years nothing changed. There was no hope, so we decided to leave for Europe, go to a European country, somewhere in the European Union to be able to have some legal status.

Albania is on the border with Greece, so we decided to come to Greece, which is in the European Union. We thought that the best thing we could do, was to go to Greece; maybe there they could give us some kind of asylum. But when we came to Greece, we realized that because of the large immigration flow here in Greece they were not giving us anything either, so we couldn't get away and life was too hard. So, when I came to Greece, I realized that if I stayed here for two more years, I was going to lose my life again, just like in Albania, where I couldn't get any kind of legal status. There was no point in staying here, because getting a refugee status was very difficult. So that's when I decided to leave Greece, of course in the illegal way. There are smugglers here who take you by plane, but of course with fake passports and stuff. And the other thing I was looking for is that I just wanted to feel safe somewhere, I wanted to be stable, I think I had the right to feel that.

There is one thing I forgot to say, when we were in Albania, because of the organization, there were also agents sent by the Iranian regime in Albania as well. Because Tirana is very small, when you walked in the streets you could see Iranian agents sitting in different places, they were taking pictures of us, I felt so unhappy there. In Albania, they were not attacking anyone, but the Iranian intelligence system was very active in Albania: They were following people, they knew everything about us, and they wanted to use us for their own benefits. So, what the Iranian regime started doing in Albania, they started bribing the people who came out of the organization. They were saying we can pay you this much, you can come with us now. But the problem was that the Iranian regime had killed two of my brothers. I had to leave my homeland because my life was threatened. I had forcibly left my elderly parents and have not seen them for seventeen years. And I think the factor of all these hardening is the dictatorship of Iran. But I had decided to stand up against the dictatorship, I always refused to surrender to their demands. I didn't want to continue this situation in Albania at all.

I did not want to repeat Albania's experience at all, and on the other hand, I thought that Greece might not be as safe for me as other European countries, such as Germany or the Netherlands. Even though I knew what I was doing was illegal and that I was using a fake passport to leave the country, it's not something correct, but I took the risk and I got arrested at the airport. There are a lot of people who do the same thing at the airports right now, but they don't arrest them in Greece, they just leave them go, on the same day. So, a friend told me that even if they stop you, they will let you go, so that's how I did it. When they arrested me there were twenty other people who were arrested for the same reason, fake passports. But it was unbelievable, because they freed everyone else, they just kept me. That was another bad luck for me, because they kept me, and they freed everybody else. So, they kept me in the airport, at the detention centre for one week and then they transferred me to another detention centre. It wasn't a prison, it was some kind of detention centre, and we were treated like prisoners. They handcuffed me like an offender, while I did not commit any crime; I just wanted to find a safe place as a refugee.

What surprised me was that when I entered a European country, I didn't think that I was ever going to face stuff like this again, because I was in a closed camp for sixteen years, I had been attacked since I was a kid I had been restricted and now I had gone back to another prison, so everything in my whole life was changing from one form of prison to another. After three days in prison, I asked for asylum there, but unbelievably, two days after I had asked for asylum, they told me that I had to sign a form, and that I would be deported, go back to Iran. I got scared there a lot, because my whole life I was running away from Iran and they were telling me, now we have to deport you back to Iran, so this was very hard. And I knew that if they were going to deport me to Iran, because I was in this organization for sixteen years, for sure they were going to execute me because they had executed my two brothers, they knew me. I would have just lost my whole life, for sixteen years I had lost everything, and they were going to deport me back to Iran. There was no way I could explain to the Greek government that I was a political person, that I had been recognized as a person of concern from the UNHCR; they didn't care, they said you have to be deported. The police just told me, 'we have to do this, and you have to go, so we are giving you this form: you have to sign it for the deportation'. There was a big fight there, I didn't sign, lawyers were coming and going, and they were making claims against the deportation.

When we were getting attacked, when we were in the camps, I was afraid of my life, it was too hard, but when I was in prison and they were telling me that I would be deported, that was a lot harder for me, because I didn't know what was going to happen to me and my future. So, from there in prison, every night I was just crying and praying to God and I was asking God, 'when are you going to finish this? Every day you bring something else on me, another disappointment, one after another, so when is it going to finish?' So, the only thing I was asking God was, 'I just want to live like any other girl in this world, I just want to be able to study, I just want to be able to have a good job, I don't want anything else. Why do you keep putting me through all these difficulties?' Because what I could see in other girls like me, is that they have suffered one time in their life, twice, maximum three times, not for sixteen years. But for me, it was the whole family history, the fact that I still hadn't achieved anything in my life: I hadn't completed my studies, I hadn't got a job, I hadn't done anything. I was still being treated harshly, I didn't have the right to do anything; I didn't even have the right to live any more.

So, it was like every step I was taking in my life I was hoping for a better future, but it was like every step, was just another mistake, so I had no future at all. So what I was thinking I would do, during the time I was in prison here in Greece, the only thing I was thinking about was that I am thirty-six now, I haven't gone to school, I haven't finished university, I don't know any languages, I don't know anything. It's too late to start a life, because you know, when you are a woman, you have to have kids, above thirty-six is going to be harder for your menopause and stuff like that, so everything was over. I was like, 'I lost my life, I don't even want to go on with my life anymore'. During the time I was in prison I was very, very hopeless, I didn't even want to continue after that, but at one point we changed the lawyer, and fortunately the new lawyer was able to bring me out; it took him a month and ten days and I came out. So, he was able to get me out very fast and when I came out, I was like, I am going to start again from this point.

In the first two months when I came out of prison, everything was very hard for me, even when I was walking in the streets and I saw a police officer I was afraid. I didn't know if they were going to come after me; psychologically, I was under a lot of pressure and I didn't really have the will or anticipation to even start a life anymore. So, I was always in the house, I was not coming out, but then at one point I decided that I needed to change everything, and I wanted to start again my life. Even though I was very old, I said, I am going to start again. I wanted to learn the language, the Greek language and then I wanted to look for a university; I was after something to start my life again here. Unfortunately, I tried a lot, I went to like everything you can imagine, every NGO, I wanted to find some kind of school to learn Greek, to learn English, I went everywhere and then I was lucky! Finally, I found Webster University and we took an exam and I got some certificates that I have gone to high school and everything and they gave me a scholarship. So, in January, I will start a course for the first two months, I have a scholarship and if I am good, they are going to support and sponsor me for the whole bachelor's degree.

When you ask me about my dreams, I have a lot of dreams because I haven't reached any of my dreams since I was born, I haven't reached not even one of them, so I have a lot of dreams. Some people might think that my dreams are nothing, but I just want to finish university. For some people, it is just like a simple thing, you turn eighteen, you go to university, but for me it's a life-long dream.

When we talk about reality, however, I don't know how my future will be here. Because after the first two months at Webster, I don't know if they will continue the scholarship here. Second, we don't even know about the asylum-seeking case here. If we are rejected and we are not going to be able to stay here, we will have to go somewhere else again. So, I don't know anything, but I am trying all I can to just start a stable life here. For the one thing that I have learnt during this process here is that there are a lot of people who get anything for free: they have their family, they reach everything they want. For me, it wasn't like this; it took thirty-six years and I didn't even have the chance to start my life. My own life is now that I can decide what to do. What

I am going to be doing, I am going to start building everything step by step, that's what I am going to try.

One person who has given her a lot of hope is Jack Ma, the founder of Alibaba. As you know, he doesn't have a higher education, he was rejected from Harvard University ten times, but now Harvard is inviting him to go and give speeches there. So, this has given me a lot of hope. One thing Jack Ma said, which has given me a lot of hope, is that when I want to employ someone, I don't ask them what's your education background. I ask them how much can you tolerate failure; how many times can you fail until you give up?

So, what I am going to be doing from now on is to start thinking positively. I know I have failed my whole life, every step, but I also know that I can fail again, and I can get up again. So, from now on, even if I fail again, I am going to get up again, I am going to try again and again. I know eventually someday, even if I am very old, I am going to reach my goals. I don't know how long I am going to live for, I don't know when I am going to die, but I have done a promise to myself that until the day I die, I am going to try and try again; even if I fail every day until the rest of my life, even if my life finishes like this, I am going to try again. Even if I am not able to change anything in my life, I am never going to give up, stop trying, I just want to live an ordinary life, reach the basic goals I have: I just want to finish university, get a good life, get married, just be legal somewhere. Once my friend told me, you shouldn't be so negative on yourself; you should know that one day God is going to reward you somehow, don't think you cannot make it. I know, everyone is going through difficult times, so given that my difficult times were my whole life, I am not thinking about something special, it is not like I got to do something more difficult than the others, I am just going to try and try. Even though my wishes and my dreams are very basic and very simple, these are my wishes and dreams and I just wanted to share them with you, it's nothing more than a certificate from the University, getting a good job and being able to support myself on my own life; I don't want someone else to keep supporting me.

One of my biggest wishes since I was a little girl is to be able to have a wedding, I want to wear a wedding dress, I want to take pictures and show them to my friends; but until now I am not legally allowed to get married, I don't have the money to be able to wear the dress, or anything, so this is one of my biggest wishes. Maybe for other people, it's not some kind of dream, but I still have the dream to somehow have a little kid, if I am still able to have it. And why I want that kid, I don't want that kid to experience what I have experienced. I want my kid to have a free life with no pressure, just that is something in my life that I want. And basically, in general, I just want to be legal somewhere, I just want to be stable, I want to be able to travel, I just want to work, just have a normal life, a simple life without tensions, that's all.

And I also hope one day even after seventeen years, I hope to see my mother and father again. My mother and father are over eighty years old now, they are very old, and they say our only reason in life is to see you before we die. But the problem is that politically they are restricted, they don't have a passport to travel and I am not allowed to go to Iran, because I will be executed, just like my brothers.

And in the end I would like to thank you for your time because I really needed to share my story with someone and I wanted to thank you for listening to me and I just expressed everything in the story, but because of the lack of time I didn't get into details, I said more general things.

Chapter 5

Thinking with Antigone
Political Narratives of Agonistic Humanism

my first brother was nineteen
when he was executed
and the second was twenty-three
so there was always this question in my mind
why were they executed?
they were so young[1]

As we have seen in the previous *Interlude,* Somi started her story memorializing the execution of her two brothers by the Iranian regime. The traumatic memory of their death marked her life from the very beginning and initiated a series of forced displacements as an effect of her civil disobedience – her decision to leave her country at the age of nineteen and join a group of Iranian dissidents in Iraq. While following the rhythms of Somi's poetics of exile, the figure of Antigone erupted in the soundscapes of her story and became a constant presence in the political narratives of my research archive. Somi had to bury her two brothers before escaping an oppressive political regime to join forces of resistance. Click a Zimbabwean freedom fighter, crossed the borders with her childhood friend to join the guerrilla army in Mozambique fighting against British imperialism, when she was only sixteen years old. Hanna, an eighteen-year-old single mother, escaped the oppressive regime of Sierra Leone, leaving her baby son behind. She had to struggle with her fear to speak publicly before becoming an ardent activist defending refugee and migrant women's rights in Greece. Elena, a Gülenist physicist, persecuted by the Turkish government, crossed the borders on foot, carrying her three-months-old baby daughter in one hand and a bag with her laptop in the other. Migrant and refugee women's stories of following *lines of flight* are unique and unrepeatable. Yet, what connects them with other stories of displacement and movement via the figure of Antigone is the desire to tell their stories as an expression of their will to rewrite their exclusion from oppressive regimes, defend their choice of civil disobedience, grasp their passage, claim their right to have rights and affirm their determination for new beginnings.

In this chapter, I am thinking of/with Antigone, a political figuration that has been invested with so many readings, interpretations, philosophical ruminations and artistic expressions. As all Greek tragedies, *Antigone* raises existential questions to its diverse audiences and readers, across multiple times and geographies, spanning 'from Greece to Australia, via Brazil, Argentina, Cuba, Puerto Rico, Nigeria, Ghana, South Africa, India, Indonesia, Ireland, Poland, Spain, Egypt, Turkey, Colombia, Mexico and beyond' Fanny Söderbäck has commented (2010, 3). In mapping Antigone's travels around the world, Moira Fradinger has observed that 'it is a challenge to one's stamina to follow the traces of this 2,500-year-young Theban princess, who looks younger every day (2010, 15). How is this possible? Tina Chanter's rationale, which links Antigone's 'youth' with her rebirth in modern South Africa, seems persuasive: 'as many times as Antigone dies, she comes alive, reborn time and again, born anew each time she enters the theatrical stage, inserting herself into a new political history' (2010, 83).

But what is it that has brought Antigone on the stage of narratives of displacement and travelling? 'Memory is crucial for the survival of political life' Söderbäck has noted in an Arendtian reading of Antigone's insistence on burying her brother as an act of memorialization (2010, 83). In doing this, however, Antigone has also inscribed herself in the scripts of history, becoming an actor and a spectator at once. It is this double subject position that I want to consider in this chapter, which unfolds in four parts. After this introduction, I look at the rich archive of feminist readings of Antigone, excavating themes and tropes that make connections with the stories of my research.[2] Antigone becomes a *narrative persona* – a conceptual figure that I converse with in the analysis of migrant and refugee women's political narratives in the third part of the chapter.[3] By way of conclusion, I revisit Arendt's famous actor/spectator separation in her analysis of life narratives in the light of uprooted women's stories of agonistic politics.

TRACES IN THE *ANTIGONE* FEMINIST ARCHIVE

unmourned by friends and forced by such crude laws
I go to my rockbound prison, strange new tomb –
Always a stranger, O dear god,
I have no home on earth and none below,
Not with the living, not with the breathless dead. (848–852 [938–942])[4]

Sophocle's *Antigone* is amongst the most discussed and analysed literary texts in the history of philosophy, feminism and political theory. Themes that often come up in its different and contended readings, interpretations and performances, include civil disobedience, the public/private divide, gender, sexuality, mourning and death, as well as the right to resist the tyranny of sovereign power.[5] I remember being taught this text as part of my Ancient Greek course in the last years of my high school. We were at the heart of the military dictatorship in Greece (1967–1974) and *Antigone* was the text [and pretext] for discussing the importance of speaking truth to power under a strict authoritarian regime. Little did I know then that the protagonist of a tragedy that was a core component of our curriculum would soon become a central figure in an emerging body of feminist literature, which has now reached the second millennium and is still bursting.[6]

My conversations with Antigone as a narrative persona, thus, emerge from my situated perspective as a student growing up during the military dictatorship in Greece. While marking my own position in the Antigone archive, I also acknowledge its constraints and limitations within a wider spectrum of figures that transgress Western mythologies in opening up spaces wherein feminist politics can be re-imagined. Having pointed to the Western origins of Antigone's influence, however, I have also been drawn to the inspiration that the play has offered to thirty Syrian refugee women in Lebanon within the wider project *Antigone of Syria*.[7] In reflecting upon her involvement in this project, Hiba Sahyl, who has lost two brothers, in the war, has said: 'I understand why Antigone does what she does. If I could go to Syria and bury my brother with my own hands, I would do it', (Ross, 2014: 2) Sahyl's claim of understanding Antigone resonates with Andrés Fabián Henao Castro's (2013) argument that 'Antigone stands for refugees, undocumented immigrants, and noncitizens in the reinvention of the play's symbolic repertoire in the twenty-first century' (2013: 309).

To return to the feminist archive on Antigone, it goes without saying that is large and still unfolding, but it is outside the scope of this chapter to do a comprehensive overview of the various debates within it. What I have done instead is to follow lines of thought that make connections with my interpretation and understanding of the stories that migrant and refugee women have shared with me. Bonnie Honig's (2013) important re-reading of the play has largely influenced my own understanding and interpretation, throwing new light on my Arendtian take of political narratives, as well as in my conversations with the figure of Antigone. In this process, I have created 'the Antigone *assemblage*', bringing together concepts, ideas and insights from a range of feminist theories and beyond, as they make connections between them, as well as with narrative lines of forced displacement. As I have already noted in previous chapters, *assemblage* thinking and diffractive readings facilitate a nuanced understanding of the complexity of entanglements between different theoretical perspectives while also allowing for reading theories through one another in understanding the difference that their difference makes.

In reviewing the early feminist readings of *Antigone*, Catherine Holland has pointed to the danger of past texts and figures overfilling the present and thus limiting our political vision and horizons: 'how can feminist political theorists "restate new possibilities" without reinstating the past?' she has asked (2010, 28). In Holland's reading, this is precisely what we can learn from Antigone: the radical possibilities of breaking with the past, by taking the difficult decision of leaving behind family ties, wedding expectations, or the promise of 'a normal life', in the pursuit of what feels to be right. But liberating the self from a paralyzing past is not easy, and the tragedy boldly exposes Antigone's fear and anger in reflecting on the material effects of her transgression.

Although driven by ethical principles in challenging the absurdity and hubris of sovereign power, Antigone is not indifferent to the fact that her body is going to suffer. It is precisely because she is sensitive to the needs of the body that she has decided not to let her brother's dead body exposed, 'his corpse carrion for the birds and dogs to tear, an obscenity for the citizens to behold' (207–207 [229–231]) in Creon's cruel edict. The tragedy itself starts with Antigone's call to the physicality of her relationship with her sister: 'My own flesh and blood – dear sister, dear Ismene' (1[1]). It is the tragedy's focus on the grammar and corporeality of the body that Adriana Cavarero highlights in her own reading of *Antigone*, pointing to the complex ways that physical and 'stately bodies' are entangled in political action, the body/polis opposition in the case of this tragedy: 'the enemy appears as pure body: a body that takes sides against the bodies of co-citizens, a warring body, a body that kills and is killed: *body politic* in a direct rather than metaphorical sense' (2002, 47).

The passage from the tragedy that has initiated this section is taken from Antigone's dirge, whilst taken to her tomb to be buried alive – the ultimate annihilation of her living body. As Judith Butler has commented, Antigone's death 'is always double throughout the play: she mourns over her imminent death, but also for the fact that she has not lived, that she has not loved, and that she has not borne children' (2000, 23). As she walks to the land of the dead, she realizes that she has already been there, since 'her punishment precedes her crime' (77), as an extension of her parents' incest, Butler has remarked:

Look at me, men of my fatherland,
    Setting out on the last road
Looking into the last light of day

The last I will ever see . . .
The god of death who puts us all to bed
Takes me down to the banks of Acheron alive –
       denied my part in the wedding-songs,
no wedding-song in the dusk has crowned my marriage –
I go to wed the lord of the dark waters. (806-816 [900-908])

Butler's turn to *Antigone* has offered two versions of the tragedy's impact on political thinking. In *Antigone's Claim*, the overarching theme is the battle over sovereignty, entangled in the paradoxical act of challenging power, while embodying its norms (2000, 10). Butler's reading and interpretation focus on Antigone's language acts, highlighting the importance of performance, particularly since *Antigone* is a play after all. In this context, Antigone's defiance of state power is double: not only does she disobey Creon's edict, but she also boldly accepts that she has done it: 'I did it. I don't deny a thing' (443 [496]) she responds to his interrogation: 'do you deny you did this, yes or no?' (442 [491]). Her defiance is even bolder when Creon asks her: 'were you aware a decree had forbidden this?' (447[496]) to which she answers back swiftly: 'Well aware. How could I avoid it? It was public'. (448[497]) In taking full responsibility for her transgression, Antigone tries to appropriate Creon's sovereignty, although in the end she fails, Butler has observed (2000, 77).

When the figure of Antigone returns in *Precarious Life* (2004) though, it is the heroine's grief and lamentation of ungrievable lives that Butler is more interested in. Antigone's act of burying her brother 'exemplified the political risks in defying the ban against public grief during times of increased sovereign power and hegemonic national unity' (46). As Henao Castro (2020) has commented, Butler's interpretation of Antigone's grief in *Precarious Life* creates 'a frame of grievability', wherein ethics and politics are interwoven. But what Butler does not consider in her analysis is the political impact of Antigone's grief over her own life, a recurring trope in the play, as I have already noted above. Antigone's lamentation is not only about her death, but also about the fact that she feels she has no home, neither with the living, nor with the dead. 'I am a stranger' (868 [956]) she bemoans, grieving over her unlived life. Antigone 'is indeed a stranger [*metoikos*] to every given order' Cavarero has commented (2002, 41). Her actions estrange her not only from the tyrannical regime of the *polis,* but also from her beloved sister – 'you are in love with impossibility' (90 [104]) Ismene tells her in the opening scene of the play. Her fiancé, Haemon, kills himself in devastation after having warned his father Creon that 'her death will kill another' (751 [842]). Antigone, however, does not refer to Haemon, not even once in the play. Her grief is over losing an important ritual in a woman's life – her wedding, not over her future husband. Within the economy of the tragedy, she has distanced herself from

Haemon, well before his unsuccessful plea to save her life. In Henao Castro's reading of the tragedy, Antigone's reluctance to connect with her fiancé can be understood as 'a refusal to compromise the ontological ambiguity of her strangeness in marriage [given] the inseparable function of marriage in organizing and regulating political membership' (2013, 316).

It is the interruption of Antigone's dirge in the canonical readings of the play within feminist theory and beyond that Honig has taken as a starting point in a new reading of the tragedy. Antigone's lamentation 'is always and inexorably political-even partisan' she has commented (2013, 120). Without denying the power of public grief in reconfiguring resistance politics, Honig points to the danger of death and lamentation taking over the force of the Arendtian notion of 'natality' and new beginnings in political theory. As Arendt has suggested, 'the lifespan of man running towards death would inevitably carry everything human to ruin and destruction if it were not for the faculty of interrupting and beginning something new, a faculty which is inherent in action' (1998, 246). In deconstructing 'lamentational politics', Honig considers *Antigone's* ongoing impact towards 'an agonistic humanism', particularly addressing the question of how to act politically in conditions of impossibility (2013, 8). Juxtaposed to a *mortalist humanism*, maintaining that 'what is common to humans is not rationality, but the ontological fact of mortality' (17), *agonistic hum*anism emphasizes 'natality and pleasure, power (not just powerlessness), desire (not just principle) and *thumos* (not just penthos)' (19). In Honig's succinct definition then, 'a humanism that calls on us to act not out of shared finitude but out of natalist commitments to worldiness is an agonistic humanism' (in Browning 2012, 135).

Seen in the context of 'agonistic humanism' Antigone is still a figure that laments her brother and takes the decision to bury his body against Creon's inhumane edict. But in doing so she is not just a conscientious objector of a tyrannical regime, a humanist lamenter of the dead or a monstrous creature of desire – three subject positions that canonical readings of the play have mostly configured for her, Honig has argued (7). Antigone laments, 'but she does so in a way that is also partisan, vengeful, not just mournful or humanist' (8). It is not only the dead that drive her action, but also her loyalty to her living sister Ismene, whom she tries to protect till the end, Honig maintains in a completely new reading of the two sisters' relationship in the play. 'Courage! Live your life. I gave myself to death, long ago, so I might serve the dead' (559–560 [630–631]) is Antigone's last address to her sister, before taken to her tomb. In doing so, she takes responsibility for Polynike's first burial – an act that remains a mystery in the tragedy,[8] but could have been performed by Ismene, Honig has suggested (2013, 161). In protecting her sister, Antigone 'enacts sorority as a different sort of citizenship' in Honig's interpretation (91) In this context, lamentation is not taken as an affective practice, expressing pain and grief, but rather as a complex political vernacular, overflowed with multiple, different and contested meanings in Honig's analysis (89). The question here is not about what lamentation is, but rather about what it does.

Against long-held readings of the play that see Ismene as an anti-political character, Honig identifies a language conspiration in the scene where the two sisters confront each other in front of Creon: 'Never share my dying, don't lay claim to what you never touched. My death will be enough' (615–617 [546–547]) Antigone responds to her sister's imploration: 'Oh, no my sister, don't reject me please, let me die beside you, consecrating the dead together' (544–545{613–615]). According to Honig's new reading then, the language conspiracy lies precisely in Antigone's dismissal of her sister's confession, as an act of protection and not as a sign of disdain for her. The sister's quarrel 'is a theatrical performance for Creon's benefit' (2013, 167), Honig argues, in dissecting aspects of political agency in both women's deeds and words. It is Honig's proposition of 'an agonistic humanism' through the prism of the politics of lamentation that I want to explore in the next section, following lines of migrant and refugee women's narratives.

Lost Lives and New Beginnings

But I still had to make a decision
if I moved to that camp
I would be free from all the pressure in Iran
but at the same time
I was giving up my life
because I had to dedicate my life
to having more activities
just to help the Iranian people
this was a decision I had to make

An Antigonean theme that runs as a red thread through Somi's story is the realization that she had to sacrifice her life in the struggle against the Iranian regime. Her brothers did not remain unburied, but were unjustly killed, so she followed Antigone's steps in civil disobedience. But reverberating Antigone's sacrifice, not only for the dead brother, but also for the living sister, Somi took the decision, to honour her two brothers' death but also to create new possibilities for the living, herself and a new generation of Iranian women:

I accepted the risks
I took the fears

and everything
and I just travelled

The lamentation of her brothers' death was not restricted to mourning, although in her story Somi admitted that there was a lot of grief in her family after her brothers' execution. It was precisely the sadness and continuous grief in her family that made Somi's decision to leave extremely difficult:

I didn't want to leave them
I knew they had already lost two kids
if they lost me too
that would be very hard on them
and yet
I didn't really have a choice
I just couldn't continue my life there

In raising the question of the impossible choice, Somi situates herself in what Alenka Zupančič has configured as the plane of the 'forced choice', in its two manifestations: the classical and the modern. (1998, 110) Seen in the light of the 'classical forced choice' Antigone will either obey the sovereign power and leave her brother unburied – an hubris to her family, the gods and the *polis,* or she will bury him fulfilling her duty as a god abiding human/sister/daughter/citizen and die. However, Antigone goes beyond this dualistic opposition in Zupančič's reading. By transgressing the subject position of the guardian of divine law or family honour, she moves into the position of creating something new: *'the ability to choose where there is no choice'* (Zupančič 1998, 110, emphasis in the text). Honig takes Zupančič's idea of creativity within the ethical realm of 'the impossible choice' further, by pointing to its political dimensions. Antigone's dirge is an *agon* over the meaning of her action, which will leave its marks in history and will appear in the public sphere of *the polis,* irrespective of her death, the dissolution of her corporeal body. This is how Honig sketches Antigone's political creativity: 'she responds to the forced choice thrust upon her by constructing for herself something like the elongated beautiful death of Homer's heroes' (2013, 175).

What I therefore, suggest is that Somi's decision to leave her family can better be understood as a 'modern forced choice' in Honig's political redeployment of Zupančič's schema. Her story unveils the long process, the how of the 'forced choice', repeatedly emphasizing how she grew up feeling like a stranger [*metoikos*] in her own country: 'wherever I went, anything I wanted to do, there was an obstacle in my way'. When she went to university, Somi found herself in a group of students who were trying to organize a resistance network:

we would write small letters
against the regime
and at night
when everybody was asleep
we used to go door to door to the dormitories
and give the letters
telling students
you should start speaking out
now
let's go to the demonstration
let's stand up
against this criminal regime

Somi's struggle was thus a continuing effort to redraw the lines of the polity that excluded and marginalized her, an Antigonean line of resistance that Chanter has succinctly traced (2010, 94). But when their activities became known to the university authorities, they were threatened with expulsion. It was then that the idea of joining a dissidents' organization outside Iran emerged: 'I was not going to tolerate the situation anymore'. Instead of being restricted to 'lamentational politics', Somi's decision to leave was turned into an Arendtian new beginning, 'so that the future generation, the other girls, wouldn't have to go through what I went through in my life'. But it seems that Somi's life seems to have unfolded as a series of disasters and new beginnings:

every step I was taking in my life
I was hoping for a better future
but it was like
every step
was just another mistake

Although Somi did not go into a tomb to be buried alive, she had to bury her dreams of living a carefree adult life. Her experience in the Iraqi dissidents' camp was fierce and violent – she was not walled up in an earth tomb like Antigone, but the refugee camp was a marginal space, which became a death trap in the wake of the Iraq war. Somi's experience during this time 'illuminates the process according to which any contingent fact [. . .] can become a ground for an exclusionary politics', Chanter has commented (2010, 93). The last part of Somi's story around her stateless condition in Albania, where she was transferred after the disbanding of the Iraqi camp, unfolds as a dirge over 'a lost life'. Its textual transposition from the prose of the preceding *interlude* to the stanzas of the rythmanalysis approach has made connections with Sophocle's tragic poetry, some trails of which we have already followed in the previous section of this chapter:

at that time
I had a lot of stress
I had lost my whole life
I was not allowed to go to university
I was not allowed to get a job
I had lost my family
I had lost everything

When Somi crossed the borders to go to Greece, she had hoped for a better future, but again she found herself in a country hit by a deep financial crisis and uncontrolled refugee flows. It took a lot of courage to undergo imprisonment when she was arrested at the airport with a fake passport and was threated with deportation back to Iran: 'when we were getting attacked, when we were in the camps, I was afraid of my life, it was too hard. But when I was in prison and they were telling me I would be deported, that was a lot harder for me.' There were many moments in her story, when Somi wept over her 'lost life', but every time her dirge turned into a vengeful defiance

I have done a promise to myself
until the day I die
I am going to try
and try again
even if I fail
every day
until the rest of my life

Somi's pledge at the end of her story, was a sign of agonistic resilience and perseverance, as I will further discuss in Chapter 6. What has particularly struck me in her story is that every time she has been rising up again, she has also been rewriting or transforming the grounds of her exclusion, as Chanter has pithily commented on Antigone's historical and political rebirths (2010, 93).

Uprooted women reflected a lot on the difficulty and pain of the decision to leave, the process of their 'forced choice' (Zupančič 1998), even when there was almost nothing to leave behind. In doing so they were continuously vacillating between the two Antigonean subject positions that Honig's analysis has identified: 'the active dissident' and 'the vulnerable lamenter' (2013, 69). Click agonized a lot over her friend's suggestion that they should leave Zimbabwe and join the guerrilla forces in Mozambique to fight for freedom.

At the time she was living with her friend's family after her father was killed in the war of independence against the British imperialism:

One day we went together to the well
to fetch some water
and then she said to me
we must
let's go and fight
we must go
I said
go?
where?
she said to Mozambique
I said
Mozambique?
what about school?
and she said
do you think all these missionaries will take care of you?
we must go and fight
I said
no
she said
you don't have a family
let's go
I said
no
she said
I thought you were my friend
I said
no, no, no, no
I can't go
But overnight
I decided
I said OK
I decided to go⁹

Click's ambivalence about joining the freedom fighters was expressed in the staccato rhythm her story sounded in my ears, but in unravelling their perilous journey, she never really clarified how and why she changed her mind overnight. In the sonics of my understanding however, it was her friend's determination and a feeling of love, care and camaraderie that gave them courage to walk through the dangerous bush for days 'without food and without water'. Her decision can be framed within the schema of sorority based democratic politics that Honig has offered in her analysis, as already discussed above. She decided to follow her friend not on the basis of a shared finitude – dying together in the war for independence – but on the basis of her Arendtian determination to live in-the-world-with-others, a 'natalist commitments to wordliness' in Honig's pity definition of 'agonistic humanism' (in Browning 2012, 135).

When the two friends finally crossed the borders of a flooded river and joined the Mozambique soldiers, they were treated with suspicion, because nobody could trust two young girls: 'they were very harsh with us'. Both Somi and Click talked about the risks of being recognized as political actors, because of their gender. 'What man alive would dare' (248 [281]), Creon wondered, when told about the violation of his edict, immediately taking the gender of the offender for granted. It took a year in the military camp before Click and her friend could start their training. And yet, they persevered and eventually actively contributed to the history of liberating their country. Echoing Antigone's political imaginary, their actions was a critique of the colonial conditions that had perpetuated suffering for their people and a call for a radical future that has yet to be realized.

Gender norms and restrictions were not only externally imposed, but also very deeply and forcefully internalized as well. When Hanna first got involved in agonistic politics in Greece, fighting for migrant women's right to claim residence status, she was confronted with her own ghosts of being afraid to speak in public, as we have already seen in Chapter 2. Hanna's decision to speak was a new beginning in her life; her own dirge was an internal process that eventually took her out of the dark holes of patriarchy and into the public sphere of appearance and action. This exit, however, has not absorbed the pain of not having seen her son for thirty years, since she left her country:

I will never forget this moment
when I was saying goodbye
to my people
and was mostly crying

Material suffering and bodily pain were at the heart of Hanna's story, narrated in full in the following *interlude*. She went through the horrible experience of assisting her childhood friend to bury her new-born baby, but she also had to bury her own dream of seeing her son grow up. Her forced displacement was unavoidable though, the only possible escape from unbearable entanglements of poverty and tyranny: 'People got sick and there were no doctors and at the same time you didn't have the right to speak or say anything. Sometimes we had to go for days without any food and I just felt I was living a nightmare that keeps returning in my dreams up until now.' Hanna's body that suffered, however, also became the body that talked back and acted against her predicament.

But while for Hanna it was political activism that opened up a new path in her life, for Elena it was science and academic writing that threw light in her dark times. Her response to my question of how she imagined her life in five years' time was unequivocal:

I want to go on with my research
I already have several publications
I actually wrote most of them
when we were hiding
it was a small house
there was only a room
and a kitchen
but I was working non-stop
as we were trying to keep sane
my research took my mind away
from all the drudgeries
that's how I published so many things
when we were hiding
when I crossed the borders
I only had a bag
with very few things
but my computer with my work was with me

A genealogy of women's involvement in science and politics has yet to be written, but there are some significant events in considering the relevance of science studies in the long durée of women's fighting for freedom and independence. (see Koblitz 1988, Tamboukou 2020) It was precisely the emancipatory aspects of scientific knowledge that have made the Gülenist movement so appealing to many young Turkish women, like Elena, as we have already seen in Chapter 3. When talking about her decision to leave Turkey and cross the borders on her own, carrying her three-months-old baby daughter, Elena remembered how difficult this decision was and how estranged and isolated she had felt, particularly so from her academic community: 'I was especially hurt by my supervisor's attitude [. . .] we had a lot of projects, and publications but when he heard that I was fired, first thing he did was to block my phone number and tell my friends that I was sick, and that they shouldn't call me.' Not knowing what to do, Elena ultimately took the decision to run away. She recounted her escape in what sounded in my ears as a slow-motion cinematic narrative:

We were four people
I was alone
with my baby
nobody accompanied me
maybe that was the hardest time for me
I could have been kidnapped
I was travelling with people we didn't know'
[. . .]
The smuggler drove us close to the border
after that
I turned my head away
and I didn't even look at him
in the eye
it was dangerous
we found ourselves at the border
and the hard journey started
I gave my baby some medicine
to make her sleep
she was sleeping
when we crossed the borders
she had no idea of what was going on now
when we crossed the river
we started walking
we could see the border
we were taking courage
there was the border
we wanted to escape from
and there was the other border
where we wanted to get caught
we were longing to see a police officer
and say
please arrest us
now

While walking between borderlines, Elena was fully aware of the life-threatening risks she was taking: 'I was crying [. . .] I could be one of those people who had either die or drowned and I could have lost my child'. Elena's dirge was over the bleak prospect of death hanging over her illegal crossing, but she also knew that 'there was only one way for us'. Her narrative brings forward the ethics and politics of 'forced choice', and it is her entanglement in the aporetic situation of making 'the impossible choice' (Zupančič 1998) that turns her passive melancholia into the creative force of becoming a fugitive.

Her lamentation over the risks of border crossing was at the same time an affirmation of a new beginning:

A new life started for me
on that day
we were in a detention centre
for three days
but of course
I understand
they had to do that
we had crossed the borders

Elena's decision to cross the borders was an act of taking back her rights of free movement. Her passport had been confiscated and the authorities had denied issuing a passport for her baby daughter. Going beyond the lamentation of having been stripped of her civil rights, Elena thus decided to reclaim them. As Balibar has aptly noted 'the whole history of emancipation is not so much the history of the demanding of unknown rights, as of the real struggle to enjoy rights which *have already been declared*' (2002, 6, emphasis in the text).

Seen in the shadow of Antigone's civil disobedience Elena's act of crossing the border can thus be made intelligible through Gabriel Tarde's idea of a philosophy of 'having': 'All philosophy hitherto has been based on the verb *Be*, the definition of which was the philosopher's stone, which all sought to discover. We may affirm that, if it had been based on the verb *Have*, many sterile debates and fruitless intellectual exertions would have been avoided'. (2012, 52, emphasis in the text). Society can be defined as a complex system of reciprocal possessions according to Tarde, to the point where the Cartesian cogito ergo sum should be replaced with '*I desire, I believe, therefore I have*'. (Tarde 2012, 52, emphasis in the text) 'Having' thus creates *assemblages* of complex systems, types and degrees of entangled possessions, which have yet to be considered, classified and catalogued in the way science has done it: 'The deep and accelerating divergence between the course of science strictly speaking and that of philosophy comes from the fact that the former, happily, has chosen for its guide the verb Have. For science, everything is explained by properties, not by entities' (Tarde 2012, 53).

What I suggest then, is that Elena's and indeed all uprooted women's passage to freedom is a forceful expression of a philosophy of 'having', rather than 'being'. The different tactics they have deployed in grasping their right for free movement materialize Honig's idea of 'an agonistic humanism that sees in mortality, suffering, sound, and vulnerability resources for some form of enacted if contestable universality' (2013, 19). Universality should not be taken here as homogeneity, since the resources that Honig refers to are various, diverse, contested and multiple. Agonistic humanism should rather be taken as an *assemblage* encompassing components of grief, mortality and suffering, but also of natality, pleasure and power, taken as *potentia*.[10] Mapped within the *assemblage* of 'agonistic humanism', lamentation is not only about shared human finitude, but also and perhaps more importantly, about vengeance, politics and the quest for sovereignty, Honig has succinctly remarked (2103, 18). Like Antigone, uprooted women are lamenting subjects, grieving over forced choices of leaving behind their loved ones, as well as cherished places and spaces. In doing so, they raise to the challenge of grappling with unprecedented difficulties, confronting life threatening risks and indeed facing death. But while lamenting, they are also reborn as political agents, who plot, conspire, manoeuvre and act politically, re-imaging their futures and opening up paths in and out of personal troubles and wider geopolitical upheavals. Through narrating their actions they finally leave mnemonic traces, and forcefully intervene in the making of future archives.

ACTING, NARRATING, REMEMBERING

Arendt's philosophical take on biography suggests that 'narratives invent stories that accompany history' (Kristeva 2001, 15). What is exactly the relationship between the 'invented story' and history? In Arendt's thought, Kristeva notes, there is a discrepancy between the actor and what constitutes a heroic action. Actors make history only if their action is recorded and becomes memorable and this memorialization is the role of narratives: 'One immortalizes one's self by becoming a "*who*" that acts within political space, thus giving rise only to a memorable narrative' (19, emphasis in the text). How is this memory constituted? 'It is *spectators* who complete the story in question, and they do so through *thought,* thought that follows upon the *act.* This is a completion that takes place through *evoked memory,* without which there is nothing to tell' (16, emphasis in the text).

Following Arendt's take on the entanglements between narratives, memory and history, Söderbäck sees political action unfolding in three steps: 'first in an action, then in the witnessing of this action, and finally in the memory and commemoration of it' (2010, 71). It is in this context that Antigone emerges in a double configuration in Söderbäck's reading of the tragedy: as an actor, transgressing the law and as a spectator of her political action, who sings it through her dirge, memorializes it and inscribes it in history. Uprooted women's narratives follow this Arendtian tripartite schema: (a) they have acted by intervening in the ethics and politics of 'forced choices', (b) they have become spectators and indeed narrators of 'impossible' actions rendered possible and (c) they are in the process of inscribing the mnemonic traces of their actions in emerging decolonial histories and feminist genealogies. As Söderbäck has eloquently commented 'Antigone's actions have not only survived in various stories for generations to come, but also continue to inspire and make possible subsequent acts of resistance' (2010, 77).

NOTES

1. Somi's story, a café in Athens, 7 December 2018.
2. Given the limitations of this chapter, I have only focused on themes that are relevant to the analysis of uprooted women's narratives. For most recent overviews of feminist literature on Antigone, see Söderbäck 2010 and Honig 2013.
3. For an extended discussion of the figuration of the *narrative persona*, see Tamboukou 2018.
4. Citations to the play indicate first the Greek lines and then in square brackets the lines from the Fagles translation (1984).
5. The background of the *Antigone's* play lies in Sophocle's previous tragedies. When Oedipus, King of Thebes, discovered that without knowing it, he had killed his father and married his mother, Jocasta, he put out his own eyes, while Jocasta killed herself. Once Oedipus gave up his throne, his two sons, Polyneices and Eteocles, agreed to alternate as king. But when Eteocles refused to give up power to Polyneices, the latter attacked the city. When the two brothers killed each other in the battle, Creon, Jocasta's brother, became the new king. In his attempt to bring order, he decided that Eteocles would be given an honourable burial, while Polyneices corpse would remain unburied on the battlefield as a punishment for attaching his home city.
6. For earlier engagements with Antigone, see Irigaray, 1974; Elshtain, 1982; Dietz, 1985; Zerilli, 1991. The current developing body of literature includes, Butler, 2000, 2004; Cavarero 2002; Sjöholm, 2004, 2010; Söderbäck, 2010; Honig, 2013; Gsoels-Lorensen, 2014; Henao Castro, 2013, 2020.
7. For more details about this project, see http://www.openartfoundation.org/antigone-of-syria
8. Creon's edict is violated twice in the play. The first time, an unknown person throws dust on the body as a symbolic burial act. The body is re-exposed by the guards, but a second burial is performed, and Antigone is caught in the act. Everybody assumes that she performed both burials, but this mystery has never been resolved. (See Honig 2013, 157–161 for a discussion of various readings and interpretations of this second burial in the *Antigone* literature)
9. Click's story, her workshop at the *Victoria Square project*, 20 March 2019.
10. In Braidotti's conceptual vocabulary, power is taken both as entrapment (*potestas*) and as empowerement (*potentia*) (2019, 33).

Interlude III

HANNA'S STORY

I will start with this, why I left my country for Greece. Things were very difficult because we were under a dictator and things were very rough. I found myself in a terrible situation, because in my family there were serious problems. My father was working, but then they fired him, because he was not a supporter of the dictator and we all had to suffer. If you were not with the part of the dictators, you were out of job and your family would suffer like that. And then there were more problem for me at school. Children got sick and there were no doctors and at the same time you didn't have the right to speak or say anything. Sometimes we had to go for days without any food and I just felt I was living a nightmare that keeps returning in my dreams up until now. Many times, I have to wake up in a state of shock, not shock, but a state that makes you feel totally depressed. Because sometimes in the night and maybe in the mornings or any time in the day, I think about this and it makes me feel depressed. Sometimes I wake up in the night or in the morning, and I can still hear people shouting. I will never forget it, how people were shouting, 'my husband is dead', 'my child is dead', and children were crying, I don't know what to say. Friends of mine were dying and during this time I was in deep depression. Our house was in front of a cemetery, so as a child, I had to watch how people were just dying, day after day. At that time, the dictator only cared about himself and his people, so if you were not with them, you just had to suffer.

At that time because of the dictatorship, you could not walk at nights and imagine if you were sick, where were they going to take you? I remember my niece, my niece broke my heart because she was sick and me and my sister were looking for a doctor, running up and down, but we couldn't find one and then she died in my hands. And then sometimes we had black outs in Sierra Leone; there are still black outs there and you had to stay in the dark all the time. One of the worst things I can remember was this dictator. Sometimes he went around, he would go to churches, visiting churches so that he could gain votes, talking to people about voting for him, there was no other party anyway. So, sometimes he came to our church. When he came, they made sure that there were lights, but when he left, we were in blackouts again. And this happened because we lived in a tropical country then, which was back to zero, you understand.

So, these things were going on, even in my school. Most of my schoolmates were just dying: How can you bear seeing your friends get sick and die? Even if you had appendicitis, people would die from appendicitis. And at that time, children of my age, because I had my son when I was sixteen years old, children like my own age, got pregnant and tried to have an abortion, not knowing what an abortion would do. So, there were people going to these rich doctors that you cannot meet, they stole the instruments from the doctors, they were not even educated, but they came and did abortions in my area, I lost many friends from that. Me, myself I nearly lost my life because of that, you understand.

So, things were going very bad, but what happened to me, I think for my own luck, was that I found a job. This job was in a Greek company. I found a job in a Greek company and I made friends with Greeks and we had holidays together and things like that. But these people worked there for a certain period. When their time was up, they had to leave. So, when some of my Greek friends were preparing to leave, I told them about our household situation; that in my family nobody was working, that I was the only one working and that I had to support all the rest of my family: my father, my sister and my son – I had a son, but I wasn't married. So, I asked them to help me so that I could support my family, because life was very bad, everything was so scarce, food was scarce, doctors were scarce. We had no doctors. It was not like now. In Africa now, we have so many aid organizations, but back then there were no organizations. We were just in the middle of a desert, not a desert but a jungle, an animal jungle. You lived there and if you survived, you survived.

I remember one day, one morning I was sleeping, I woke up in the morning and one of my friends, she was fourteen to fifteen years old like me, and she was knocking on my window. She said, 'please Hanna, open the door, I have a problem'. I said, 'what problem?' She asked me, 'do you have a hoe?' You know this tool that we use to dig the plants. I said, 'what do you want it for?' She said, 'I want to bury my baby because I've just had a baby and I want to bury it.' I said, 'What? What are we going to do with the baby now?' You understand? So, I advised her to go out and find some adults so that we could ask for help; we couldn't just go and bury the baby like that. And that's what we did. But you can just imagine that everybody was responsible for this situation. You could see women get pregnant. When they were pregnant what could they do? I lost a lot of friends. When you were pregnant there was 70 per cent chance that you would die. And that's going on up till now. When you hear that somebody is pregnant, you know what might happen. Child death rates are also very high.

I come back to my story now, to the place I was working. So, I asked, I begged these Greek friends of mine to help me leave the country. But at the same time, it was very difficult for me, I had my son, my son was then one year old. How could I leave him? Do you understand? But I decided, I said, either I stay here, and we are all dead, or I go away to help, you understand. So, I decided, I talked to these Greek friends and then they said, 'Ok, when we go to Greece, we will see what we can do for you. We will help you.' And really, it was my luck, really, I was very lucky. When they went to Greece, they sent me a ticket to travel to Greece. At that time, we had a Greek consulate in my country, not now. So, I went to the Greek consul, he was a businessman. I said, 'I have this ticket to go to Greece'. And then he said to me, 'How can you go to Greece? You don't have a passport'. Yes, I did not have a passport, because I didn't know you needed one. And then he said, 'you also have to have 500 dollars and you also need to have a return ticket, to show that you are coming back'. I said, 'oh my god, how can I go? How can I go to Greece?' OK, I was crying of course, as this was my only opportunity to escape. When they sent me the ticket for Greece, I said 'I am going to leave now'. But when I went to the consulate, I found out that I needed huge things, like a passport, traveller cheques of 500 dollars and a return ticket. Where could I get this return ticket? What could I do?

So, I was crying, and I went to see some of my friends. I told them that I had a ticket and that some good friends in Greece were trying to help me. But the consul had told me that I also needed a passport, where could I look for passports? In my country, I didn't know how to do it with my government; I had no idea, I had never thought of it, do you understand? So, what could I do? I went to my friends and then they told me, 'send a telegram to these people in Greece'. So, I sent a telegram to Greece and the next day they sent the ticket to me, the return ticket, the next day. Just as if they were waiting for me in Greece, the next day they sent me the return ticket. Now how did I manage to find the 500 dollars? Well I found it. This is what happened: I went to my house and I sold *everything* that I had. I *sold everything* and then I had 590 dollars. And then I met the consul and he said 'bravo, how did you find it?' In a one-week time, I had found everything that he had asked from me. I wasn't paid a lot, I only got five dollars a month. But how did I manage to find 500 dollars? Because I took *everything* in my house and sold it and the house was like when you move, nothing inside.

But I was having another problem. I was born an activist, because my father was a creole – these old slaves that they freed – and my mother was a country woman, she was not educated, so they always discriminated against me. So, since I was a child, I was fighting, and this made me become an activist. So, when this government, this dictator's government came to power, I was talking to people, 'why is this happening?' My father was all afraid of that, because in that place, when you talk, you are punished. So, my family was afraid because this dictator had spies everywhere; and they reported you every time you talked.

So, what happened to me was that I had all these dollars, I had the dollars, I had the ticket to come to Greece, I was supposed to transit in Paris, but when I was at the airport, they arrested me, they arrested me at the airport. How could I go to Greece? The plane was about to leave, everybody was inside, and I was at the police station. But, luckily for me, my father was with me and he had a distant relative who was the head of the police at the airport. I didn't know him, as my father was not in touch with him because of his ties with the dictator. So, my father asked to see this man and said, 'what has happened? My child was arrested, and the plane is leaving, she will not go'. And this man helped me, I was the last to go inside the airplane, and then they closed the door. And when I was going inside the plane, I climbed the steps and then I stood up, I turned and said, 'you will never see me here again, the dictatorship is finished, F... you!' And then I left, you understand, I just said, 'F... you, I am leaving', and the door closed, and I left Sierra Leone for Paris. From Paris, I came to Greece alone.

When I came to Greece, I did not know the language, I was in a different planet, I did not know anybody, and I had said goodbye to my people. The one scene that I remember was when I was saying goodbye to my people. All my soul was crying, you won't believe how I felt. Up until now, when I see a movie where they say goodbye, I will cry, up until now. I will never forget this moment when I was saying goodbye to my people and was mostly crying. So, when I arrived in Greece, I did not know anything, I didn't speak a word, I only knew how to say Alpha, Beta, Gama (ABC). So, when a policeman asked me something at the airport, I just showed my passport and then I said, 'Alpha, Beta, Gama', I didn't know anything else'. And then these people who helped me had come to the airport to meet me, but the plane that I was supposed to come was not the plane I eventually came, so they waited and then they had to leave. I was all alone, but since I had the address of the place that I was going, I took a taxi and it took me to these people.

Everybody was happy, they kept me for around six months before I was able to find my own place and a job. But the next problem that I faced when I left my country was that I was not aware of this immigration system and how it worked – trying to get a residence permit, you understand, that was another problem. I tried to ask for political asylum and they said, 'there is no way you can do that'. At that time there was no Internet to see photos of what was happening. Now you know what is happening around the world, but back then there was no Internet and no proof to say what was happening in my country, that we had this dictator, you understand. And that man was killing people. I remember that one day he killed about ninety-five people. It was ninety-six people he was supposed to kill, but he freed one of them and this person was the one who started the civil war years after, you understand? He was the one who started the civil war. So, I was not having any proof to show that I was from a dictatorship country and that I needed political asylum, and nobody cared, you understand. So, I accepted it, I said 'I have to live my life, I won't go back, I won't go back to Sierra Leone.' The conditions of life in Sierra Leone were unbearable, so I had to live somewhere, I had to help my son, I had to help my family; so, I stayed.

I started looking for a job. I went to find some people from my country; I asked them what they were doing, and the women told me, 'we are doing house jobs'. Believe me, I said, 'OK I can do this house job' and they advised me that the best way was to find a job where I could live in people's houses, so this is what I did. I found a job that I had to live inside a Greek family house. That was also very good for me because I got to know the Greeks very well, you understand. Because sometimes you think, you look at something bad, but if you look closely, you can find something good inside. The good thing that I found was that I got to know the Greek family. That's why when I go to give a speech at some place now, I tell them, 'we know you, but you don't know us. You just see us like immigrants, but we know you, we've been in your house, we have worked in your houses, we know how you live'. That's why in our organization I always tell the women who come: this is our own house, come and know us the way we know you. You understand, because some people they just stay there, and they say 'the immigrants.' You don't know the immigrants! Try to know them, you understand.

But while I was working, I didn't find how I could have my residence permit; it was very difficult for me. But luckily for me at that time, the police were not harassing people, so I just lived and worked in some family houses. But you don't know how difficult it is not to have a residence permit; it is a very difficult thing. Sometimes I worked for a month with some bad family and then I left, but I was afraid to go back and ask for my money. You know, sometimes, I would leave my wages, because I was afraid that they would find me and deport me to my country. Some even threaten you, 'if you call me, for your money again, I will report you', because all the time people knew that I didn't have a residence permit. So, they could deport you, I have even seen two women from my country being deported with their children. So, in Greece we didn't have a Human Rights Organization at that time. It is now that you have Human Rights Organizations, but at that time, nobody knew, you understand. So, when I worked in a house and they treated me badly and I wanted to leave, I just left and I was leaving my money as well, you understand.

So, for years I was working at people's houses and then in 1998, they decided to legalize all immigrants. I submitted my papers and I was legalized, so then I became more independent, I could stop working in people's houses and live with them. For the first time in my life, since I came to Greece, I had my residence permit, for the first time! But what happened is that I was working in a house and then somebody that I was taking care of, died. And at this time the Greek government was asking us to give them papers from our boss, as a guarantee for the fact that we were working. Because my employer had died, I was in danger of losing my residence permit and being sent back to my country as a consequence. But this is what I said to myself: 'there is no way I will lose my residence permit, no I will not take it easy, there is something I can do, they can't keep treating us like that'. So, I had to find a new way. Somebody advised me that there was a woman lawyer, who was an advocate for immigrant women, and they gave me her address. Somebody said, 'go to her and tell her about your problem, maybe she can help you'. I found her phone, I called her, and I went to her office.

When I went there, I was just crying. She was asking me what had happened, and I was just crying. I don't know what to say because I was living in Greece for seventeen good years without a residence permit and then I got it, but was I to lose it again? I had no money in my hand, my passport had expired, I was having nothing! So, I decided, I said 'NO, there is something going on, let me see what I can do'. And then I went to this woman and I was just crying. She said, 'what happened?' Before she could get me to talk, several minutes passed, but then I finally explained what had happened to me. She told me, 'for me now, I cannot help you, but what will happen is that I know a women's organization and I will take you to them, so you can talk. I said, 'ok, let's go'.

But for me, for African women, it is very difficult to speak in public because in Africa when I was there, everything you do, they tell you, 'shut up, you are a woman, what do you want to say?' So, we have been used to this society in Africa. And then she took me to this organization, but when they asked me to get up and speak in public, I said, 'I cannot do that, I cannot do that', two times. But the second time, when I got home – because, whenever I have a problem, I talk to myself, I talk to myself *really* – I said, 'look, what do you want now? Are you going to speak in public, or are you going to leave without a residence permit? Just think about that. I told myself, '*decide*, here is not Africa, *decide*, what are you going to do?' And then I *decided*, I said, 'no problem, I *will speak this time*'.

And then, the lawyer took me to another organization, I forgot their name, but it was a feminist organization, and she took me there. On that day, I said:

'Hana, *this is it*'. Either you stay without a residence permit and then they get you and send you back to Sierra Leone and then you and your son and your family die, or you can *decide* otherwise'. And then I *decided*, I began to speak, I began to speak out. And what I found out was that when I began to speak out, by doing that, it made me feel safe. I began to know people, everywhere people used to say oh, this was what I was supposed to do. So, this is how I began to speak. But one day when I was at one of these European Women's organization meetings, I started wondering. I began to think 'Look at that, why can't we as African women, have something like this to talk about our problems? Why?' I was alone in the streets at night and I said to myself, 'why can't we do that? If we have our own organization, we can talk, we can do anything we want to do'.

I was thinking about that, if I tell you, for more than seven months. But I didn't know how to approach African women, you understand. I decided to call a meeting, but how? And this is what happened: I was going to this women's organization and one day there was a political rally, or something, I am not sure what it was exactly. But these women introduced me to a political leader, who was also an MP. I didn't know anything about this political party and what they were doing. But this MP invited me to go to Parliament and I went there – this women's organization took me there. But can you believe it, when I got there, all television channels were there, and instead of showing men speaking, they were showing *me*, everywhere, *everywhere*. I didn't even have a clue about that, that they were showing me. I was thinking I would speak and that was that.

But that helped me, so after that, the next day I was walking in the street and met some African women and they were saying, oh we saw you at the Parliament. And then I said, we need to talk about our problems, let's have a meeting. I gathered them all, well, most of the African women I knew. I said, 'let's have a meeting' and then I gave them the dates. But they listened to me, they believed me because they had seen me in Parliament, so it helped me. And then when I called the meeting, all of them came and I explained to them about my own problem, I said, 'this is what has happened to me'. I asked all women to talk about their own problems as well and after the meeting, we found out that this is what we were waiting for, to talk and listen to each other. At the end of the meeting, we found out that most of the women were having problems with their children's citizenship. So, we founded this organization and we started a campaign about the children's citizenship rights, and it was very successful, but I think I will end my story here.

Chapter 6

Education, Art and Radical Hope

'Being poor, African and non-Greek I do not have access to Higher Education. I want to follow postgraduate studies, but I cannot afford it. Since I do not have Greek citizenship, I cannot have access to other European Universities either' (Noor, in Louka 2020, np). Noor is a young African woman striving to follow post-graduate studies in Greece, but she is also a member of The United African Women Organization – Greece (UAWO), that Hana founded, as we have already seen in the previous *interlude*. Noor's bitter observation about the impossibilities of following graduate studies in Greece was included in a report of an important academic event that took place in Athens between 11 and 13 October 2019. Centred on the theme 'Sisterhood and Struggle: Writing Black Women's Political Leadership', the event was organized by UAWO in collaboration with The European Network of People of African Decent (ENPAD). It included workshops, women's circles, reading groups and public talks and its aim was 'to address issues concerning the politics of space, and function as a platform to access knowledge and histories of political struggle often unacknowledged in many activist spaces in Greece and elsewhere.'[1] The central speaker of this three-day event was Carole Boyce Davies, Professor of English and African Studies at Cornell University, who excavated a long genealogy of marginalized Black women's activism.[2]

This event did not emerge out of the blue, but rather as a culmination of UAWO's ongoing study of Black and Afrofeminist traditions, including a Black Feminist Skillsharing workshop, which run for five weeks in Athens between October and November 2018. When I visited Athens for the first leg of my research in December 2018, I had the chance to meet some of the wonderful women from UAWO and interview its founder. What struck me at the time and continues to do so is that these important intellectual events are happening outside the formal structures of academic institutions in Greece – Perhaps, this is why they are so vibrant and interesting.

It was in the context of crossing the borders of academia that I got involved with the 'Feminist Researchers Against Borders' (FRAB) network of academics and activists[3] and participated in the summer school of the *Feminist No Borders* short course, 'Inhabiting the Borderlands' organized in collaboration with the 'Feminist Autonomous Centre'[4] in Athens in June 19–21 2020.[5] Both of these networks have been working with the UAWO, as well as with other feminist activist groups and grass-root organizations of migrant and refugee women in Athens. Having visited all these organizations and centres and having interviewed some women in them I had the chance to see new channels of knowledge formation and new pedagogical relations emerging that keep challenging what education is (in the process of becoming). What has also struck me with these community and grass-root organizations is the entanglement of different art practices and expressions in migrant and refugee women's education.

Drawing on such experiences of re-imagining education within border situations, in this chapter, I theorize entanglements between education and art as a plane of 'radical hope' (Lear 2008), for new beginnings in uprooted women's life. As Jonathan Lear has put it, radical hope emerges from the limits of human existence and it is directed 'toward a future goodness that transcends the current ability to understand what it is.' (2008, 103) Indeed, women's attachment to and belief in the power of education runs as a red thread through their narratives, without the need to be fully grasped or understood. As always in women's histories all over the world, education is also an agonistic area, a field that women have been struggling to get access to, before, throughout and at the end of their tortured and agonizing journeys. Moreover, educational activities and practices have opened up heterotopic spaces in the dystopias of the refugee camps, as we will further see in this chapter. 'Radical hope anticipates a good for which those who have the hope, as yet lack the appropriate concepts with which to understand it', Lear has pithily commented (2008, 103).

The chapter unfolds in four parts: Following this introduction, I map the emerging field of refugee and migrant women's education within current debates around re-imagining what education is and what it can do. Here, I make connections between Lear's notion of 'radical hope' (2008) with Geert Biesta's take of education as 'a beautiful risk' (2013), opening up possibilities for new beginnings through the Arendtian quest for 'feeling at home in this world', a theme that we have already discussed in Chapter 3. In doing this, I revisit 'the art/education *assemblage*' that I have theorized elsewhere in my work (Tamboukou 2008, 2017), particularly focusing on entanglements between ethics, aesthetics and politics through the Rancièrean notion of dissensus. In the third part, I turn again to the narrative archive of my research, taking women's stories as inscriptions and traces of experiences and actions within the wider movement of decolonizing education and re-imagining it as 'a space of solidarity for knowledge exchange' (Aparna and Kramsch 2018, 93). By way of conclusion I consider how the analytics of this chapter make connections with current transnational educational policies. In looking at recent debates around refugee education, I point to the need of moving beyond debates and practices of what I call 'academic philanthropy', to consider the potential of re-imagining migrant and refugee education on the plane of radical politics. My aim in this concluding section is to explore how 'education as action' (Tamboukou 2016c) within conditions of displacement and violence can 'transgress the here-and-now' (Lotz-Sisitka 2019) and open up radical futures in migrant and refugee women's lives and beyond.

THE AESTHETICS AND POLITICS OF EDUCATION UNDER CONDITIONS OF FORCED DISPLACEMENT

This is how I arrived here [Lesvos]
and then I found myself in Moria
I slept on the floor for 8 days
there was no bed
no mattress
only cartons
every day I had terrible pains
in my back and waist
all over my body really
I thought I had got rid of my troubles in Somalia
but now I was going through new ones
then I met some people
from the écoles-en-*boîte* [schools-in-a-box]
I wanted to go to these UNICEF schools
not so much for the lessons
 but just to be in a clean space
this is the only thing I wanted
to be in a space
with clean air and oxygen
for two hours
and then after five
I would go back to Moria
to sleep on the floor
again[6]

In recounting the story of how she survived the Moria refugee camp, Warda, a young Somalian woman whose torturous journey we have already followed in Chapter 3, said that the reason she got enrolled in the UNICEF écoles-en-*boîte*[7] was not because she was interested in educating herself. Going to school was a mere survival tactic. But although it was the clean space that made her go to school, it was a 'lovely teacher from California' who helped her get over the bodily and psychological scars of her darkest moments before her escape. Warda acknowledged how much she had learnt from her teacher, but she also fondly remembered how it was through the help of her teacher that she sought medical treatment for the FGM operation in Somalia: 'I didn't tell my friends anything about this new operation; I stayed in hospital for two days and my teacher came to be with me and help me'. It was also through her teacher's intervention that she eventually left the Moria camp and found accommodation in a flat for vulnerable groups in Mytilini. As we have already seen in Chapter 3, Warda went on to enrol to mainstream secondary education with plans to become an airhostess and also joined the intercultural adult choir *CANTAlaloun* [CANTAλαλουν]. Her story of finding hope in her life through education was one of many in the archive of my research that have revolved around Lear's (2008) notion of radical hope. As Honig (2015, 625) has pithily commented, 'radical hope' raises the question of how to act hopefully while immersed in hopeless situations, by reclaiming the democratic right 'to constellate affectively around shared objects' – the UNICEF school-in-a-box objects in the case of Warda's story above.

Public things are at the heart of democratic life for Alexis de Tocqueville, whose classic analysis of *Democracy in America* (1840) has influenced Arendt's political theory.[8] If democratic life needs shared and common things, education is surely one of them. But apart from the lamentation and critique of how 'public things' have disappeared in the democratic crisis of neoliberal regimes (Honig 2015), the question of who is included in the 'demos' (see Brown 2015) is crucially important when it comes to migrant and refugee women's education, even in countries where education is still considered to be 'a public thing'. What is also important here to acknowledge is that as 'a public thing', education is inevitably a site 'of confrontation and encounter, enjoyment and conflict', as Honig has pithily observed (2015, 624).

While Warda has presented her decision to go to school as a mere desire for a clean space, away from the catastrophic environment of the Moria camp, education has done much more for her. Even in the context of the refugee condition, education responds to our 'shared need for public things around which to constellate, gather, and differ', in Honig's political poetics (625). It was through the channels of education that Warda's courage to leave the black holes of patriarchy in her native country was resignified and redirected within the ruins of the Moria refugee camp. The UNICEF educational box thus became a shared object that enabled Warda to manage the trauma of forced displacement in adapting to the reality of the refugee condition, at the same time of imagining a future that was both unknowable and elusive.

In this light, radical hope through education has offered Warda some sense of stability in moving through the abyss of the borderlands but has also mobilised her *lines of flight*. As Honig observes, 'radical hope is a key element in anyone's repertoire of resilience' (2015, 627), but it is also through the affective channels of radical hope that subjects negotiate existential and political strategies of survival and resistance, treading the thin line between messianism and despair. Such a stance towards a world that falls apart 'is a daunting form of commitment to a goodness in the world that transcend one's current ability to grasp what it is' Lear notes (2008, 100). This remark brings into mind Arendt's famous *amor mundi,* care and love for the world, as I will further discuss in connection with Geert's (2015) Arendtian configuration of education as 'a beautiful risk'.

Weakness is 'the very condition that makes education possible' Biesta provocatively argues, while inviting us to re-imagine education as a slow process full of risks and uncertainties, but also bursting with possibilities for new beginnings (2013, 4). Here he draws on Arendt's notion of 'natality' as the human faculty of making new beginnings (1994, 321). I have already discussed the importance of 'natality', as a constitutive component of political action in Chapter 5, but what I want to highlight here is that new beginnings for Arendt are also closely interrelated with freedom: 'because [he] *is* a beginning, [man] can begin; to be human and to be free are one and the same (Arendt 2006, 165–6, emphasis in the text). This link between education and freedom via Arendt goes through what Biesta calls 'emancipation as a lifelong challenge', juxtaposed to the discourses of lifelong learning (2013, 75). But such new beginnings for knowledge are always unpredictable, precarious and full of risks, as they interweave in the weak fabric of what education should be. As Tyson Lewis pithily observes however, what remains undeveloped in Biesta's thesis of 'the beautiful risk of education' is the aesthetic dimension of risk: 'beauty only arrives at the beginning of the book (in the title) and the end (actually, in the appendix) without any intervening analysis of justification' (2014, 305). It is this missing link between education and aesthetics that I now want to take up.

Elsewhere in my work I have theorized the 'art/education *assemblage*' making connections between Foucault's power relations and Deleuze's forces of desire within a range of socio-historical and cultural planes (Tamboukou 2008, 2017). What I have argued is that art and education are tightly interwoven in women's lives and beyond, gearing their *lines of flight*. In doing so I have drawn on Jacques Rancière's (2004) influential theorization of the relation between aesthetics and politics, as well as Foucault's

(1986) notion of the *ethics and aesthetics of the self* as transformative forces in the constitution of the subject. Here it is important to note however, that questions of aesthetics cannot be reduced to art. For Rancière, 'aesthetic practices are forms of visibility that disclose artistic practices', while artistic practices 'are ways of doing and making that intervene in the general distribution of ways of doing and making as well as in the relationships they maintain to modes of being and forms of visibility.' (2004, 13) In Rancière's configuration then, aesthetic practices are wider than artistic practices. As Cecilia Sjöholm has aptly commented, 'we experience aesthetic phenomena in our everyday lives, in nature, in the sciences and so on' (2015, x). It is, thus, on Rancière's famous thesis of the role of aesthetics in disrupting 'the distribution of the sensible' that I want to draw in considering the aesthetics of risk.

In Rancière's analysis, societies are structured alongside 'the distribution of the sensible', a hierarchical system, which 'reveals who can have a share in what is common to the community based on what they do and, on the time, and space in which the activity is performed' (2004, 12). The 'distribution of the sensible' is, therefore, a system where inclusion and exclusion work hand in hand defining the grounds, subjects and implicit laws of certain communities of practice and thought. As Rancière has lucidly noted above, time and space are crucial in 'the distribution of the sensible' and in this sense, we can see how migrant and refugee women amongst other marginalised groups are automatically thrown in its blind spots and grey areas. This is why Rancière rigorously argues that 'there is "an aesthetics" at the core of politics' (2004, 13), linking his understanding of aesthetics to the way Foucault (1986) has theorized entanglements between ethics, aesthetics, politics and pedagogical practices.

In taking up the concept of *aesthetics* as central in the formation of subjectivities, Foucault (1986) has highlighted the need for an *aesthetics of existence* to be cultivated through education, learning and agonistic practices, pointing to the empowering and transgressive possibilities of art. Foucault sees the *aesthetics of existence* as a sensibility towards what is happening around us, a sort of an aesthetic rationality, founded on a capacity to perceive, through an openness to experience. This sensibility is not limited to the private sphere. It extends to the public, what is out there that one cannot stand, a sensibility to what is intolerable and unacceptable. Such *an aesthetics of existence* also implies the development of an ability to judge, having the flexibility to change and have various options and criteria, for reconstructing oneself, ultimately *the ethics of the self*. In its relation to aesthetics, ethics is thus conceived as the reflexive form of freedom; 'what is ethics if not the practice of freedom, the conscious practice of freedom?' Foucault has asked (1991b, 4).

Foucault's link of ethics and aesthetics via the Kantian route of aesthetic judgement makes connections with Arendt's writings about the role of sensibility and aesthetic judgment in politics, as well as her bold argument that Kant's third critique was actually his political treatise. In Arendt's reading, 'since Kant did not write his political philosophy, the best way to find out what he thought about this matter is to turn to his "Critique of Aesthetic Judgement", where in discussing the production of artworks in their relation to taste, which judges and decides about them, he confronts an analogous problem' (1982, 61). While Kant did not write his political philosophy, Arendt did not produce an aesthetic theory. However, 'there is an aesthetics hidden in Arendt's writings', when the archive of her unpublished notes and her philosophical diary is carefully studied, Sjöholm has argued (2015, xi). In thus reconstructing an Arendtian approach to aesthetics and politics, Sjöholm has highlighted four themes: (a) public appearance; (b) permanence and resilience to commodification; (c) plurality through judgement and (d) action. It is alongside these four themes that I map Arendt's take of education as a political and therefore aesthetic process whose aim is to make human beings 'feel at home in the world'.

Conceptualizing education as an aesthetic process is a genealogical trail in the histories of the discipline that goes back to the early nineteenth century but has only recently taken up again from the perspective of radical pedagogies (see Lewis 2012). An aesthetics approach to education enhances the freedom of action for all actors – those who 'teach' and those who 'learn', while blurring the boundaries between teaching and learning in the pedagogical process. It is in this context that Arendt has highlighted responsibility and love as two components of the educational praxis: 'education is the point at which we decide whether we love the world enough to assume responsibility for it' (2006, 193). As I will further discuss in the last section of this chapter, Arendt's take of education as action makes connections with Whitehead's idea of education as adventure. But since risk is always part of any adventure, we can now come full circle to Biesta's neglected consideration of aesthetics in his Arendtian take of education as 'a beautiful risk'.

In reconsidering the aesthetics of risk, Rancière's take of politics as *dissensus* also becomes critical. For Rancière, politics is never more than a moment, a political event that disrupts *the status quo* and makes visible what the social order wishes to cover and keep invisible. There are connections between Rancière's idea of politics as dissensus and Arend's take on politics as action in concert. The two thinkers part ways, however, in that Arendt's take on the political focuses on the creative capacity of new beginnings, plurality and action, while for Rancière everything that is not *dissensus* is not politics, but police. As Samuel Chambers (2013) has observed, Rancière uses 'police,' 'policing' and 'police order' to name any order of hierarchy, including the state, political bodies, architectural constructions and I would add institutions, such as education. Police is a symbolic constitution of the social for Rancière, while the political only comes about because of the irruption of politics within a police order (Chambers 2013, 60).

We can, thus, see the link between politics and aesthetics: they come together in enacting dissensus. Although I do not agree with Rancière's thesis that 'the essence of politics and of aesthetics for that matter, is the manifestation of dissensus', I still think that 'dissensus' is an important component, downplayed in Arendt's take on politics. What I think is unique in Rancière's approach to the politics of aesthetics is the idea of discerning the power of artistic practices to unveil and flag up the disruptive forces of aesthetics. It is in this context that Rancière's politics of aesthetics has been taken up in educational theory and research from a wide range of sometimes conflicting perspectives (see Tyson 2012). In following tracks and traces of adventures and risks in the archive of the stories that migrant and refugee women generously shared with me, I will, therefore, make a new cartography of ethics, aesthetics and politics in the education of uprooted women.

DECOLONIZING EDUCATION IN BORDERLAND SITUATIONS

In April 2020, I received a message from Somi, whose full story we have followed in the second *interlude,* sharing with me her excitement for receiving a prestigious honorary award: an invitation to become a member of the Webster University Lambda Kappa Chapter of the Delta Mu Delta International Honor Society in Business, as a recognition of her outstanding academic achievement. Somi's admission in the Athens campus of Webster University to study 'Management in Human Resources' was an event that threw light in some of the darkest moments of her refugee experience and turned a whole new page in her long and tough struggle to survive the borderlands. Since our encounter in December 2018, we have been in regular communication about her studies. Somi proudly sent me her first university student identity card in February 2019, while later in April she shared with me one of her essays for which she had received full marks. Her brilliant essay was peer reviewed and has now become part of the archive of knowledges of the overall research project, 'Revisiting the nomadic subject', which underpins the writing of this book.

Somi's amazing achievements in pursuing university studies is not unique; it is rather a bright moment in a chain of academic successes that I have traced in the archive of my research, but I have also seen emerging as a trend in the wider field of migrant and refugee higher education worldwide, including UNHCR's Albert Einstein German Academic Refugee Initiative (DAFI)

Programme,[9] the Connected Learning in Crisis Consortium (CLCC),[10] as well as the Refugee Education Initiatives [REIs], a European project a funded by the *Erasmus and Social Inclusion* programme.[11] All these refugee education programmes are supported by national and international institutions in the context of the Article 26 of the Universal Declaration of Human Rights, which stipulates that 'higher education shall be equally accessible to all on the basis of merit' and that: 'education shall be directed to the full development of the human personality and to the strengthening of respect for human rights and fundamental freedoms'.[12]

Despite such forceful assertions however, the United Nations High Commissioner for Refugees (UNHCR) estimates that only 3 per cent of refugees now have access to tertiary education and that the Sustainable Development Goal Four (SDG4) 'won't be achieved if we don't prioritize refugee education'.[13] Higher Education has indeed become a priority for UNHCR as outlined in their education strategy, *Refugee Education 2030: A strategy for refugee inclusion.*[14] In, thus, addressing harsh inequalities in the field of Refugee Higher Education and beyond, the UNHCR has devised a tripartite schema of action: (a) inclusion of refugees in the national education systems of host countries; (b) funding from donor governments and (c) involvement of the private sector and individuals. In this context, their targeted contributors include 'governments, intergovernmental and regional organisations, donors within multi-lateral and bi-lateral organisations, international non-governmental organisations, private sectors and foundations, national civil society organisations, academic networks and individual philanthropists'.[15] Social movements are not listed in the UNHCR education strategy, but I suppose they could be linked to national civil society organizations. What definitely emerges from this strategy is that refugee education is an undisputable human right, but the fact that it is also a contested field is not discussed in the public documents of refugee educational policies.

Thus, apart from the fact that only 3 per cent of refugees have access to tertiary education, even when they do, they face barriers that seriously hinder and jeopardize their progress. Within a wider context of hostility geared by media representations of the refugee condition in Australia and the UK, Jaqueline Stevenson and Sally Baker (2018) have identified a range of systemic problems in Refugee Higher Education including, restricted access to widening participation structures, limited language classes for academic purposes, unaffordable fees, scarce and highly competitive scholarship opportunities, invisibility within the system, as well as curricula and pedagogical practices that alienate refugee students, eventually constituting them as 'the other' (21). Stevenson's and Baker's (2018) critical investigation of the state of Refugee Higher Education in Australia and the UK aligns with some of the challenges that Loo, Streitwieser and Jeong have identified (2018) in their overview of higher education responses in Canada, the United States, Sweden and France. Having chosen four countries that are rich in economic, human, cultural and social resources the authors have pointed to similarities and differences, but they have also flagged up two areas of concern that need to be addressed: cost and language barriers.

Situated in a country severely hit by a wave of intertwined economic and political crises, Somi's success story emerges from intersections of synergies between academic networks and NGO's. She initiated her studies in January 2019, having won a first-term scholarship from Webster University, Athens Campus and after achieving top marks in the first term, she got a full scholarship to complete her degree from LERRN [Love Elevates Refugees Relief Network], an American NGO.[16] But here it is important to note that only two candidates were awarded this scholarship. Although Somi's success is not unique, it is still exceptional and rare, and her pathway should be considered within the wider picture of only 3 per cent of refugees having access to Higher Education worldwide. For Elina, a young Syrian woman, who escaped the war after the death of her parents and the failure of her marriage, university education has now become her 'wildest dream' in the prose version of her imaginary narrative:

> What I want now is to reunite with my son and then stay in Greece and study. I want to learn Greek and English and to go on with university studies and become a doctor. This is my dream. I don't want to get married again; I only think of my studies. When I was in Syria after finishing school, I trained as a nurse, and then I worked in a hospital for 2 months. That's why I want to follow medical studies. It is my wildest dream.[17]

The dream of studying to become a doctor has indeed sustained Elina during the darkest moments of her refugee experience, particularly so when she was trying to cross the Syrian Turkish borders: 'I tried to cross the borders six times, but the Turkish police would be there, and they were shooting people.' Her sea passage to Greece was also 'difficult and dangerous' as 'again the Turkish police would come, arrest people and send them to prison'. When she finally reached Greece, she had to endure the dreadful experience of the Moria camp for five months, before she was transferred to a flat in Mytilini, where I met her through Iliaktida. At the time of the interview, Elina was still waiting to reunite with her son, who had left Syria seven months before her. Seeing her son again and studying to become a doctor were the flickering lights she was waiting to see at the end of the tunnel.

Things were even more difficult for Shachnaz, however, a thirty-six-year-old Afghan woman who left her country after the killing of her husband, because 'in Afghanistan it is not safe when you are a woman alone'.[18]

Shachnaz was herself wounded by a bomb and lost her job as a teacher because of her disability. 'The whole journey was difficult, but the most horrible experience was the sea voyage' she told me, as 'I really felt I would die'. On arriving at Lesvos with her toddler son, who also has a disability, she went through the Moria experience, before being granted a flat in the Iliaktida structure. Being a teacher herself, she was fully aware of the importance of education but there was no provision for single mothers, and she felt helpless. I heard her story in the staccato rhythm of the cadence of difficulties she faced in the refugee condition:

The situation in Moria camp was very difficult
I had to join long ques
waiting for food
with my leg problems
this was such a difficult thing to do
I also couldn't go to school
to learn English and Greek
I couldn't leave my kid alone
in the tent
it is dangerous
when I moved from Moria to the Iliaktida apartment
here in Mytilini
I tried to go to a school here
but they told me that I had to go on my own
how can I do that?
he is a baby
I can't just leave him
so I haven't been able to follow any class up until now
If you are alone
you always feel uncomfortable
I was always in tears
because I didn't have anybody to talk to
it is so difficult to be alone

Schachnaz's story is not an exception. Adult refugees' education in Greece is a huge problem since the few courses that are available mostly through civic organizations' and NGO's channels become immediately oversubscribed and things are even more difficult for single mothers, like Shachnaz. As Ourania Tzoraki has noted 'in 2015, the Greek government was unprepared to face the refugee influx in terms of both procedures and infrastructures' (2019, 13) and although a lot has been done since then, in relation to refugees' children integration in the Greek education system, adults' education, as well as access to Higher Education, are still considered to be huge challenges. And yet the dream of making a new beginning through education runs as a red thread throughout all of the stories that refugee women shared with me. Having gone through the hell of domestic violence with her in-laws in Cameroon, Hanielle escaped her country, only to find herself in the hands of traffickers in Turkey, but she concluded her story opening up her dark times to the poetics of radical hope and new beginnings:

Now that I am here
I feel safe
I have been here for two years
I have a home
I don't have any problems
I feel good
I go to school
to Mosaik[19]
to learn English and Greek
I want to continue my studies in Information Technologies
which I had started when I was still in Cameroon
I want to find a good job in Athens
perhaps in tourism
as a hotel receptionist
or something like that
I also want to bring my daughter over here
I have already asked for our reunification
my dream is to be here
to stay here in Greece
to be free
It is very important for me
to make a new beginning[20]

Refugee women's stories of gathering hope by re-imagining themselves through education reverberates with many of the observations that Kolar Aparna and Olivier Kramsch have made in relation to 'the Asylum University movement' [AU]: 'our refugee friends for the first time had the chance to use their minds, the dignity to engage in the world as thinking beings, rather than as 'bodies' awaiting a decision from the Dutch state as to their asylum procedure.' (2018, 100) The AU movement is an initiative of the Nijmegen Centre for Border Research (NCBR) at Radboud University, that emerged in the Dutch/German borderland of Nijmegen (in the Netherlands) and Kranenburg, Kleve (in Germany) and has now been extended to other locations in Belgium, Italy, Denmark and Kenya. What is crucial for this movement is that it has also sprung from grass roots and community activism within academic circles and beyond, following the patterns we have seen in the beginning of this chapter. According to its founders then,

> The Asylum University (AU) emerges as a movement bringing together academics, students, activists, volunteers, citizens, 'undocumented migrants' (whose asylum application has been rejected), refugees (those waiting for the asylum procedure as well as those with 'legal status'), and just people to find ways to collaborate with each other in an informal manner. (Aparna and Kramsch 2018, 94)

Apart from the obvious reasons that makes the Asylum University so different from the official education institutions and policies, its configuration as 'a movement' is of particular importance for the discussion of this chapter. Its existence and activities have shaken the legalities of borders and border practices, particularly as they are implemented in Higher Education across Europe through policing and tracking international students' mobility and status within a system of 'technologies of everyday bordering' (see Yuval Davis et al., 2018). In doing so, they have inevitably challenged the institutional structures of the neoliberal university, wherein education ceases to be the 'public thing' that democracy needs and becomes an irregular commodity that cannot possibly serve the laws of the free market it is supposed to follow: 'AU emerges as a movement to transform everyday processes of knowledge exchange within university walls as well as within walls of asylum procedures and walls confronted by those who are "out-of-procedure"' (Aparna and Kramsch 2018, 94)

Moreover, when extracted from the particular geopolitical context of its emergence in the Dutch/German borders, the Asylum University movement is much wider and multifaceted and has an interesting genealogy that goes back to the radical histories of popular education and its strong links with international social movements (see Grayson 2014). Elsewhere in my work, I have looked at transnational histories of women workers' education, wherein migrant workers have taken the lead (Tamboukou 2017). As we have further seen in Chapter 3, migrant and refugee women workers are alive and kicking all over the world, with radical education projects being at the heart of their grass-root organizations and activism.

Click's story is striking in this context, as it unravels as an assemblage of agonistic politics, educational aspirations entangled with art practices, as well as experiences of forced labour. Readers should remember Click as a Zimbabwean freedom fighter, from Chapter 5, but here we will follow more folds of her unbelievable story. I met Click through the Refugee Legal Support-Athens and I listened to her story in March 2019, at her workshop in the *Victoria Square Project*, a community-based art society.[21] Click's story has been narrated from many angles, in different contexts and across a range of media, including journal and newspaper articles, online platforms, videos,[22] as well as in *Flame,* a 1996 war film, which was 'a tribute to the Zimbabwe African National Liberation Army's many female guerrillas'.[23] After the war, Click spent six months in prison as a consequence of her decision to leave the army. She did it because she wanted to study history:

If you wanted to resign
they would put you in prison for six months
because they were thinking
you were against the government
I said
I can go to prison
I don't have a problem with that
I went to prison for at least six months
When I got out
I finished my school
and then I went to college
I became a history teacher
yea
I was teaching history
I was the first guerrilla fighter to be at university

It was then that she met her husband, who was amongst the many journalists who had interviewed her at the time, about her decision to leave the army and become the first guerrilla fighter to follow university studies. But when her husband died, Click started knitting to complement her meagre income and provide for her four children. It was then that her career as a textile artist begun, although knitting goes back to her childhood; 'I started knitting when I was 7 years old and I have been doing it every day since then' she has said in one of her many interviews.[24] Her talent as a textile artist took her to Greece but she had to undergo a period of working as a domestic worker under conditions of modern slavery, before she was able to take up her art again. When I visited her textile art workshop in Athens, she took me to the basement, to show me some pieces of her textile artwork, which includes knitting, embroidering and sewing. Moreover, Click is a singer, dancer and a wonderful teacher: she runs weekly art workshops in the neighbourhood, as part of the *Victoria Square Project* communal activities and many migrant and refugee women follow them, amongst other attendees.[25] Before joining the *Victoria Square Project,* Click was one of the co-founders of Melissa,[26] a network of migrant and refugee women in Athens, housed in a colourful and beautiful space that I also visited as part of my research in April 2019. The following extract from an article published by Amnesty International beautifully depicts the ethics, aesthetics and politics of this space:

> A woman with a white scarf slung around her head is singing in Farsi. Her voice is soon joined by other women sitting around a wooden table. A colorful blanket hangs on the wall behind them, and a white door with green shutters opens up into a terrace filled with lush, green plants. Birds are chirping loudly in the background. When we close our eyes, it's hard to believe that we're in a building in the centre of the Greek capital Athens. The contrast is stark to the refugee camps in or near the city, where thousands of people are living difficult and uncertain lives after European countries closed their borders. (Christensen 2017)

Founded in 2014, initially as a migrant women's' network, Melissa has importantly been at the fore front of the refugee support movement in Athens from 2015 onwards. It was the time when hundreds of refugees would camp out at Victoria Square for a week or two, before moving on to other European countries. As Click narrated it in her story, the women of the Melissa network begun by preparing breakfast for children, since refugees were only getting one meal per day at 3 o'clock: 'we thought about all the kids that were there from morning till 3 o'clock: what were they going to eat?'. The local community helped them by donating food and thus they started creating back packs with food in the beginning, but when kids were ready to leave following their parents' passages to the borders, they also though of preparing back packs with toys, ball points, crayons and books for the children. It was then that Click came up with the idea of putting a journal in the backpack:

you never know
one of the kids might write a story
which will be useful
and sometimes
he or she can discuss
and say
you know
during the war
we came
we passed by a country called Greece
and then
we met women
they were also migrants
and they gave us this
and then they gave us

a journal
such things
they can be writing
in their story
you never know

Thus, the initial idea of putting a journal in the children's backpacks as an informal educational intervention of inspiring memory writing, was later transposed into a wider project of creating a space for refugee women 'to learn, take art classes and prepare for the next phase in life' (Deutsche Welle 2019). As Hadell, an eighteen-years-old Syrian woman simply put it: 'Here, it's good. I feel at home. I tried to go to Greek school, but I couldn't relax. So, I come here to learn'. We are reminded here, of the importance of education within the Arendtian context of 'feeling at home in the world'. As Sjöholm has commented, aesthetic sensibility in Arendt's work 'underlies all forms of political reflection, producing possibilities, as well as constraints' (2015, x). It is this feeling that grass-root organizations like Melissa can nurture and cultivate as a necessary condition for moving to the next step of more formal education that can be accessed through national and international higher education institutions. In this context, art goes hand in hand with education in changing something in women's lives. In talking about her engagement with photography as part of her art lessons in Melissa, Khaterch Ahmadi, a fifteen-year-old Afghan refugee, who was born and grew up in Tehran, spoke forcefully about how she moved from sadness to hope through art:

> In the beginning I was taking photos of the sea and of sunsets. Sunsets are like our lives: the sun sets, as our life sets, this never changes. This is how it is when you are a refugee: our lives cannot change, except if we manage to change them ourselves. When we do art, our mind flies away from our problems, even if it is for a short time. It was when I started teaching children in our camp painting and photography, that my way of thinking changed, and I began to hope for the future. We became very close with the children and we depended on each other. (Huffington Post 2019)

Khaterch's powerful argument of the need to 'change our lives' and of art as a pathway to freedom, makes connections with the experiences of many migrant and refugee women in the archive of my research and beyond (see Hakki 2018; Martiniello 2019). Her poetic reflections on the sunsets of our lives forcefully express the sadness of a fifteen-year-old young woman and confirm a plethora of research findings showing that refugees in Greece experience psychological distress, while living through 'the frozen transit' (see

Bjertrup et al., 2018). Art education initiates a healing process that leads to new beginnings, as beautifully expressed in Asma's free verses from a poetry workshop at Melissa:

She's the new life.
She is the greatest She.
What do I describe?
She gives birth to women who can live.
She brings them to life and takes care of them.
She is full of emotions.
She carries the smell of the Lilly.
She makes you feel like a lost child who finds her mother.[27]

Warda's choir singing, Click's textile art, Khaterch's photography and paintings and Asma's free verses are just moments that crystallize Rancière's (2004) entanglements of artistic and aesthetic practices, as I have discussed them in the previous section. It is through knitting, dancing, singing, art photography, painting and poetry writing, amongst other artistic practices, that migrant and refugee women keep disrupting 'the distribution of the sensible' in the refugee camps and other sites of living the experience of forced displacement. These art practices disclose the ways that these women experience aesthetic phenomena in their everyday lives – the sea, the sunset – but they also create new forms of visibility and understanding. In displaying their artistic practices, these women open up themselves to the world, escaping the isolation and confinement of the refugee status. We, thus, return here to the four themes that Sjöholm (2015) has identified in the Arendtian link between aesthetics and politics: (a) public appearance; (b) permanence and resilience; (c) plurality through judgement and (d) action.

Here, it is also important to remember the link between ethics, aesthetics, politics and pedagogical practices in Foucault's configuration (1986). It was through teaching children how to draw that Khaterch's aesthetic sensibility erupted as a force that took her out of the misery of 'the frozen transit' and deterritorialized her from the black holes of the refugee experience. Migrant and refugee women's aesthetics of existence geared their *lines of flight*, their desire to change themselves and ultimately their will to freedom. But education as an agonistic site of freedom is also, always a territory, where uprooted women are continuously challenged to take risks. Nadia's experience of striving for an opportunity to get some education after more than three years working in conditions of forced and unfree labour in the Istanbul textile industry, throws light in Biesta's (2013) idea of 'the beautiful risk of education':

I saw there was a scholarship
from the American College of Greece
an English learning programme
for young refugees
I became very excited
and I said
it's a good opportunity
[. . .]
I asked the social worker
who helped me to register
to show me
how to fill in the application
because I didn't have any degree
or any certificate
nothing
she said
there are very few chances for you
but I said
it's ok
even if there are few chances
let's try

Nadia's brave decision 'to try' is a tangible expression of 'radical hope', a force that kept her alive and moving through the dark times she went through as we have already seen in the *interlude* of her story. Within the archive of the stories of my research and beyond, education has been perceived as an adventurous process, full of risks and failures. This is how Somi put it in her story: 'I know I failed my whole life, every step, so I know I can fail again and I can get up again, so from now on, even if I fail again, I am going to get up again, I am going to try again and again.' While listening to her story, I remembered Samuel Becket's famous saying: 'Ever tried. Ever failed. No matter. Try again. Fail again. Fail better.' (2012, 81) I shared these thoughts with Somi, and after the interview I sent her a thank you message, where I wrote amongst others: 'I was deeply moved by your story, which confirmed my trust in women's strength and force to go on struggling and living!' (personal communication, 8 December 2018).

But why is it important to conceptualize education as an adventure full of risks and failures? Running in parallel with Arendt's configuration of education as a critical site at the heart of the political, education for Whitehead (1967) is an art and an adventure whose object should be to create affective conditions for imaginative learning. Here it is important to remember that imagination is also a process for Whitehead: it can never be crystallized, condensed or conserved, let alone commodified in any sort of knowledge exchange economy or market, notions and structures that we simply take for granted in contemporary educational discourses and policies. Instead of supporting the certainty of analysis, knowledges and ideas, education should instead encourage and facilitate creativity, as 'the actualisation of potentiality' (1967, 179). It is in the realm of sustaining and supporting creativity that education takes up artistic dimensions and becomes the art of inspiring ideas.

Creativity, however, is precisely the field where universities and other national and international education structures and institutions have failed: not only can they not advance the adventure of ideas and the risks that it entails, but they are actually directed towards eliminating risks in the pursuit of delivering predefined 'objectives' and 'learning outcomes', that stifle and suppress creative forces. And yet, it was within the colourful and relaxed spaces of the Melissa network in Athens or the Mosaik centre in Lesvos, that migrant and refugee women could 'feel at home in this world' and it was in these familiar spaces that affective forces for imaginative learning were unleashed. In this context refugee's education aligns with the wider movement of decolonizing knowledges, discourses and practices within education and beyond, as I will further discuss in the concluding section.

EDUCATION AS ACTION: TRANSGRESSING THE BOUNDARIES OF THE POSSIBLE

In launching the project *Futures of Education: Learning to become*, UNESCO has underlined the need for re-imagining education as a process that emphasizes potentials, rejects determinism and expresses a flexible openness to the new as a global response to current conditions of poverty, exclusion, displacement and violence.[28] This project is a transnational mile stone within a wider field of debates and discussions about how education can be and most importantly act, within dark times of precarity, crises and risks. As Heila Lotz-Sisitka has succinctly put it in her keynote address at the European Educational Research Association Conference [ECER] at Hamburg University in September 2019: 'Should education be about acculturation in order to "progress", "cope" and "adapt" according to pre-framed scripts, or should education be about transgression of the here-and-now in order to "stay with the trouble" (Haraway, 2016) and re-constitute life more organically under hot, messy, uncertain conditions?' (Lotz-Sisitka 2019) Pointing to Biesta's 'beautiful risk of education', Lotz-Sisitka has highlighted the role of educational praxis in fighting against 'dehumanization tendencies' and has suggested action towards 'a humble yet possible relation between education, political subjectivity and transformative agency' (2019).

Lotz-Sisitka's suggestion of education as a transgressive praxis shows that things have not really moved very fast in the past twenty-five years since bel hook's important book, *Teaching to transgress* (1994), where she configured the pleasure of teaching as both an act of resistance and performance, 'countering the overwhelming boredom, uninterest and apathy [. . .] of the classroom experience [. . .] offering space for change, invention, spontaneous shifts' (1994, 10–11). What migrant and refugee women's experiences have shown is that dehumanizing trends in education, particularly along the lines of what Al-Amoudi has configured as the *dehumanisation of subalterns* (2019, 182) are components of wider *assemblages* of power relations, striated institutional practices and colonial discourses, wherein education is not recognized as 'a public thing' anymore. To put it simply, the sore state of refugee's education is a symptom and effect of the overall demise of the idea of inclusive education, which 'isn't dead, it just smells funny', as Roger Slee (2018) has wittily put it.

In re-imagining inclusive education, 'we need to rethink the very foundations of what we currently do' (Lotz-Sisitka et al. 2015, 73), since the question is not about optimization anymore. UNHCR's tripartite schema of action towards Refugee's Higher Education, as outlined earlier on in the chapter, is limited within discourses of optimization – doing what we do better. It is precisely on this restrictive optimization level that I situate moments of what I have called 'academic philanthropy' in the form of scholarships, university collaborations within the Erasmus and Social Inclusion programme and other academic initiatives, as already discussed in the first part of this chapter. Without denying the usefulness of such programmes what I argue is that they mostly offer individual and temporary forms of relief and do not really address the wider problems of dehumanization and exclusion. Moreover, such academic philanthropic practices are often instrumental: modalities of 'civic engagement' and 'outreach activities' that the neoliberal university needs to demonstrate its 'usefulness' to society, following guidelines and requirements of public and private funding bodies. Such interventions of 'academic philanthropy' ultimately become components of what Stephen Ball (2008, 747) has discussed as 'governance [which] is accomplished through the "informal authority" of diverse and flexible networks', that are diffused in the private, public and voluntary sectors, on national, international and transnational levels. What I want to suggest here is that such interventions of academic philanthropy shake the structures and discourses of the neoliberal university, at the same time of being limited within its restrictions.

As we have already seen in the previous section, the Asylum University Movement has precisely attempted to break down the recognized/undocumented divide by including undocumented migrants and asylum seekers in its courses and extracurricula, as well as extramural activities, since, 'speaking especially about borders and migration in our classrooms without being engaged with embodied practices outside the campus relevant to such work, raises questions of how disconnected to everyday realities university knowledge production processes are.' (Aparna and Kramsch 2018, 97). When I visited the University of Iceland in May 2019 to participate in the Nordic Journal of Feminist and Gender Research-NORA Conference on 'Border Regimes, Territorial Discourses and Feminist Politics', I found myself embroiled in a protest against the University's involvement in performing physical age examinations on unaccompanied refugees, organized by academics and activists of No Borders Iceland, a community based organisation, whose goal is 'the deconstruction of all borders'.[29] As a result of these protests, a statement was released by the participants of the conference, where we asserted our support for No Borders Iceland and their intervention at the NORA Conference. The statement also flagged up our strong belief 'in the accountability, responsibility and non-neutrality of researchers to engage in the political struggles and lived experiences taking place in the environments in which they exist [standing] for research that is put into action.'[30] What I want to highlight here by referring to just one of many interventions across the globe is the importance of enacting agonistic politics in the field of refugees' education, if we are to move beyond 'academic philanthropy' to transforming education and re-imagine what it can do.

In the sphere of action them, it is not accidental that transgressive possibilities within refugees' education and beyond, only seem to unfold beyond the striated spaces of the academy and in alliance with migrant and refugee social movements and grass-root organisations, as I have already shown earlier on in this chapter. As a matter of fact, we are currently witnessing the emergence of the 'academic abolitionism movement', which started as a protest against institutional racism and sexism within universities (see Lomax 2015, Ahmed 2016, Maldonado and Guenther 2019), but has important ramifications within 'the slow science movement' (Stengers 2013, Mountz et al. 2015), as well as various strands of decolonizing the university (Bhambra et al. 2018).

Crossing academic borders and boundaries has also led to hybrid formations, such as the Asylum University Movement that we have already discussed, as well as the Campaign for the Public University (Holmwood 2011), which erupted after the 2010 financial crisis. Sometimes, however, exiting academia altogether and acting outside its 'walls' might be inevitable. 'When we try to shake the walls of the house, we are also shaking the foundations of our own existence. But what if we do this work and the walls stay up?' Sara Ahmed has asked before walking out (2016). Her decision to leave 'the walls' resonates with Tamura Lomax's bitter observation that black women's lives don't matter in academia, a realization that made her resign because 'we sometimes *have* to walk away from the institution in order to tell the truth about it – not for only our lives but those beyond our own' (2015, np.).

Resisting academic spaces and acting outside its walls has an interesting genealogy that goes back to the sixteenth and seventeenth centuries when Spinoza repeatedly rejected the prestige and security of academic positions and preferred to work as an optical lens grinder, as a route to maintain the freedom to write and think. In doing so he followed a wave of thinkers, including Leibniz, Bacon and Erasmus, who were not members of university faculties as the imaginative and creative force of their thought could not develop within the restraints and limitations of the university milieus of their era (see Whitehead 1967, 59).

Arendt's intellectual career was very similar to the experience of this philosophical stance vis-à-vis the academy. Although she took up temporary university positions in the United States, she persistently refused to get a tenure as she could not bear the stifling atmosphere and meaningless administrative loads of universities. In reflecting upon the crisis of education, of her geographies and times, Arendt tried to see it not as a problem, but rather as an opportunity for action (2006, 171). Education has been historically related to politics she has noted: not only has it become 'an instrument of politics', but also and perhaps more importantly 'political activity itself was conceived of as a form of education' (2006, 173). What I want to suggest then in concluding this chapter is that it is precisely the Arendtian configuration of education as action that runs as a red thread within contemporary and historical migrant and refugee social movements, unleashing creative forces and political imaginaries of radical hope.

NOTES

1. See https://www.africanwomens.gr/?p=602 [Accessed 25 May 2020].
2. See https://africana.cornell.edu/carole-boyce-davies [Accessed 25 May 2020].
3. See https://frabnet.wordpress.com/about-frab/ [Accessed 25 May 2020].
4. See, https://feministresearch.org
5. See, https://feministresearch.org/events/inhabiting-borderlands/ [Accessed 25 May 2020].
6. Warda's story, *Iliaktida* premises, Mytilini, Lesvos, 11 April 2019.
7. For details of these schools, see https://www.unicef.org/french/supply/index_40377.html and https://www.unicef.org/supply/reports/school-box-guidelines-use
8. In a letter to Seymour Drescher dated 12 March 1959, Arendt acknowledged the 'great influence' of Tocqueville on her thought. (Hannah Arendt papers, 1898-1977, Library of Congress, Box 9).
9. See, amongst others, refugee students' testimonies of the DAFI Programme Report 2018, https://www.unhcr.org/uk/5d7f61097 [Accessed 24 May 2020].

10. See https://connectedlearning4refugees.org [Accessed 24 May 2020].
11. See https://www.refugeeeducationinitiatives.org [Accessed 20 May 2020].
12. See, https://www.un.org/en/universal-declaration-human-rights/ [Accessed 24 May 2020].
13. See, https://www.unhcr.org/uk/tertiary-education.html [Accessed 24 May 2020].
14. Ibid.
15. See, https://www.unhcr.org/5d651da88d7 [Accessed 24 May 2020].
16. For more details, see https://loveelevatesnetwork.com [Accessed 25 May 2020].
17. Elena's story, a café in Mytilini, Lesvos, 11 April 2019.
18. Shachnaz's story, a flat in Mytilini, Lesvos, 11 April 2019.
19. Mosaik is a project run by Lesvos Solidarity, a local activist group, run by volunteers in the spirit of solidarity. See: https://lesvosmosaik.org for more details of this support centre.
20. Hanielle's story, a flat in Mytilini, Lesvos, 8 April 2019.
21. See https://www.facebook.com/pg/VictoriaSquareProject/about/?ref=page_internal [Accessed 25 May 2020].
22. See amongst others: 'Meet Click: Artist, Mother of Four, Guerilla Fighter, Ted Talker, Survivor of Modern Slavery', at https://asseenfromthesidecar.org/blog/2017/12/14/meet-click-artist-mother-four-guerrilla-fighter-ted-talker-survivor-modern-slavery/ ; 'Imprisoned in Athens [Φυλακισμένη στην Αθήνα], https://video.vice.com/gr/video/imprisoned-in-athens/5be03a80be407767cd5e64ca [Accessed 20 June 2020].
23. The film was directed by Ingrid Sinclair and was 'the first Zimbabwean film since independence set during the Rhodesian Bush War'. See https://www.youtube.com/watch?v=BufnnzLrIxo [Accessed 20 June 2020].
24. https://www.debop.gr/deBlog/athens-of-foreigners/click-ngwere-mia-polytaladi-gynaika-apo-ti-zibaboue-stin-athina- [Accessed 20 June 2020].
25. See, https://www.lifo.gr/videos/on_air_lifo_talks/166873 [Accessed 20 June 2020].
26. See, https://melissanetwork.org [Accessed 25 May 2020].
27. Assma, a thirty-year-old Syrian woman as part of a poetry workshop with A.E Stallings, https://melissanetwork.org/migrant-stories/ [Accessed 20 June 2020].
28. See, https://en.unesco.org/futuresofeducation/ [Accessed 27 June 2020].
29. See, https://www.facebook.com/nobordersiceland/
30. See https://www.facebook.com/nobordersiceland/posts/2293968324002948 for full and visual details of the protest and the statement.

Chapter 7

Imagining the Non-Nomad

> The non-philosophical process of describing and rigorously explaining a reality is one that observes the effects of the real, reacts to the 'workings of the real' which resides behind the conceptual or discursive phenomenon that represents it, and builds its own syntax, which is then subjected to the real. (Kolozova 2014, 3)

Embarking on the theoretical journey of Francois Laruelle's 'non-philosophy', Katerina Kolozova has provoked us to challenge philosophical thought's colonization of 'the real'; instead, she has urged us to approach the subject (amongst other concepts), not as a construed figure or even map of positions that can only think itself, but rather as a radical concept, 'an instance' that can enable thought to align with the real, instead of absorbing it in the totality of any system of linguistic representation and/or meaning.

But how can one 'correlate only with the real and in an immanent way' (4) within and beyond nomadic theories? Throughout this book, I have interrogated the figuration of 'the nomadic subject' trying to open up dialogic spaces between philosophical abstractions and narratives of 'the real'. What I have argued is that although nomadic theories have seemed to facilitate non-static ways of theorizing the subject and his/her relations to the world and to other, the nomads of the real world and their torturing wanderings today have challenged the romance of unregulated movement and have forced us to problematize our situated positions in the cartography of feminist theories. In this context, the figuration of the nomad has been overstressed to the point that it has lost the reality of its reference. Dana's story, which erupted from my last encounter with migrant and refugee women in Athens, has forcefully shown what it means to have lived all your life paperless and stateless, as an effect of a nomadic lifestyle and culture:

my country is Kuwait
I was born in Kuwait
my father was from Kuwait
the problem is that
we were never given
identity papers
we had to pay for everything
even for education
and we didn't have any money

let me clarify
we are biduns
a tribe without recognised nationality
and they call us
biduns
which means
'without'

but we deny a life like that
you cannot live
without papers
that's why we took to the streets
demonstrating peacefully
for our rights
last demonstration was in 2014
when they arrested my husband
my son is still wanted by the police
my husband has completely disappeared
nobody can reach the police headquarters
and up until now
we haven't heard any news from him[1]

Dana is a bidun woman from Kuwait in her late forties. I met her through the Diotima Centre and her story was told in their premises in Athens. When she started narrating her story, I couldn't believe my ears. Quite out of the blue, I had met a nomad of the real world, but her story was hardly related to the nomadic theories that had fired up my imagination since the days of my Ph.D., back in the early 1990s. Dana's story emerges from one of 'the best-and-least known cases' (Manby 2018) of stateless people in the Gulf States: the biduns constitute a minority group – 10 per cent of the people in Kuwait – and they have been living in a legal limbo for the past thirty to fifty years. Their name, bidun, carries the semantics of their condition: 'bidun jinsiyya', means 'without nationality' in Arabic, as Dana has pointed out in the beginning of her story. They are officially considered as 'alien' residents, despite the fact that they have been living in Kuwait for many years and many of them, like Dana, were actually born and grew up in this country. What were the conditions of possibility for this 'ghost population' (Beaugrand 2018, loc.236) to emerge in the interstices and margins of the Kuwaiti society?

The biduns originate from semi-nomadic tribes living in the interior of Kuwait and the surrounding areas of the settled (hadar) Kuwait port city. According to Claire Beaugrand's (2018) important study, the biduns were the effects of the Kuwaiti modern state-making process, which created a tripartite hierarchical system of citizenship: first, second and stateless. Those who could prove continuous residence in Kuwait since 1920 were granted citizenship and full political rights as 'original Kuwaitis'. With the advent of the oil economy, the old nomadic tribes in the peripheries of Kuwait were forced to settle and the majority of them became labourers in the oil industry. Some of the Beduins (badu) and other foreigners were granted naturalization within the terms of the 1959 Nationality Law in Kuwait, but without political rights. Finally, it was the people, who were left behind. Beaugrand claims that one of the factors that left the biduns in the margins of the Kuwaiti state project was their badu origins as nomads: They either arrived in the country after the completion of nationality granting in 1965, or they just failed to register 'because they were unaware either of the process or of the idea of nationality altogether' (loc.267).

In Beaugrand's analysis then, the case of the biduns in the history of the Kuwaiti state making was a project that merged citizenship with class: While overseas migrants became ethnic outsiders, the biduns became class outsiders to a nation with a globalised bourgeois class (see Vora 2018, 2). As paperless people and illegal aliens, the biduns have been denied basic civil and human rights, including access to education and health, the right to work, as well as official identity documents. They work in low-waged and low-skilled jobs and live in poverty in shanty towns on the outskirts of Kuwait City. On the aftermath of the Arab spring revolution, the biduns organized their own protests, demanding an end to their stateless status, free education, free health care and the right to work. As one of the protesters forcefully put it: 'it is not about naturalisation, it is about existing'.[2] Although the initial bidun movement was mostly comprised of young and middle-aged men, in April 2012, Group 29, the first all-female Kuwaiti organization was created, particularly focusing on the rights to education.[3] But beyond Kuwait and the specificities of the biduns origins and trajectories, there is a wider use of the term bidun 'for a term of foreignness that denotes lack of papers, but also of rights in general, despite their ties of work, which makes possible a stable existence', Agier has observed (2016, 67)

Dana's story is a testimony of the bidun's on-going oppression and struggles: It carries traces of the hardships of nomadic provenance and experience in a country that privileges settled [hadar] perspectives, policies and ways of life. Her narrative is, thus, an instance of philosophical thought's 'colonization of the real', as already discussed above. It throws light to what Laruelle has identified as an 'amphibology' between thought and the real to the point that not only do they become indiscernible from each other, but they also cancel each other's meaning, as Kolozova has aptly commented (2014, 6). Here, it is important to note that in its Ancient Greek etymology, the prefix 'amphi' [ἀμφί] means 'on both sides, at both ends, of both kinds and around'[4]: just consider, amphibians and amphitheatre as two striking examples of its use. In this sense, it is the first compound of the Greek word *amphibolia* [ἀμφιβολία], which means ambiguity and doubt. Laruelle, thus, uses the term 'amphibology' [amphibologie] to refer to any ontological ambiguity between the real and its linguistic construction and representation (see Galloway 2014, 10). Dana's story is a narrative trace of such an amphibology, between the lived experiences [le vécu] of the biduns and 'the nomadic subject' as a figuration of feminist philosophy. Not only is there an ontological ambiguity in their relation, but also an ethical and a political one. To put it in a Foucauldian modality of interrogation: who speaks of the nomad, from what position and with what effects?

In raising Foucauldian questions around discourse and power relations enfolding the nomad, what is also important to consider today as a component of the *mobility assemblages* that I have discussed throughout the book is an unprecedented backlash on women's rights around the world. Such attacks range from women's overall marginalization in the global economy, threats to abortion rights, gender-based violence and rape culture, forced and unfree labour, trafficking and sexual slavery, and an overall culture of suspicion and moral anxiety. The abject figure of the derailed male refugee and/or economic migrant has become not only the enemy of the state, but also women's enemy par excellence! As Bonnie Honig has succinctly remarked, xenophobic feelings and attitudes often pass through 'concerns' for women, whose rights and bodies are in danger and need to be protected (2001, 65). Indeed, the media abound with horror stories and gender atrocities.[5] What they convey is a culture of what I configure as 'gender-based fear', which is expressed through a return to women's spatial and mobility restrictions, an issue over which so much feminist ink has already been spilt. As feminist geographers have persistently argued however, escaping confinement is a constant theme in the long durée of feminist histories. To return to Dana's story, it was because of her persecution and confinement that she eventually took the decision to leave:

The police came to my house
to arrest me
because of my husband
they searched everywhere
they beat me
they even beat my fifteen-years-old son
who is now with me
but he was only eleven years old
back then

that's why
I put my children in hiding
with my sister
I stayed at home
as I couldn't leave
the truth is that
every time the police took me
they brought me back
but after all this pressure
I decided to leave
and to take one of my sons
who was suffering
from mental health problems
after what had happened to him
I have eight children
and I couldn't take them all
so I only took this son of mine
I decided to take him
and leave

For Dana, then, leaving into the unknown was a fearful and yet not unfamiliar situation of being in the world. While in Kuwait, she fought against the predicament of her nomadic fate by demanding civil and human rights as a Kuwaiti citizen: 'bidun until when? Kuwaitis! Kuwaitis! Death rather than humiliation! Freedom! Dignity' were the leading slogans of the 2011 bidun uprising (Beaugrand 2018, loc.3827). But when her situation became untenable, once again she took nomadic routes of escape, flying away to the unknown:

we got our passports,
fake of course

through the smuggler
they took us from my country
to Iraq first
I think
and then
to Turkey
there were some incidents in Turkey:
we would go into the woods
the police would chase us
we tried to leave
through a dinghy
they would put
sixty to sixty-five people
in each boat
we were trying to escape
but the police would come
and we had to go back
we would hide
in the woods again
and it was very difficult
to find an escape route
in the end
when we were finally exhausted
we said
whatever happens
happens

Fear and hope are folded in Dana's decision to cross liquid borders, particularly as 'somewhere waits a ferryman whose face can't be seen' Kapka Kassabove has poetically written (2018, i). Throwing herself in the uncertainty of 'whatever happens, happens', the figuration of the nomad still carries real and symbolic possibilities for resistance in the ways I have already discussed in the previous chapters of this book. Discarding nomadism altogether, therefore, carries the risk of losing a strong concept that has opened up radical ways of thinking women in non-static ways, outside the boxes of domesticity, as non-place bound, and as not necessarily and essentially linked to 'motherlands' and 'fatherlands' of all sorts and renditions of nationalist discourses and practices. What is to be done then? How can we still imagine women following *lines of flight*? And last but not least, how exactly can a non-philosophical approach to the concept of nomadism keep its relation to the real in all its unfolding complications and contingencies? These are the questions that I will explore in this chapter, which unfolds in three parts.

After this introductory section, I follow trails of Laruelle's non-philosophy, particularly focusing on Kolozova's reconfiguration of female subjectivity through the lenses of the real [le Réel], radical solitude and the Stranger. In doing so, I discuss the challenges that a different conceptualization of the real can bring to the project of revisiting the nomadic subject. In the third part, I suggest the concept of the 'non-nomad' as a figuration that retains the radical possibilities of unregulated and free movement of nomadic theories, while responding and reacting to the material conditions of displaced women's urgent precariousness.

FEMINIST TRAILS IN NON-PHILOSOPHY

Since its beginning, western philosophy has sought to set the premises and foundations within which to envision the real. But the paths it has followed have ended up in totalizing ways of grasping and defining the real. In Laruelle's critical stance, philosophical debates have often followed their own discourses to the point of having confused the object of their quest – experience and the real – with forms of thought that have revolved around them. In this way, philosophical thought has distanced itself from the real of which it speaks: in producing knowledge, it constantly reproduces itself, asserting its self-sufficiency and efficiency in defining [and confining] subjects, objects and their relations. In levelling this critique within the project of non-philosophy, Laruelle is careful to acknowledge other non-philosophical traditions that go back to Kant's search for the conditions of possibility of philosophical though. Since Kant then, philosophical thought has attempted to chart its limits and abilities, by demarcating 'a non-philosophical margin that it tolerates, circumscribes, reappropriates, or which it uses in order to expropriate itself: as beyond or other to philosophical mastery' (Laruelle 2013, 2). But what differentiates these other 'non-philosophical' histories from Laruelle's project is that such trends still operate within philosophy. As Anthony Paul Smith helpfully explains: 'philosophy always appeals to something outside of philosophy in order to complete it, but philosophy itself remains untouched' (2016, 11).

For Laruelle though, it is philosophy itself that becomes the 'object' of non-philosophical inquiries (2013, 3). In this context, the project of non-philosophy is about destabilizing the problematic relation between philosophy and the real (le Réel). But non-philosophy for Laruelle 'only claims to succeed the faith and authority of philosophy, never to deny its reality, nor to refuse it at least a "relative" autonomy' (2013, xxi). In this light, 'non-standard philosophy' is another term that Laruelle has used to configure his theoretical work, pointing to its emergence from the philosophical grounds of 'radical immanence' (xxi). In doing so, Laruelle proposes a unified theory of science and philosophy, wherein the real 'is *immanent to itself rather than to a form of thought*' (5, emphasis in the text). As Mullarkey and Smith have noted, Laruelle's idea is that 'thought should think of itself as immanent to the real' (2012, 2). In this context, instead of pretending to represent, become or transcend the real of which it speaks, non-philosophy admits that while it will never ultimately reach the real, it will maintain certain relations with it: will walk along it, will speak to it, will try not to lose sight of it and will finally attempt to transform it:

> Non-philosophy must remain an explicative theoretical hypothesis: it does not confuse itself with its object, with experience [but] it must at least also transform experience [. . .] it is in a perpetual state of producing novelty; of opening and rectifying a specific space of knowing without confusing itself with the reality to be described. (Laruelle 2013, 11)

Kolozova has followed Laruelle's non-philosophy in conceptualizing the real, as 'that which is outside interpretation, outside the cognitively created reality' (2014, 155). In Kolozova's non-philosophical analytics, the real is always grounded in specific space/time/matter conditions: It is neither an abstraction, nor a substance, but rather a status (2). It is on these premises that she theorizes the subject in its relation to the corporeal real, beyond the era of post-structuralist fragmentation:

> the sense of inescapable situatedness in one's own body, the organic self-enclosure and corporeal self-circumscription, is the most direct experience of the real of one's inevitable situatedness in oneself. It is in the body that one is bound to persist in and survive as one(self)'. (153)

What she further suggests is that although the real continuously leaves its marks on bodies, thoughts and lived experiences, it cannot be subsumed to any forms of thought or figurations, no matter how complex and nuanced they can be: 'the real of my reality is elusive to naming and conceptualization, and it is irreducible to a meaning' (146).

Kolozova's assertion that the real is essentially indifferent to the attempts of philosophical thought to name it and tame it, chimes with my critique of the nomadic subject, both as a descriptor and as a figuration of migrant and refugee women's lived experiences. However, I have found that the non-philosophical debates have created their own abstractions that have interfered in their supposedly dialogic relation with the real (le Réel). In engaging with questions of the real, I draw on Alfred North Whiteheads' organic awareness of reality (1985). In Whitehead's realism, and his famous thesis against 'the bifurcation of nature', there is no gap between the scientific conception and the subjective experience of the world (1964, 30). As we emerge from the world and not the world from us, the real that has conditioned our being-in-the-world and our very ability to think, is continually urging us to respond to the questions it raises and to react to the necessities it creates, no matter how chaotic or ungraspable they are. Indeed, I think that the project of non-philosophy would benefit from some traditions of process philosophies, particularly around questions of what I call 'the material real', within the cartography of new materialism genealogies (see Tamboukou 2020, 169-170).

Situated within the genealogical terrain of new materialisms then, the figuration of the nomad encompasses components of a radical conceptualization of subjectivity, but it is still outside 'the syntax of the real'. As Kolozova explains, the latter is a process in Laruelle's 'non-philosophy' that attempts to chart the real in a rigorous way; it is affected by the immanence of the real and rejects a–priori philosophical decisions or gestures that would obscure and ultimately substitute it (2014, 9). Engaging with Laruelle's non-philosophy might, therefore, be a way of addressing the limitations and constraints of using the nomad as a descriptor, without altogether rejecting the philosophical figuration and the radical paths it has opened in feminist theorizations of subjectivity.

When Braidotti writes that 'in my work on nomadic thought I adopt a creative redefinition of thinking that links philosophy to the creation of new forms of subjectivity' (2012, 5) she seems to conflate her figurations with the objects/subjects of which she speaks, even when she claims to take them as embedded and embodied. How can philosophy create new forms of subjectivity? Philosophical thought can only respond to or walk along new forms of subjectivity that emerge from their entanglement in the world, not the other way around. As Isabelle Stengers insists, we need to develop sensibilities towards 'the experience as we experience it' (2008, 109).

WALKING ALONGSIDE THE REAL: THE *NON-NOMAD*

Given the centrality of the philosophy/science relationship in Laruelle's theorization, attending to the emergence of the real and tracing its unfolding is at the heart of the non-philosophical project. In devising a research project wherein, I have asked migrant and refugee women to narrate their experiences of travelling to Greece, I have, thus, attempted to build a bridge between an influential figuration in feminist philosophy and the real in the subject of which it speaks. While my take of the real follows Whitehead's organic realism (1985), I nevertheless agree with Laruelle and Kolozova that the real can never be fully grasped, mirrored or represented. The real is in a continuous process of becoming, but as it passes, it leaves tracks and traces in bodies, objects, as well as novellas and stories, both told and written. It is to these stories that I have turned in my attempt to see how philosophical figurations can walk along the real. What these stories have brought forward are different cartographies and modalities of nomadism that I have mapped drawing on Glissant's philosophical poetics (2010). Dana's story of fleeing to Greece carries traces of such different modalities of nomadism, including her poem story, whose meaning kept erupting in the intermezzo:

my son told me
you know how to swim mum
because we have beaches in Kuwait
he was afraid about me
I was afraid about him
the smuggler didn't come with us
the boat was driven
by the passengers in turn
it was very easy
for anything to happen
like get drowned
whatever

it was night
there was fear
and you didn't know
whether you would reach Greece
or not
after six hours in the boat
we reached a beach in Samos

there was a woman there
who run a restaurant
and she helped us
we brought wood
and set up a fire altogether
and then
the police came
we stayed in Samos
in tents
this was a bit difficult
there was no water
you had to walk one hour

to get water
it was really a very difficult situation
even food was difficult
there was no money of course

The sea, the boat, the beach and the tent in Dana's story become material components of the geopolitical conditions underpinning different modalities of 'nomadisms of escape', as I have already mapped and discussed them in the previous chapters. But even when taken as a diverse cartography of nomadism, such space/time/matter conditions do not necessarily create a plane for 'a nomadic subject' to emerge as a figuration that can encompass the precarity of migrant and refugee women's travels today. As I have shown throughout the book, nomadism, alongside *errance* [errantry] and other modalities of wandering, yet to be charted, are components of entangled relations within *mobility assemblages* at work. In grappling with the aporias that the figuration of the nomad raises in moving alongside the real what I therefore suggest, is a radical encounter between the nomad and 'uprooted women travelling alone'. What emerges from this encounter is the *non-nomad*, a figuration that retains the radical possibilities of unregulated and free movement while responding and reacting to the material conditions of displaced women's urgent precariousness. In bending Braidotti's figuration, I follow here her suggestion that constructing 'intellectually mobile requires an ethic of differential coding for the various modes and forms of mobility' (2012, 10).

In experimenting with the notion of the *non-nomad*, I take insights from the project of non-philosophy and particularly Kolozova's deployment of non-philosophical tools in theorizing female subjectivity: 'the means of non-philosophy have enabled me to think the real and conceptualize a form of realism that [. . .] represents an extension, supplementation, or expansion of the possibilities created by postructuralist [. . .] feminist philosophy'. (2014, 11) In the same vein, while I still situate myself within the plane of nomadic theories, I also point to the possibility and indeed necessity of critiquing their western privileged conditions of possibility. Dana's story is an instance of both keeping some of the radical possibilities of nomadic becomings, while at the same time pointing to its margins and limitations:

because my son was underage
they looked after us
and one and a half month later
they sent us to Athens
they put us in a camp
again

but there were many problems in this camp
again
these problems were from the residents
not the organizations
when they took us to the camp
there were some people who were threatening me
because I was witness to an incident in the camp
there was a gang
who were trying to rape African young women
there was a commotion in the camp
and they came and threatened me
they told me
that they would burn my container
together with my son
who was sleeping there
I was not afraid of course
this incident happened at the weekend
and when the NGOs came on Monday
we reported it
Diotima helped me at the time
and this is when they took me out of the camp
they took me and my son at the same time
they put us in a hotel
and then we came to Athens

The verses of Dana's poem story, chart *lines of flight*, as she recounts her experience of escaping a country in which she could not get rid of her nomadic identity, only to become a fugitive nomad again. What I, therefore, argue is that through her story Dana constitutes herself as a *non-nomad*. Here, the 'non' in nomadism is taken as a *transposition*, 'an intertextual, cross-boundary or transversal transfer, in the sense of a leap from one code, field or axis into another' (Braidotti 2006, 5). Dana's oppression within the real existence of being a nomad in Kuwait has created conditions of possibility for resistance. But her revolt could only be materialized through the nomadic route again: her deterritorialization from the unwanted position of the bidun to the reterritorialization to the position of a refugee woman travelling in the wilderness. Acting within the immanence of her nomadic condition, Dana knew how to survive within unknown territories: She knew how to swim, how to light a fire, put up tents, fetch water and be fearless. But while being immersed in the nomadic condition, she still wanted to disentangle herself from the constraints of this position and claim her right to a recognized citizenship, whether in Kuwait, Greece or any other territorial state in the world.

The condition of the *non-nomad* then, does not negate nomadism, but rather points to its shadows and margins. As an emerging figuration, the *non-nomad* reassembles lines of flight within the restrictions of the real; she demythologises fictions of free movement without shattering its political imaginaries.

In configuring the *non-nomad* as an instance of 'the syntax of the real', I thus make connections between the critical possibilities of a radical strand in feminist philosophy with the urgency of decolonizing the 'stubborn facts' of its past and its becomings, a theme that I will come back to the conclusion. Kolozova's notion of 'radical solitude' is crucial in mapping the positions, affects and practices of the *non-nomad*. 'Grief is a state of being exposed in one's constitutive dependence' (49) Kolozova notes in a fine summary of Butler's late work on the political significance of grief (2004). But in doing so, she bypasses Cavarero's influence upon Butler's position.

Indeed, Cavarero's philosophy is strikingly absent from Kolozova's theorization of female subjectivity as a radical unity, perhaps because Cavarero is not included in the spectrum of post-structuralist feminist philosophies that she discusses and criticizes. And yet Cavarero's thought is very much alive, kicking and present in Butler's late work. Drawing on Arendt's political philosophy Cavarero has also written about the uniqueness of the *Who*, as well as the political significance of the corporeal voice (2005) of 'the One' that Kolozova wants to re-insert in the conceptual and linguistic vocabularies of feminist post-structuralist theories. It is in her Arendtian exposition of the relational *Who*, as a figure constituted within the sphere of politics, that Cavarero points to the force of grief: the moment when amongst his tears Ulysses remembers the continuity of himself through listening to his story at the court of the Phaecians:

> Ulysses is moved to tears. Not only because the narrated events are painful, but because when he had lived them directly he had not understood their meaning [. . .] before hearing his story Ulysses did not yet know *who* he was: the story of the rhapsod, the story told by an 'other', finally revealed his own identity. (Cavarero 2000, 18)

For both Cavarero and Butler then, grief 'exposes the constitutive sociality of the self' (Butler 2004, 19). But while agreeing with Butler about the political force of grief, Kolozova argues that grief is also, an instance of 'radical solitude' par excellence, encompassing 'the hard labour of self-preservation performed by the 'I' in the face of the dread of its possible annihilation (2014, 49). No matter how mobile or transient the self is, it works hard on preserving its continuity. This hard labour, the force of the Spinozist 'conatus', creates a state that is for Kolozova, 'an irrevocably solitary one' (50). Moreover, there is something acutely poignant in the refugee's solitude: 'a solitude born in/

with the multitude is a solitude that remains potentially populous – utterly singular and yet collective, always crowded with other solitudes', Trinh has remarked (2013, 50), while pondering on the thought of a refugee: 'never does one feel as solitary as when fleeing in the midst of millions' (50).

It was such moments of 'radical solitude' that have left their traces in the *non-nomadic* narratives of the archive of this research: 'I remember when I was working in the textile, everyone was busy with the stitching and when I was walking around, so nobody could see me, my eyes were always full of tears, I was always crying, I was not happy at all'.[6] I was quite drawn in the way Nadia recounts tearful moments of despair shortly before taking the decision to go away. As Kolozova writes, radical solitude encompasses instances of 'a self-enclosed reality of mere labour at a point where the organic and the sense of selfhood merge into each other' (2014, 50). Nadia's tears, as an embodied expression of pain merge here with a sense of who she wanted to be or rather to become. Her tears become material components of her self-preservation that is elusive to the authority of language, as well as to any philosophical figuration that attempts to grasp and theorize it.

Such stories of radical solitude have released forces of communication and correspondence, 'the real of the pure, non-reflected experience of being human' (Kolozova 2014, 108). It is here that Laruelle's notion of 'the Stranger' becomes crucial: 'one lives the destiny of the world through the solitary experience of living one's individual destiny of a Stranger' Kolozova has noted (150). In Laruelle's conceptualization, we all become Strangers to our non-reflected lived experiences, *le vécue,* since at the very moment we start grappling with the world and attempt to map ourselves within it, we initiate a process of self-alienation from the real. Nadia's poem story has left traces of this process of becoming 'a Stranger':

life was not easy
you have to fight with life,
I learnt this
otherwise
I could not have got out
of all those situations
I had to confront in my life
at some point
I felt I would kill myself,
because
when you don't have a home
when you don't have anything
you think
your life is useless

Autoalienation is repetitive and as it keeps going it leaves behind crystallized formations, psychosocial and material residues, memories and embodied habits, 'the stubborn fact of the past' (Whitehead 1985, 129) that gradually gives form to what we come to see and recognize as 'the self' or 'the subject'. There is, thus, a distinction between the real and 'the Stranger', which should not be taken as a split or as a duality, but rather as a parallel movement of self-differentiation, Kolozova pithily notes (2014, 115) As already noted above, the body is the immediate locus of the Stranger in his/her continuous interaction with and differentiation from the real, 'the site of that mute persistence of the self' (153).

Feeling themselves as 'Strangers' in the radical solitude of grappling with the world, displaced women cannot escape the regulatory hold of mobility restrictions: their wanderings will be severely limited, impeded and even annihilated. Yet, it is in the very act of autoalienation and self-differentiation that displaced women are provisionally crystallized as *non-nomads,* restricted in their actual mobility but free in their radical immanence to imagine a different position in the world and act on it: dare live *for* the world and not *in* it, as Laruelle and Anne Françoise Schmid have aptly put it (2003, 55).

RE-IMAGINING LANGUAGE AND THE SUBJECT

In addressing the aporias that the real of the current refugee crisis and particularly women's position within it has raised to the way we understand the subject of feminism, in this chapter I have experimented with the figuration of the *non-nomad* as an emergent language game that retains the subversive potentialities of nomadic theory, while pointing to its margins, shadows and exclusions. What I have suggested is that the *non-nomad* can bridge gaps between thought and the real. In doing so, I have followed some trails of Laruelle's non-philosophy, particularly as it has been deployed in Kolozova's theorization of gendered subjectivities. I have done so, while taking non-philosophy as a site of experimentations and not as a doctrine or a closed theoretical framework.

In suggesting this nominal play between the nomad and the *non-nomad*, I have followed Christine Koggel's suggestion that such imagining points to 'the endless possibility and variety of language games but also demonstrates just how complicated the description of some activities can become' (2002, 239). If we accept Wittgenstein's argument that language games are practices that do more than denote or describe, creating a political vocabulary that is more sensitive to the demands of the real might contribute to the overall project of changing the real, by pointing to its shadows and exclusions, both real and nominal.

NOTES

1. Dana's story, Diotoma Centre, Athens, narrated in Arabic, 23 April 2019.
2. Dr Abd al-Hakim, member of a youth bidun movement called *Al Muwatinum* [citizens], in Beaugrand 2018, loc.3811.
3. See Beaugrand 2018 for an extended study of the biduns mobilization, particularly Chapter 6.
4. Collin's dictionary, https://www.collinsdictionary.com/dictionary/english/amphi [Accessed, 22-2-2020].
5. See for example, http://www.dailymail.co.uk/news/article-3390168/Migrant-rape-fears-spread-Europe-Women-told-not-night-assaults-carried-Sweden-Finland-Germany-Austria-Switzerland-amid-warnings-gangs-ordinating-attacks.html [Accessed, 12-2-2020].
6. Nadia's story, a café in Athens, narrated in English, 25 July 2018.

Conclusion
Decolonizing Feminist Theories

My husband had many problems in Iran, so he left and came to Greece on his own. He picked up his things and left at midnight from our house. We didn't hear from him for a long time but then he phoned me and told me that he had arrived in Greece. Seven months later he suggested that the whole family should leave and join him in Greece. My father did not agree, and he did not want us to make this journey. He was telling me, 'how can you do that with a little six years-old child in tow'? This will be very difficult'. But my daughter kept asking me, 'I want to go to my dad, where is my dad?'. However, my father insisted, and he told me, 'if you decide to leave you can never come back here.' But despite all this, I did set out for my journey. They had warned us that we could drown while on the boat crossing the sea. But we did manage to reach Turkey and after a few days we found the smugglers, but we were in Turkey for two months and every time we were trying to cross the borders, the police would come and arrest us. We thus tried five times and on the sixth attempt we finally crossed the borders. While in Turkey I went through immense difficulties. We were moving from one house to another all the time, I run out of money, I thought of finding a job there. I know a little Turkish, but I didn't really know what to do, so that we would not be arrested by the police. We would travel for seven hours to the borders, around fifty people in one car, we were overcrowded, and my daughter almost suffocated once from all these people thrown in a small van. I told my husband that it was almost impossible to cross the borders. But he told me you should wait till my application is accepted and I get the asylum and then you can come here legally, or you can go back to Iran. But then I tried for one last time and I managed to cross the borders after two months in Turkey. While in Turkey it was getting worse and worse day after day and I could not ask for help from my father, because he had warned me against leaving in the first place. He had told me that I would have huge difficulties, but I hadn't listened to him. It was such a difficult journey and one of the biggest difficulties I had was the men's gaze towards a woman who was travelling alone. If you are a woman alone with a child and nobody can help you, this is terrible. (Ilya's story)

I met Ilya at the Kara Tepe refugee camp in April 2019. She was amongst those women who listened to my talk first and then decided to share her story, as I have already discussed in Chapter 2. Her story struck me from the very beginning as a struggle in an entanglement of antagonistic heteropatriarchal power relations: her father, her husband, the state, the smugglers and the men's intruding gaze. It is a story that powerfully weaves together many threads of the analytical lines that I followed throughout this book to propose that what emerges from the encounter between theoretical abstractions and women's lived experiences is the need to decolonize feminist theories. In doing this, I have responded to Linda Martín Alcoff's argument that feminist philosophies keep creating 'false universalizations', even when they trouble the social constructions of gender. In her view, 'decolonizing feminist philosophy requires being prepared to do philosophy differently [and] this involves challenging universalist deconstructionist agendas, but also universal conceptualizations of gender and gender related forms of oppression' (2017, 33–34).

Chandra Mohanty's influential essay 'Under Western Eyes' originally published in 1984 drew attention to the role of Western feminist scholarship in reproducing exclusive hierarchies of knowledge and has initiated a rich body of literature in decolonial feminist studies.[1] Writing the preface of Margaret McLaren's 2017 volume on *Decolonizing Feminism, Transnational Feminism and Globalization,* more than thirty years later, Mohanty has further pointed to the need for the notion of the 'transnational' to be disentangled from the normalizing discourses and settings of the neoliberal university and has raised some critical questions around the need to decolonize transnational feminism in the context of globalization.

In a close reading of Mohanty's *Feminism without Borders* influential book (2003), Gaile Pohlhaus (2017) has suggested the idea of 'knowing without borders' through the decolonizing process of 'epistemic gathering'. Instead of simply challenging the subject of knowledge through the questions of 'who knows' and 'whose knowledge counts', Pohlhaus has suggested that we should rather ask 'with whom am I knowing and with what effects?' (2017, 50). Following Pohlhaus' suggestion that 'knowing is not something that we do on our own', (50) in writing this book I have tried to experiment with methodologies that could advance a decolonizing feminist approach, particularly focusing on the importance of listening as a way of learning and understanding with others. As Sonali Kolhatkar has simply put it in criticizing western feminist approaches to Afghan women's experiences: 'isn't it imperative and a little bit obvious that when we speak of Afghan women and their rights, we must listen carefully to what they themselves have to say about it?' (2002, np). Reflecting on the politics of listening through the prism of feminist Indigenous philosophies, Allison Weir points to 'the need to engage in a politics of self-transformation through listening, to become capable of a politics of mutual recognition' (2017, 258). It is analytical lines, traces and themes that emerge from my immersion in the soundscapes of uprooted women's stories that I now want to reassemble in this concluding chapter.

DECOLONIZING RELATIONS WITHIN THE HETEROPATRIARCHAL ASSEMBLAGE

There were many and significant differences even amongst the small group of twenty-two women, who participated in this study, including age, ethnic origin, race, religion, social class, educational background, personal status and disability amongst others.[2] Their social, political and embodied differences confirm Mohanty's argument that the projected unity of experiences amongst women, even amongst critical feminist approaches, is in itself a false universalization, 'an ahistorical, universal unity between women based on a generalized notion of their subordination' (2003, 31). Situated within different contexts, all stories, however, recounted *lines of flight* from a heteropatriarchal *assemblage*. To put it simply, all women were running for their lives, escaping violence at the hands of men, whether soldiers, rapists, traffickers, smugglers, or their fathers, husbands, brothers and uncles, and sometimes even their 'rescuers'. Uprooted women's common ground of struggling against heteropatriarchy confirms Kelly Oliver's suggestion that, 'focusing on women refugees as a group with shared interests, and yet acknowledging vast differences in cultural, social, historical, and material conditions amongst the world's refugee women, demonstrates the need for transnational feminisms that go beyond national sovereignty, beyond universal human rights discourse, and perhaps even beyond feminism itself' (2017, 179).

But what also emerges from uprooted women's stories is that subjects and relations are not pre-existing but rather emerge through complex intra-actions enacted within various *assemblages*, as I have already discussed throughout the book. In this context 'families' were very differently configured and experienced in uprooted women's narratives. Melina, a Turkish woman who spent a whole year in jail because of her involvement in the Gülenist movement was really disillusioned by the way her relatives and friends reacted to her predicament: 'while we were in jail, our families were excluded from society. Our relatives and neighbors turned their backs immediately.' But Melina, as indeed many displaced women created a new network of relations in solidarity with other refugees trying to survive while waiting for her asylum application in Athens:

while I am here
I try to help other people
because although my English is not very good
it is better than other Turkish people here
so I am helping them with their English
I also try to join social activities
with my friends
and I am waiting
I feel lucky
that I have friends
who support me
but I also know
that some of our friends
and family
didn't give support
some of them
didn't even want to see us[3]

The heteropatriarchal family as a unity of kinship relations was irreparably challenged in migrant and refugee women's narratives. It is from family members that they were escaping – whether uncles, fathers, brothers or in-laws – but it was also with family members that they were trying to reunite while on the move, usually their children, mothers and in some fewer cases, husbands. Perceived within *assemblage* thinking, families were, thus, configured through relations of exteriority: what escaped them was perhaps more important than what was unfolding within their boundaries. Women's agential movements and cuts were, therefore, conditioned, but not determined by their families. Moreover, their subjectivities as *assemblages* of positionalities emerged through relations within 'communities of choice' (Friedman 1989), within a context of relational ontologies, epistemologies and ethics.

As I have already written in the introduction, what struck me from the beginning of this research was the various media and policy reports representations of uprooted women as 'women travelling alone'. What I have argued throughout the book is that the discourse of loneliness is a Western construction deeply rooted in the Enlightenment idea of an autonomous individual, often represented through the image of the adventurous wanderer/traveller/nomad/flâneur or even flâneuse in its various feminist appropriation and renditions (see Wolff 1990). Uprooted women's stories have radically and decisively challenged such Eurocentric constructions of individuality by forcefully expressing the notion of 'transindividuality' as a modality of being- in the world-with others. In Balibar's influential reading of Spinoza, 'transindividuality' (1997) is understood as the mutual constitution of individuals and collectivities within specific socio-political, historical, economic and geographic situations. Balibar's notion of transindividuality chimes with feminist and indigeneous relational ontologies, but the latter include the Earth, as well as non-human entities. What my analysis of uprooted women's stories through the lenses of *assemblage* thinking and new materialist approaches has shown is that subjectivities do not pre-exist relations, but rather emerge through their intra-actions and that they are never fully realized within these relations.

DECOLONIZING FREEDOM

It is within *mobility assemblages* that decolonized practices of freedom were also enacted. As Allison Weir has suggested in proposing the notion of relational freedom, 'we are free only in and through our relations with others, including all creatures in an animate universe' (2017, 268). Such situated practices of freedom challenge liberal individualistic approaches that are still dominant in Western political theory. Uprooted women's political activism has been seen and discussed through the figure of Antigone in this book. What I have argued is that while lamenting their vulnerability and the loss of their beloved, migrant and refugee women have also transposed their stories in political narratives of resistance. It is through narration as action (Tamboukou 2018) that migrant and refugee women have rewritten their exclusion and marginalization, have defended their decision to transgress authoritarian border regimes of the nation state sovereignty and have opened up possibilities for transnational connections. In this context, there were two planes on which I mapped *lines of flight* in the context of relational freedom: labour activism and education.

As it has been widely acknowledged and documented, uprooted women's labour has contributed significantly to historical and contemporary formations of racial capitalism. In this book I have looked closely at the discussion and discourses of gendered and racialized labour relations under conditions of forced displacement. But what I have also argued is that it is from the conditions of their exploitation that migrant and refugee women's deep and passionate involvement in labour activism has also emerged, and it is still alive and kicking. In tracing agonistic genealogies of gendered and racialized labour relations, I have challenged the construction of the uprooted woman as a helpless victim in need of protection and humanitarian aid, but have also pointed to her marginalization within the histories and structures of the labour movement, which reaches our own days. Migrant and refugee women's struggles bring forward new modalities of relational freedom and force us to revisit the Western foundations of social movements and agonistic politics.

Re-imagining the self through education has also been a strong theme that has woven together the various stories of this research. Education has been mapped not only as a site of struggles, but also as a realm of 'radical hope' that continues to open up future imaginaries. What I have argued in this book is that in unleashing creative forces in uprooted women's lives, the art/education assemblage interrogates its neoliberal configuration as a commodity, as well as its transposition to a humanitarian aid within the discourses of new philanthropies. Thus, 'the right to education' under conditions of forced displacement has pointed to the cracks of the dominant human rights discourses, as I will further discuss in the next section.

DECOLONIZING RIGHTS: CARCERAL HUMANITARIANISM AND 'RESCUE POLITICS'

Is the human rights framework a useful approach to understand and support uprooted women's condition? McLaren has asked (2017, 2), juxtaposing the individualistic and universalizing premises of the dominant human rights discourses to collective struggles and social movements. As Oliver has persuasively argued the abstract concept of human rights, which has its roots in the Enlightenment idea of cosmopolitanism is seriously challenged by the uprooted women's condition (2016, 55). Indeed, the stories I heard unfolded on the plane of what Wendy Brown (2000) has configured as 'suffering rights as paradoxes': the fact that displaced women were granted special rights as a vulnerable group has reinforced and solidified their vulnerability, while doing nothing to address the conditions that shaped their vulnerable situation in the first place. By being grouped together under the label of 'vulnerable subjects' these women were homogenized under the gaze of the western humanitarian eyes. In Oliver's analysis then, the refuge woman is a creation of the political technologies of what she configures as *carceral humanitarianism*:

> contemporary detention centers and refugee camps are part and parcel of a system of carceral humanitarianism and 'rescue politics' that turns refugees into criminals and charity cases simultaneously, which, in turn, becomes the troubling justification for 'rescuing' them in order to lock them in, increasingly in dangerous, disease-ridden, sorely inadequate conditions. (2016, 6)

'Rescue politics' (Tazzioli 2015) is then part of the predicament of the refugee woman and not its solution, as it is often presented within dominant 'human rights' discourses, institutions and organizations. Since it is nation states and their border practices that 'create refugees and then pay humanitarian aid organizations to take care of them' it is within transnational decolonizing practices that we need to rethink the condition of the refugee woman, Oliver has argued (2016, 13). She has further remarked that the traditional categories of *indigeneous* and/or *settlers*, as they are deployed in some strands of decolonial feminisms are not always adequate in understanding 'the special plight of the refugee woman' (2017, 180). Moreover, even intersectionality cannot fully respond to the condition of leaving home with nothing in Oliver's analysis (194). Adding to the inadequacies of the intersectional approach, here I would also point to the difficulty of pinning down uprooted women in a single occupation, social class, family position, or even physical appearance, given the fluidity of their mobile condition and the recurrent changes of their status. In recounting the moment of going through the procedures of the Red Cross photograph recognition, Nadia was devastated not to be able to identify her mother:

I looked at all the photos
but I couldn't see my mother
yes
it was more than three years
that we had got separated
in the same way
that I had changed
physically and mentally
they had also changed
so
I didn't recognise my mother

Throughout this book, I have deployed the notion of the assemblage not only to address the complexities of migrant and refugee women's condition, as already discussed above, but also to make 'cartographies of struggles' (Mohanty 2003). What I have argued is that these women have enacted the Arendtian 'right to have rights' (1943) by grasping their passages and moving in-between worlds. While having charted their *lines of flight* however, I have also pointed to the need to decolonize the ways we theorize mobility in general and the nomadic subject in particular.

DECOLONIZING MOBILITIES: NOMADISM AND ITS DISCONTENTS

'There is a forcible affect of language, which courses like blood through its speakers', Denise Riley has written (2005, 1), pointing to the force of language to wound beyond consciousness, recognition and analytical thinking. Moreover, feminist theorists have persuasively argued that naming is a political act, one that is based on mutual recognition (see Sheman 1983, Braaten 2002). What they have argued is that the names that we deploy not only express, but also constitute the real. Drawing on Ludwig Wittgenstein's philosophy of language, Jane Braaten has succinctly observed however, that there are no literal or fully determinate meanings of words and sentences and, therefore, viable alternatives are always. possible (2002, 176) Since naming is an important political form of recognition, albeit not fully determinate, what I have contemplated in this book is the necessity or desirability of a shift in naming as a way of recognizing migrant and refugee women's right to have a place to live.

In light of the above, I have problematized the nomadic subject, both as a concept and as a name – a descriptor of a subject position. My argument has been that despite its radical genealogy in feminist theory and politics, the figuration of the nomad cannot correlate with the lived experiences of displaced women in the current geopolitical context. Although nomadism is still a component entangled in current *mobility assemblages*, its cartographies unveil different modalities of wanderings, other tracks, traces and sea crossings to be followed and understood. In charting situated contexts of uprooted women's mobility, I have drawn on Édward Glissant's (2010) notion of the *errance*-errantry as a line of thinking, decolonizing histories and geographies of nomadism.

Glissant's notion of the *errance* encompasses the wanderings of the slave ships in the openness of the Atlantic, but the closeness of the Mediterranean Sea and the proximity of the Greek islands to the shores of Turkey has created geographical conditions for new modalities of nomadism, yet to be charted. While I have traced lines of 'arrowlike nomadisms of escape' in some of the stories that comprise the archive of my research, my argument is that every story needs its own cartography, if we want to really make sense of continuously emerging and changing *mobility assemblages* of our geographies and times. Moreover, the geopolitical conditions underpinning particular modalities of nomadism do not necessarily create a plane for 'a nomadic subject' to emerge as a figuration that can encompass the precarity of migrant and refugee women's travels today. Nomadism, alongside *errance* and other modalities of wandering, are rather taken as components of entangled relations within *mobility assemblages* at work. In further recognizing the constitutive character of names and words, as well as the political effects of 'language games', I have suggested that the figuration of the *non-nomad* as an attempt to interrogate the conceptual vocabularies of feminist theory and point to their detachment of the real, migrant and refugee women's lived experiences in the case of this research.

While doing so, however, I have also recognized my own partial view and situated perspectives throughout this book. It was my own engagement with nomadic theories since the days of my Ph.D. that eventually came to haunt me in a critique of the concept that I have used throughout my work of writing feminist genealogies. It was my involvement in the second wave feminist movement in Greece that created conditions of possibility for being trusted, when organizing the fieldwork of this research and being introduced to women who were willing to share the gift of their story with me. It is my scholarship in narrative research from an Arendtian perspective that has triggered my inquiries in the existential uniqueness, of migrant and refugee women's experiences. It is my interest in the project of rewriting feminist labour histories that has inspired me to follow genealogical trails in migrant and refugee women's work experiences and activism in the global garment industry. It was my experiences of growing up as a student in Greece during the military dictatorship (1967–1973) that brought the figure of Antigone in my understanding of uprooted women's political narratives. Finally, it is my on-going involvement in the histories, philosophies and politics of gender and education that has led me down the analytical path of the refugee women's education as a radical hope. I hope that the acknowledgement of my partiality, as well as the mapping of my positionality can contribute to the wider project of decolonizing feminist theory and politics in shattering universalist agendas, while forging transnational relations and connections.

WOMEN'S STORIES WITHIN MEMORY ASSEMBLAGES

I can only imagine what the protagonists and narrators of these stories would think of seeing their stories through my analytical lens, but also in concert with other women's, in a Bacchant chorus of what Honig has configured as 'a feminist theory of refusal' (2021). What I do know, however, is that all of them wanted their stories to be out in the wide wild world, which is what I have tried to do, by highlighting the importance of listening to these stories in grounding abstract theorizations and sketching feminist political imaginaries. As Susan Bickford (1996) has powerfully argued, being listened is interwoven in processes of political recognition: I am heard, therefore I exist as a political subject. It is this desire to be heard that I have tried to interweave in the textual transposition of refugee women's stories, knowing that it is only traces of their experiences that we will ever be able to discern.

And yet these pigments of lived experiences of displacement, violence, lines of flight and new becomings become components of 'memory assemblages' (Chidgey 2018) around uprooted women's resilience, perseverance and struggles. What I have argued is that women's stories have created an archive of existential experiences that act as counter memories, of who they are, how they act and what they can become. I see these stories as contributing to an on-going process of intense memory work against a wider background within which they only figure as victims and powerless subjects. As Sophie van den Elzen has succinctly put it, 'memory work does not just make the past present, but also textures the present into a meaningful narrative, connecting disparate contemporary events into shared history' (2021, 24). Here, as elsewhere in my work (see Tamboukou 2015, 2016a), I have deployed insights of new materialist philosophies to throw light on how uprooted women's stories act as agents of memory, thus intervening in *assemblages* of meaning making and understanding. In doing so, I have highlighted the dynamics of gendered mnemonic practices through tracing agential cuts in uprooted women's stories as they are inserted in the wider book of feminist histories, yet to be written.

NOTES

1. See amongst others, Mohanty et al., 1991; Narayan and Harding 2000; Mohanty 2003; Lugones 2008; Arvin et al., 2013; McLaren 2017; Runyan 2018.
2. Look at Tables 1 &2 in the Introduction for an overview of the twenty-two participants.
3. Melina's story, a café in Athens, 18 April 2019.

References

Adorno, Theodor. 1992. *Mahler: A Musical Physiognomy,* Edmund Jephcott (trans). Chicago: University of Chicago Press.

Agier, Michel. 2016. *Borderlands: Towards an Anthropology of the Cosmopolitan Condition.* Cambridge: Polity Press.

Ahmed, Sara. 2016. 'Resignation is a feminist issue'. Retrieved from Feminist Killjoys, August 27, https://feministkilljoys.com/2016/08/27/ resignation-is-a-feminist-issue [Accessed 4-7-2020].

Al-Amoudi, Ismael. 2019. 'Management and dehumanization in late modernity'. In Al-Amoudi, Ismael and Morgan, Jamie (eds.) *Realist Responses to Post-Human Society: Ex Machina.* London: Routledge, 182–194.

Alcoff, Linda, Martín. 2017. 'Decolonizing feminist philosophy'. In McLaren, Margaret, A. (ed.) *Decolonizing Feminism: Transnational Feminism and Globalization.* London: Rowman & Littlefield International, 21–36.

Anzaldúa, Gloria. 1987. *Borderlands = La Frontera : The New Mestiza.* San Francisco: Spinsters/Aunt Lute.

Anzaldúa, Gloria. 1990. 'Haciendo Caras, una entrada/an Introduction'. In Gloria Anzaldúa (ed.) *Making Face, Making Soul/Haciendo Caras: Creative and Critical Perspectives by Feminists of Color,* xv–xxviii. San Francisco: Aunt Lute Press.

Anzaldúa, Gloria. 2009a. 'Border Arte, *Nepantla, sl Lugar de la Frontera*'. In AnaLouise Keating (ed.) *The Gloria Anzaldúa Reader.* Durham: Duke University Press, 176–186.

Anzaldúa, Gloria. 2009b. 'Let us be the healing of the wound'. In AnaLouise Keating (ed.) *The Gloria Anzaldúa Reader.* Durham: Duke University Press, 303–317.

Aparna, Kolar and Kramsch, Olivier. 2018. 'Asylum University: Re-situating Knowledge-exchange along Cross-border Positionalities'. In Gurminder K. Bhambra, Dalia Gebrial, and Kerem Nişancıoğlu (eds.) *Decolonizing the University.* London: Pluto Press, 93–107.

Arendt, Hannah. 1943. We Refugees. *Menorah Journal* 31 (1), 69–77.

Arendt, Hannah. 2018 [1960]. 'Action and "The Pursuit of Happiness"'. In Jerome Kohn (ed.) *Thinking Without A Banister.* New York: Shocken Books, 201–219.

Arendt, Hannah. 1982. *Lectures on Kant's political philosophy.* Edited by Ronald Beiner. Brighton: The Harvester Press.

Arendt, Hannah. 1994. *Essays in Understanding 1930–1954: Formation, Exile and Totalitarianism.* Edited by Kohn J. New York: Schocken Books.

Arendt, Hannah. 1998 [1958]. *The Human Condition.* Chicago: University of Chicago Press.

Arendt, Hannah. 2006 [1961]. *Between Past and Future: Eight Exercises in Political Thought.* London: Penguin Books.

Arvin, Maile, Eve Tuck, and Angie Morrill. 2013. 'Decolonizing Feminism: Challenging Connections between Settler Colonialism and Heteropatriarchy'. *Feminist Formations* 25 (1), 8–34.

Baaten, Jane. 2002. 'The Short Life of Meaning'. In Naomi Scheman and Peg O'Connor (eds.) *Feminist Interpretations of Ludwig Wittgenstein.* Philadelphia: Pennsylvania State University Press, 176–192.

Bache, Ian. 2003. 'Governing through Governance: Education Policy Control under New Labour'. *Political Studies* 51 (2), 300–14.

Baker, Nancy. 2002. 'Wittgenstein, Feminism, and the Exclusion of Philosophy'. In Naomi Scheman and Peg O'Connor (eds.) *Feminist Interpretations of Ludwig Wittgenstein.* Philadelphia: Pennsylvania State University Press, 48–64.

Balibar, Étienne. 1997. *Spinoza: From Individuality to Transindividuality.* Delft: Eburon.

Balibar, Étienne. 2002. *Politics and the Other Scene,* Christine Jones, James Swenson and Chris Turner (trans.), London: Verso.

Ball, Stephen, J., 2008. 'New Philanthropy, New Networks and New Governance in Education'. *Political Studies* 56, 747–765.

Barad, Karen. 2007. *Meeting the Universe Halfway: Quantum Physics and the Entanglement of Matter and Meaning.* Durham: Duke University Press.

Beckett, Samuel. 2012. *Company III Seen III Said Worstward Ho Stirring Still.* Edited by Dirk Van Hulle. London: Faber and Faber

Benjamin, Walter. 1973. *Illuminations,* Hannah Arendt (ed.), Harry Zorn (transl.). London, Jonathan Cape.

Beaugrand, Claire. 2018. *Stateless in the Gulf: Migration, Nationality and Society in Kuwait.* London: I.B. Tauris, e-book.

Bhabba, Jacqueline, Giles Wenona, Mahomed, Faraaz (eds.). 2020. *A Better Future: the Role of Higher Education for Displaced and Marginalised People.* Cambridge: Cambridge University Press.

Bjertrup, Pia Juul, Malika Bouhenia, Philippe Mayaud, Clément Perrin, Jihane Ben Farhat, and Karl Blanchet. 2018. 'A Life in Waiting: Refugees' Mental Health and Narratives of Social Suffering after European Union Border Closures in March 2016'. *Social Science and Medicine* 215, 53–60.

Biesta, J. J. Gert. 2013. *The Beautiful Risk of Education.* Boulder and London: Paradigm.

Bickford, Susan. 1996. *The Dissonance of Democracy: Listening, Conflict and Citizenship*. Ithaca. New York: Cornell University Press.

Birey, Tegiye, Cantat, Celine, Maczynska, Ewa and Sevinin, Eda (eds.). 2019. *Challenging the Political Across Borders: Migrants' and Solidarity Struggles*. Budapest: Central European University Press.

Blommaert. Jan. 2006. 'Applied Ethnopoetics'. *Narrative Inquiry* 16 (1), 181–190.

Blackledge, Adrian., Creese, Angela and Hu, Rachel. 2016. The Structure of Everyday Narrative in a Citymarket: An Ethnopoetics Approach. *Journal of Sociolinguistics* 20 (5), 654–676.

Boer, Inge 1996. 'The World Beyond Our Window: Nomads, Travelling Theories and the Function of Boundaries'. *Parallax* 3, 7–26.

Boswell, Christina, Geddes, Andrew, and Scholten Peter. 2011. 'The Role of Narratives in Migration Policy-Making: A Research Framework'. *The British Journal of Politics and International Relations* 13 (1): 1–11.

Boudreau, Laura, Heath, Rachel and McCormick, Tyler. 2018. 'Migrants, Information, and Working Conditions in Bangladeshi Garment Factories', Working Paper, International Growth Centre. Retrieved from https://cgeg.sipa.columbia.edu/sites/default/files/cgeg/WP76Boudreau.pdf [Accessed 14-2-2020]

Bowie, Andrew. 1990. *Aesthetics and Subjectivity, from Kant to Nietzsche*. Manchester: Manchester University Press.

Boyarin, Jonathan. 1993. (ed.) *The Ethnography of Reading*. Berkeley: University of California Press.

Bozalek, Vivienne and Zembylas Michalinos. 2017. 'Diffraction or Reflection? Sketching the Contours of Two Methodologies in Educational Research'. *International Journal of Qualitative Studies in Education* 30 (2), 111–127.

Braidotti. Rosi. 2002. *Metamorphoses : Towards a Materialist Theory of Becomings*. Cambridge: Polity.

Braidotti, Rosi. 2011. *Nomadic Subjects: Embodiment and Sexual Difference in Contemporary Feminist Theory*. 2nd edition. New York: Columbia University Press.

Braidotti, Rosi. 2019. 'A Theoretical Framework for the Critical Posthumanities'. *Theory, Culture and Society* 36 (6), 31–61.

Brown, Wendy. 2000. 'Suffering Rights as Paradoxes'. *Constellations* 7 (2), 230–41.

Brown, Wendy. 2015. *Undoing the Demos: Neoliberalism's Stealth Revolution*. Zone Books.

Brown, Wendy. 2017. *Walled states, waning sovereignty*. London: The MIT Press.

Bronwyn, Davies. 2016. 'Emergent Listening'. In Norman K. Denzin, N. K., and Michael, D. Giardina (eds.), *Qualitative Inquiry Through a Critical Lens*, London: Routledge, 73–84.

Browning Gary. 2012. 'A Conversation with Bonnie Honig: Exploring Agonistic Humanism'. In Gary Browning, Raia Prokhovnik, and Maria Dimova-Cookson (eds.), *Dialogues with Contemporary Political Theorists. International Political Theory series*. London: Palgrave Macmillan.

Burrell, Kathy. 2017. *Moving Lives: Narratives of Nation and Migration among Europeans in Post-War Britain*. London: Routledge.

Butler, Judith. 2000. *Antigone's Claim: Kinship Between Life and Death.* New York: Columbia University Press.
Butler, Judith. 2004. *Precarious Life: the Powers of Mourning and Violence.* London: Verso.
Cantú Norma Elia. 2013. 'Sitio y lengua: Chicana Third Space Feminist Theory'. In Imelda Martín-Junquera (ed.) *Landscapes of Writing in Chicano Literature.* Basingstoke: Palgrave, 173–187.
Carastathis, Anna , Aila Spathopoulou, Myrto Tsilimpounidi. 2018. 'Crisis, What Crisis? Immigrants, Refugees, and Invisible Struggles'. *Refuge* 34 (1), 29–38.
Castles, Stephen. 2006. 'Global Perspectives on Forced Migration'. *Asian and Pacific Migration Journal* 15, 17–28.
Cavarero, Adriana. 2000 [1997]. *Relating Narratives: Storytelling and Selfhood,* Paul A. Kottman (transl.). London: Routledge.
Cavarero, Adriana. 2002. *Stately Bodies: Literature, Philosophy and the Question of Gender,* Robert de Lucca and Deanna Shemek (trans.), Ann Arbor: The University of Michigan Press.
Cavarero, Adriana. 2005. *For More than One Voice: Toward a Philosophy of Vocal Expression.* Paul A. Kottman (transl.). Stanford: Stanford University Press.
Cixous, Hélène. 1976. 'The laugh of the Medusa'. Keith Cohen and Paula Cohen (transl.). *Signs: Journal of Women in Culture and Society* 1 (4), 875–893.
Chambers, Samuel. 2013. *The Lessons of Rancière.* New York: Oxford University Press.
Chan, Huiying B. 2019. 'How Chinese American Women Changed U.S. Labor History'. Retrieved from Asian American Writers' Workshop, https://aaww.org/chinatown-garment-strike-1982/ [Accessed 14-2-2020].
Chan, Sucheng. 1986. *This Bittersweet soil: The Chinese in California 1860–1910.* Berkeley and Los Angeles: University of California Press.
Chan, Sucheng. 1991. 'The Exclusion of Chinese Women 1870–1943'. In Chan (ed.) *Entry Denied: Exclusion and the Chinese Community in America, 1882–1943.* Philadelphia: Temple University Press, 1991.
Chanter, Tina. 2010. 'The Performative Politics and Rebirth of Antigone in Ancient Greece and Modern South Africa'. In Frandiger, Moira. 2010. 'Nomadic Antigone', in in Fanny Söderbäck (ed.) *Feminist Readings of Antigone,* New York: State University of New York Press, 83–98.
Chidgey, Red. 2018. *Feminist Afterlives: Assemblage Memory in Activist times.* Basingstoke: Palgrave Macmillan.
Christensen, Lenen. 2017. A safe haven for refugee women in Greece. *Amnesty International,* https://melissanetwork.org/2019/08/01/amnesty-org-a-safe-haven-for-refugee-women-in-greece/ [Accessed 20-06-2020].
Clean Clothes Campaign. 2009. 'False Promises: Migrant Workers in the Global Garment Industry'. Discussion Paper. Retrieved from https://cleanclothes.org/file-repository/resources-publications-migrant-workers-internal.pdf/view [Accessed 14-2-2020].
Cohn, Dorrit. 1999. *The Distinction of Fiction.* Baltimore, MD: John Hopkins University Press.

Couldry, Nick. 2010. *Why Voice Matters. Culture and Politics after Neo Liberalism.* London: Sage.

Crimmins, Gail. 2020 (ed.) *Strategies for Supporting Inclusion and Diversity in the Academy: Higher Education, Aspiration and Inequality.* Basingstoke: Palgrave.

Daniel, Valentine E. and Knusden, John Ch (eds). 1995. *Mistrusting Refugees.* Berkeley: University of California Press.

Davies, Bronwyn. 2016. 'Emergent Listening'. In Norman K. Denzin and Michael D. Giardina (eds.) *Qualitative Inquiry Through a Critical Lens.* London: Routledge, pp. 73–84.

Debaise, Didier. 2017. *Nature as an Event: The Lure of the Possible,* transl. Michael Halewood. Durham and London: Duke University Press.

deCerteau, Michel. 1984. *The Practice of Everyday Life,* Steven Rendall (transl.). Berkeley: University of California Press.

de Soldatenko, María A. Gutierrez. 2002. 'ILGWU Labor Organizers: Chicana and Latina Leadership in the Los Angeles Garment Industry", *Frontiers: A Journal of Women Studies* 23 (1), 46–66.

de Tocqueville, Alexis. 1840. *Democracy in America, Volume II.* New York: J. & H.G. Langley.

Deleuze, Gilles 1992. *Expressionism in Philosophy: Spinoza.* New York: Zone Books.

Deleuze, Gilles. 1997. 'One Less Manifesto'. In Murray, Timothy (ed.) *Mimesis, Masochism and Mime: The Politics of Theatricality in Contemporary French Thought,* Timothy Murray and Eliane dal Molin (trans.). Michigan: University of Michigan Press.

Deleuze, Gilles. 2001 (1969). *The Logic of Sense,* Mark Lester & Charles Stivale (transl.) London: Continuum.

Deleuze, Gilles and Guattari, Felix. 1988 [1980]. *A Thousand Plateaus: Capitalism and Schizophrenia,* Brian Massumi (transl.). London: The Athlone Press.

Deleuze Gilles and Parnet Claire. 2002. *Dialogues II,* Hugh Tomlinson and Barbara Habberjam (transls.) London: Continuum.

Deutsche Welle: 'Melissa Network – A hive built by migrant women' https://melissanetwork.org/2019/09/21/melissa-network-a-hive-built-by-migrant-women/ [Accessed 20-06-2020]

Dietz, Mary, G. 1985. 'Citizenship with a Feminist Face: The Problem with Maternal Thinking'. *Political Theory* 13 (1), 19–37.

Dowling, C. William. 2011. *Ricoeur on Time and Narrative: An Introduction to Temps et Recit.* Notre Dame, IN: University of Notre Dame Press.

Duras, Marguerite. 1973. *Nathalie Granger.* Paris: Gallimard.

Duron, Clementina. 1984. 'Mexican Women and Labor Conflict in Los Angeles: The ILGWU Dressmakers' Strike of 1933'. *Aztlan: International Journal of Chicano Studies Research* 15 (1), 145–161, p. 150.

Eastmond, Marita. 2007. 'Stories as Lived Experience: Narratives in Forced Migration'. *Journal of Refugee Studies* 20 (2), 248–264.

Elshtain, Jean Betcke. 1982. 'Antigone's Daughters'. *Democracy* 2 (2), 39–45.

Esin, Cigdem and Lunasmaa, Aura. 2020. 'Narrative and ethical (in)action: creating spaces of resistance with refugee-storytellers in the Calais 'Jungle' camp'. *International Journal of Social Research Methodology* 23 (4), 391–403.

Farinati Lucia & Firth Claudia. 2017. *The Force of Listening*. Berlin: Errant Bodies Press.

Fisher, R. Walter. 1989. *Human Communication as Narration: Toward a Philosophy of Reason, Value, and Action*. Columbia: The University of South Carolina Press.

Folbre, Nancy. 2002. *The Invisible Heart: Economics and Family Values*. New York: New Press.

Fong, Patricia M. 1975. 'The 1938 National Dollar Strike'. *Asian American Review* 2 (1), 183–200.

Foucault, Michel. 1986. 'On the Genealogy of Ethics: An Overview of Work in Progress'. In Rabinow, P. (ed.) *The Foucault Reader*, Harmondsworth: Peregrine, 340–372.

Foucault, Michel. 2003 [1997]. *"Society Must Be Defended", Lectures at the College de France 1975–1976*, eds. Mauro Bertani and Alessandro Fontana, David Macey (transl.). New York: Picador.

Frandiger, Moira. 2010. 'Nomadic Antigone'. In Fanny Söderbäck (ed.) *Feminist Readings of Antigone*. New York: State University of New York Press, 15–23.

Friedman, Marilyn. 1989. 'Feminism and Modern Friendship: Dislocating the Community'. *Ethics* 99 (2), 275–290.

Fudge, Judy. 2018. 'Slavery and Unfree Labour: The Politics of Naming, Framing, and Blaming'. *Labour / Le Travail* 82, 227–244.

GAATW [Global Alliance Against Traffic in Women]. 2019. 'Feminised Migration and Deteriorating Conditions of Employment in the Garment Industry in Cambodia: Perspectives of Workers Organised by CATU. A Feminist Participatory Action Researh'. Retrieved from https://gaatw.org/publications/Safe_and_Fair_FPAR/FPAR_Report_CATU.pdf [Accessed 14-2-2020].

Gabaccia Donna. 1999. 'Is Everywhere Nowhere? Nomads, Nations, and the Immigrant Paradigm of United States History'. *The Journal of American History* 86 (3) (The Nation and Beyond: Transnational Perspectives on United States History: A Special Issue), 1115–1134.

Gabaccia, Donna and Iacovetta, Franca. 1998. 'Women, Work, and Protest in the Italian Diaspora: An International Research Agenda'. *Labour / Le Travail* 42, 161–181.

Galloway, Alexander. 2014. *Laruelle: Against the Digital*. Minneapolis: University of Minnesota Press.

Gedalof, Irene. 1996. 'Can Nomads Learn to Count to Four? Rosi Braidotti and the Space for Difference in Feminist Theory'. *Women: A Cultural Review* 7 (2), 189–201.

Gedalof, Irene. 2000. 'Identity in Transit: Nomads, Cyborgs and Women'. *European Journal of Women's Studies* 7, 337–354.

Gee, James. 1991. A linguistic approach to narrative. *Journal of Narrative and Life History/Narrative Inquiry* 1 (1), 15–39.

Gee, James. 2015. *Social Linguistics and Literacies* (Fifth Edition), London: Routledge.

Gergerlioğlu Ömer Faruk. 2021. 'Imprisoned Women and Children in Turkey: Human Rights Violations Under the State of Emergency'. In Aydin Hasan and Langley Winston (eds.) *Human Rights in Turkey. Philosophy and Politics - Critical Explorations*, vol. 15. Springer, Cham. https://doi.org/10.1007/978-3-030-57476-5_18

Glissant, Édouard. 1996 [1981]. *Carribean Discourse. Selected Essays,* Michael Dash (transl.). Charlottesville: University of Virginia Press.

Glissant, Édouard. 2010 [1990]. *Poetics of Relation,* Betsy Wing (transl.). Ann Arbor: The University of Michigan Press.

Gluck, Sherna, Berger. 2014. 'Why do we call it Oral History? Refocusing on Orality/Aurality in the Digital Age'. In Douglas, A. Boyd and Mary A. Larson (eds.) *Oral History and Digital Humanities.* Basingstoke: Palgrave, 136–189.

Goodman Joyce. 2019. 'Willystine Goodsell (1870–1962) and John Dewey (1859–1952): History, Philosophy and Women's Education'. *History of Education* 48 (6), 837–854.

Grayson, John. 2014. 'Migration and adult education: social movement learning and resistance in the UK'. *European Journal for Research on the Education and Learning of Adults* 5 (1), 177–194.

Green, André. 1990. *La folie privée. Psychanalyse des cas-limites.* Paris: Gallimard.

Green, Nancy. 1997. *Ready to Wear, Ready to Work: A Century of Industry Immigrants in Paris and New York.* Durham and London: Duke University Press.

Griffin, Susan. 1978. *Woman and Nature: The Roaring Inside Her.* New York: Harper and Row.

Gsoels-Lorensen, Jutta. 2014. 'Antigone, Deportee'. *Arethusa* 47 (2): 111–144.

Guttiérez Rodríguez, Encarnación. 2018. 'The Coloniality of Migration and the "Refugee Crisis": On the Asylum-Migration Nexus, the Transatlantic White European Settler Colonialism-Migration and Racial Capitalism'. *Refuge* 34 (1), 16–27.

Hacking, Ian. 1986. 'Making Up People'. In Thomas C. Heller, Morton Sosna, and David E Wellbery (ed.) *Reconstructing Individualism: Autonomy, Individuality and the Self in Western Thought.* Stanford: Stanford University Press, 222–236.

Hakki, Bayan. 2018. 'Using Art Tools with Older Syrian Refugee Women to Explore Activated Development'. *Intervention: Journal of Mental Health and Psychosocial Support in Conflict Affected Areas* 16 (2), 187–194.

Haraway Donna. 1992. 'The Promises of Monsters: A Regenerative Politics for Inappro-priate/d Others'. In Lawrence Grossberg, Cary Nelson, and Paula Treichler P (eds.) *Cultural Studies.* New York: Routledge, 295–337.

Haraway, Donna. 1997. Modest_Witness@Second_Millennium. FemaleMan_Meets_ OncoMouse: Feminism and Technoscience, New York: Routledge.

Hayles, N. Katherine. 1997. 'Voices Out of Bodies, Bodies Out of Voices: Audiotape and the Production of Subjectivity'. In Adelaide Morris (ed.) *Sound States: Innovative Poetics and Acoustical Technologies.* Chapel Hill and London: University of North Carolina Press, 74–96.

Headley, Clevis. 2015. 'Glissant's Existential Ontology of Difference'. In John, E. Drabinsky and Marisa Parham (eds.) *Theorizing Glissant: Sites and Citations,* London: Rowman & Littlefield International, 53–83.

Henao Castro, Andrés Fabián. 2013 'Antigone Claimed: "I am a Stranger!" Political Theory and the Figure of the Stranger". *Hypatia* 28 (2), 307–322.
Henao Castro, Andrés Fabián (2020) 'Can the Palestinian Antigone Grieve? A Political Re-Interpretation of Judith Butler's Ethical Turn'. *Settler Colonial Studies* 10 (1): 94–109.
Herbart, Johann Friedrich. 1896 [1804]. *The Science of Education and the Aesthetic Revelation of the World,* Henri Felkin and Emmie Felkin (trans). Boston: D.C. Heath.
Hesford, Wendy. 2011. *Spectacular Rhetorics: Human Rights Visions, Recognitions, Feminisms.* Durham: Duke University Press.
Holland, Catherine, A. 2010. 'After Antigone: Women, the Past, and the Future of Feminist Political Thought'. In Fanny Söderbäck (ed.) *Feminist Readings of Antigone.* New York: State University of New York Press, 27–43.
Holmwood, John. 2011. *A Manifesto for the Public University.* London: Bloomsbury Academic.
Honig, Bonnie. 2001. *Democracy and the Foreigner.* New Jersey: Princeton University Press.
Honig, Bonnie. 2013. *Antigone Interrupted.* Cambridge: Cambridge University Press.
Honig, Bonnie. 2015. 'Public Things: Jonathan Lear's Radical Hope, Lars von Trier's Melancholia, and the Democratic Need'. *Political Research Quarterly* 68 (3), 623–636.
Honig, Bonnie. 2021. *A Feminist Theory of Refusal.* Cambridge MA: Harvard University Press.
hooks, bell. 1994. *Teaching to Transgress: Education as the Practice of Freedom.* London: Routledge.
Huffington Post Greece. 2019. 'The Other Women': A Young Refugee Woman, Khaterch Ahmadi Narrates Her Story [Οι "Άλλες" γυναίκες: μια νεαρή πρόσφυγας, η Χατερέ Αχμαντί, αφηγείται την ιστορία της], https://melissanetwork.org/2019/07/03/οι-άλλες-γυναίκες-μια-νεαρή-πρόσφυ-2/ [Accessed 20-06-2020].
Huzar, Timothy. 2021. 'Apprehending Care in the Flesh: Reading Cavarero with Spillers'. *Diacritics,* forthcoming.
Hyndman, Jennifer. 2019. 'Unsettling Feminist Geopolitics: Forging Feminist Political Geographies of Violence and Displacement'. *Gender, Place and Culture* 26 (1): 3–29.
Hyndman, Jennifer, and, Wenona Giles. 2011. 'Waiting for What? The Feminization of Refugees in Protracted Situations'. *Gender, Place and Culture* 18 (3): 361–379.
Hyvärinen, Matti, Hydén, Lars-Christer, Saarenheimo, Marja and Tamboukou, Maria. 2010. 'Introduction'. In Matti Hyvärinen, Lars-Christer Hydén, Marja Saarenheimo, and Maria Tamboukou (eds.) *Beyond Narrative Coherence.* Amsterdam: John Benjamins Publishing, 1–15.
ILO [International Labour Organization], 2017. 'Working Conditions of Migrant garment Workers in India'. Retrieved from https://www.ilo.org/wcmsp5/groups/public/---ed_norm/---declaration/documents/publication/wcms_554809.pdf [Accessed 14-2-2020]
Irigaray, Lucy. 1974. *Speculum de l'autre femme.* Paris: Les Éditions de Minuit.

Jones, Emma. 2020. *Can the Colonizer Listen? Ethnographic Encounters with Empowerment.* PhD Thesis, University of East London, UK.

Jung, Tobias, Phillips, Susan, D. and Harrow, Jenny. 2016. *The Routledge Companion to Philanthropy.* London: Routledge.

Kabeer, Naila. 1994. *Reversed Realities: Gender Hierarchies in Development Thought,* London: Verso.

Kabeer, Naila. 1999. 'Resources, Agency, Achievements: Reflections on the Measurement of Women's Empowerment'. *Development and Change* 30 (3), 435–464.

Kabeer, Naila. 2005. 'Gender Equality and Women's Empowerment: A Critical Analysis of the Third Millennium Development Goal'. *Gender & Development* 13 (1), 13–24.

Kolhatkar, Sonali. 2002. 'Saving' AfghanWomen. ZNet, retrieved from http://www.rawa.org/znet.htm

Kaplan, Caren. 1987. 'Deterritorializations: The Rewriting of Home and Exile in Western Feminist Discourse'. *Cultural Critique* 6, 187–198.

Kassabova, Kapka. 2017. *Border: A Journey to the Edge of Europe.* Minneapolis: Graywolf Press.

Kaya, A. & Kıraç, A. 2016. *Vulnerability Assessment of Syrian Refugees in Turkey.* Support to Life Association. Retrieved from https://data2.unhcr.org/ar/documents/download/54518. [Accessed 14-2-2020]

Kessler-Harris, Alice. 1976. 'Organizing the Unorganizeable: Three Jewish Women and their Union'. *Labor History* 17(1), 5–23.

Kinkaid, Eden. 2020. 'Can Assemblage Think Difference? A Feminist Critique of Assemblage Geographies'. *Progress in Human Geography* 44 (3), 457–472.

Klein, Michael L. and Reyland Nicholas. Eds. 2012. *Music and Narrative since 1900.* Bloomington: Indiana University Press.

Koblitz, Ann Hibner. 1988. 'Science, Women and the Russian Intelligentsia : The Generation of the 1860s'. *Isis* 79 (2), 208–226.

Koggel, Christine M. 2002. 'Using Wittgensteinian Methodology to Elucidate the Meaning of Equality'. In Naomi Scheman and Peg O'Connor (eds.) *Feminist Interpretations of Ludwig Wittgenstein*235–258. Philadelphia: Pennsylvania State University Press.

Kolozova, Katerina. 2014. *Cut of the Real: Subjectivity in Postructuralist Theory.* New York: Columbia University Press.

Korkmaz, Emre Eren. 2019. 'Syrian Refugee Garment Workers in the Turkish Supply Chain of Global Corporations'. In Gaye Yılmaz, İsmail Doğa Karatepe, and Tolga Tören (eds.) *Integration through Exploitation: Syrians in Turkey.* Augsburg, München: Rainer Hampp Verlag, 42–54.

Kristeva, Julia. 2001. *Hannah Arendt: Life is a Narrative,* Frank Collins (trans.). Toronto: University of Toronto Press.

Laruelle, François. 2013 [1996]. *Principles of Non-Philosophy,* trans. Nicola Rubczak and Anthony Paul Smith. London: Bloomsbury.

Laruelle, François and Anne Françoise Schmid. 2003. 'L' identité sexuée'. *Identities* 2 (3), 49–61.

Lear, Jonathan. 2008. *Radical Hope: Ethics in the Face of Cultural Devastation*. Boston: Harvard University Press.

Lee, Catherine. 2010. '"Where the Danger Lies": Race, Gender, and Chinese and Japanese Exclusion in the United States, 1870–1924'. *Sociological Forum* 25 (2), 248–271.

Lefebvre, Henri. 1991 [1974]. *The Production of Space*, Donald Nicholson-Smith (trans.). Oxford: Blackwell.

Lefebvre, Henri. 2004. *Rhythmanalysis: Space, Time and Everyday Life*, Stuart Elden and Gerald Moore (transl.). London: Continuum.

Lewis, Tyson E. 2012. *The Aesthetics of Education: Theatre, Curiosity, and Politics in the Work of Jacques Rancière and Paulo Freire*. London: Continuum.

Lewis, Tyson E. 2014. 'Book Review: The Beautiful risk of Education'. *Educational Theory* 64 (3), 303–309.

Ling, Huping. 1998. *Surviving on the Gold Mountain: A History of Chinese American Women and their Lives*. New York: State University of New York Press.

Lomax, Tamura. 2015. 'Black Women's Lives Don't Matter in Academia Either, Or Why I Quit Spaces That Don't Value Black Women's Life and Labor'. Retrieved form Academic Abolitionism. https:// academicabolitionism.wordpress.com/2015/05/30/tamura-a-lomax-black-womens-lives-dont-matter-inacademia-either/ [Accessed 4-07-2020]

Loo, Bryce, Streitwieser, Bernhard, and Jeong, Jisun. 2018. 'Higher Education's Role in National Refugee Integration: Four Cases'. In World Education News + Reviews (WENR), available on line, https://wenr.wes.org/2018/02/higher-educations-role-national-refugee-integration-four-cases [Accessed 25-05-2020]

Louka, Maria. 2020. 'African Women in Greece Share Their Experience of Oppression and Their Passion for Life' [Οι Αφρικανές γυναίκες στην Ελλάδα μο ιράζονται το βίωμα της καταπίεσης και το πάθος για ζωή], retrieved from https://popaganda.gr/stories/i-afrikanes-ginekes-stin-ellada-mirazonte-to-vioma-tis-katapiesis-ke-to-pathos-gia-zoi/ [Accessed 25-05-2020]

Lo, Ester Shauna. 2008. 'Chinese Women Entering New England: Chinese Exclusion Act Case Files, Boston 1911–1925'. *The New England Quarterly* 81 (3), 383–409.

Loo, Bryce, Streitwieser, Bernhard, and Jeong, Jisun. 2018. 'Higher Education's Role in NationalRefugee Integration: Four Cases'. In *World Education News and Reviews* [WENR], retrieved from https://wenr.wes.org/2018/02/higher-educations-role-national-refugee-integration-four-cases [Accessed 4-07-2020].

Lotz-Sisitka, Heila. 2019. Educational Research Responses to Dehumanzation Tendencies in a Context of Risk'. Keynote address, ECER Conference, Hamburg 4 September, 2019, retrieved from https://eera-ecer.de/ecer-2019-hamburg/programme/keynote-speakers/heila-lotz-sisitka/ [Accessed 4-07-2020]

Lotz-Sisitka, Heila, Wals, Arjen, EJ, Kronlid, Davidand McGarry, Dylan. 2015. 'Transformative, Transgressive Social Learning: Rethinking Higher Education Pedagogy in Times of Systemic Global Dysfunction'. *Current Opinion in Environmental Sustainability* 16, 73–80.

Lugones, María. 1990. 'Playfulness, World-travelling, and Loving Perception'. In Gloria Anzaldúa (ed.), *Haciendo Caras, Making Face, Making Soul: Creative* and *Critical Perspectives of Feminists of Color*. San Francisco: Aunt Lute Press, 390–402.

Lugones, María. 2008. 'The Coloniality of Gender'. *Worlds & Knowledges Otherwise* 2, 1–17.

Luste, Boulbina, Seloua. 2013. 'La décolonisation des savoirs et ses théories voyageuses'. *Rue Descartes* 78 (2), 19–33. DOI : 10.3917/rdes.078.0019. URL : https://www.cairn.info/revue-rue-descartes-2013-2-page-19.htm

McCaffery, Isais James. 1999. 'Organizing Las Costureras: Life, Labor and Unionization Among Mexicana Garment Workers in Two Borderland Cities-Los Angeles and San Antonio, 1933–1941'. PhD diss., University of Kansas.

McLaren, Margaret, A. 2017. (ed.) *Decolonizing Feminism: Transnational Feminism and Globalization*. London: Rowman & Littlefield International.

Manby, Bronwen. 2018. 'Book Review – Claire Beaugrand's "Stateless in the Gulf: Migration, Nationality and Society in Kuwait"'. Available at: https://blogs.lse.ac.uk/mec/2018/07/23/book-review-claire-beaugrands-stateless-in-the-gulf-migration-nationality-and-society-in-kuwait/ [Accessed 26-2-2020]

Manning Erin and Massumi Brian. 2014. *Thought in the Act: Passages in the Ecology of Experience*. Minneapolis: University of Minnesota Press.

Martiniello, Marco. 2019. *Art and Refugees: Multidisciplinary Perspectives*. Basel: MDPI, open access at: https://doi.org/10.3390/books978-3-03921-406-8

Maldonado, Marta Maria and Guenther, Katja M. (eds.) 2019. Critical Feminist Exits, Re-Routings, and Institutional Betrayals in Academia'. Special issue of *Feminist Formations* 31 (1), free access at: https://muse.jhu.edu/issue/40305

Maryns, Katrijn. 2006. *The asylum-speaker: language in the Belgium asylum procedure*, Manchester: St Jerome Publications.

Mason, Jennifer. 2018. *Affinities: Potent Connections in Personal Life*. Cambridge: Polity Press.

Maus, Fred Everet. 1991. 'Music as Narrative'. *Indiana Theory Review* 12 (Spring and Fall), 1–34.

Mezzadra, Sandro. 2011. 'The Gaze of Autonomy. Capitalism, Migration and Social Struggles'. In Vicki Squire (ed.) *The Contested Politics of Mobility: Borderzones and Irregularity*. London: Routledge, 121–143.

Mezzadra, Sandro. 2019. 'At the Borders of Europe. Discussing with Étienne Balibar. Inserito *da Redazione | Mag 28, 2019,* retrieved from http://www.euronomade.info/?p=12089 [Accessed 20-3-2020]

Mildford, Jarmila and Kinzell, Till. 2016. Eds. *Audionarratology: Interfaces of Sound and Narrative*. Berlin: De Gruyter.

Mohanty, Chandra Talpade. 1984. 'Under Western Eyes: Feminist Scholarship and Colonial Discourse'. *Boundary 2* 12 (2), 333–358.

Mohanty, Chandra Talpade. 2003. *Feminism Without Borders. Decolonizing Theory, Practicing Solidarity*. Duke: Duke University Press.

Mohanty, Chandra Talpade. 2017. 'Preface: Towards a Decolonial Feminism for the 99 Percent'. In McLaren, Margaret, A. (ed.) *Decolonizing Feminism: Transnational Feminism and Globalization*. London: Rowman & Littlefield International, vii–x.

Mohanty, Chandra Talpade; Russo, Anne; and Lourdes M. Torres, eds. 1991. *Third World Women and the Politics of Feminism*. Bloomington: Indiana University Press

Moraga, Cherríe, Anzaldúa, Gloria, eds. 1981. *This Bridge Called My Back : Writings by Radical Women of Color*. Watertown, MA: Persephone Press.

Moten, Fred. 2018. *Stolen Life*. Durham: Duke University Press.

Mountz, Alison, Anne Bonds, Becky Mansfield, Jenna Loyd, Jennifer Hyndman, Margaret Walton-Roberts, Ranu Basu, Risa Whitson, Roberta Hawkins, Trina Hamilton, and Winifred Curran. 2015. "For Slow Scholarship: A Feminist Politics of Resistance through Collective Action in the Neoliberal University". *ACME: An International Journal for Critical Geographies* 14 (4), 1235–1259. https://www.acme-journal.org/index.php/acme/article/view/1058.

Mullarkey, John and Anthony Paul Smith, eds. 2012. *Laruelle and Non-Philosophy*. Edinburgh: Edinburgh University Press.

Narayan, Uma and Harding, Sandra, eds. 2000. *Decentering the Center: Philosophy for a Multicultural, Postcolonial, and Feminist World*. Bloomington: Indiana University Press.

Navia, Luis E. 2005. *Diogenes The Cynic: The War Against The World*. Amherst, NY: Humanity Books.

Oliver, Kelly. 2016. *Carceral Humanitarianism: Logics of Refugee Detention*. Minneapolis: University of Minnesota Press.

Oliver Kelly. 2017. 'The Special Plight of Women Refugees'. In McLaren, Margaret, A. (ed.) *Decolonizing Feminism: Transnational Feminism and Globalization*. London: Rowman & Littlefield International, 177–200.

Paterson, Wendy. 2013. 'Narratives of Events: Labovian narrative analysis and its limitations'. In Molly Andrews, Corinne Squire, and Maria Tamboukou (eds.) *Doing Narrative Research*. London: Sage, 27–46.

Pesotta, Rose. 1958. *Days of Our Lives*. Boston: Excelsior Publishers.

Pesotta, Rose. 1987 [1944]. *Bread Upon the Waters*. Ithaca: Industrial and Labor Relations Press.

Pohlhaus, Gaile, Jr. 2017. 'Knowing without Borders and the Work of Epistemic Gathering'. In McLaren, Margaret, A. (ed.) *Decolonizing Feminism: Transnational Feminism and Globalization*. London: Rowman & Littlefield International, 37–54.

Portelli, Alessandro. 1991. *The Death of Luigi Trastulli and Other Stories: Form and Meaning in Oral History*. Albany, NY: State University of New York Press.

Portelli, Alessandro. 1994. *The Text and the Voice: Writing, Speaking, and Democracy in American Literature*. New York: Columbia University Press.

Portelli, Alessandro. 1998. 'Oral History as Genre'. In Mary Chamberlain and Paul Thompson (eds.) *Narrative and Genre: Context and Types of Communication*. London, Routledge, 23–45.

Rancière, Jacques. 2004. *The Politics of Aesthetics*. Translated by Gabriel Rochill. London: Continuum.

Rancière, Jacques. 2001. 'Ten Theses on Politics'. Translated by Rachel Bowlby and Davide Panagia. *Theory & Event*, 5.3: n.p.

Ricoeur, Paul. 1984. *Time and Narrative*, Volume 1. Kathleen McLaughlin and David Pellauer(transl.). Chicago: University of Chicago Press.

Ridge, Natasha, Y. and Terway, Arushi. 2019. *Philanthropy in Education: Diverse Perspectives and Global Trends*. Cheltenham: Edward Elgar.

Riessman, K. Catherine. 2005. 'Exporting ethics: a narrative about narrative research in South India. *Health. An Interdisciplinary Journal for the Social Study of Health, Illness and Medicine* 9 (4), 473–490.

Riessman, K. Catherine. 2008. *Narrative Methods for the Human Sciences*. Los Angeles, London, New Delhi, Singapore: Sage Publications.

Riessman, K. Catherine. 2012. 'The Pleasure of the Text: Sensual and Seductive Aspects of Narrative Inquiry'. *Rassegna italiana di sociologia* 53 (4), 553–572.

Riley, Denise. 2005. *Impersonal Passion: Language as Affect*. Durham and London: Duke University Press.

Ross, Tabitha. 2014. 'Syrian Refugee Women in Lebanon Take Heart from Antigone-in Pictures'. *Guardian*, 10 December 2014, available on-line, at: https://www.theguardian.com/global-development/gallery/2014/dec/10/syrian-refugee-women-lebanon-antigone-sophocles-in-pictures [Accessed 25-10-2020]

Rowlands, Jo. 1997. *Questioning Empowerment: Working with Women in Honduras*. Oxford: Oxfam.

Runyan Anne Sisson. 2018. 'Decolonizing Knowledges in Feminist World Politics'. *International Feminist Journal of Politics* 20 (1), 3–8.

Salvaggio, Ruth. 1999. *The Sounds of Feminist Theory*. New York: State University of New York Press.

Said, Edward W. 1992. *Musical Elaborations*. London: Vintage.

Samuel Raphael. 1972. 'Perils of the Transcript'. *Oral History Journal* 1 (2), 19–22.

Sanchez, George J. 1993. *Becoming Mexican-American: Ethnicity, Culture and Identity in Chicano Los Angeles, 1900–1945*. New York: Oxford University Press.

Scheman, Naomi. 1993. *Engenderings: Constructions of Knowledge, Authority and Privilege*. New York: Routledge.

Sheng Lu. 2019. WTO reports world textile and apparel trade in 2018. Retrieved from: https://shenglufashion.com/2019/08/16/wto-reports-world-textile-and-apparel-trade-in-2018/ [Accessed 14-2-2020]

Scherrer, Christoph. 2019. 'Foreword'. In Gaye Yılmaz, İsmail Doğa Karatepe, and Tolga Tören (eds.) *Integration through Exploitation: Syrians in Turkey*. Augsburg, München: Rainer Hampp Verlag, xi–xii.

Schuetz, Alfred. 1944. 'The Stranger: An Essay in Social Psychology'. *American Journal of Sociology* 49 (6), 499–507.

Sjöholm, Cecilia. 2004. *The Antigone Complex: Ethics and the Invention of Feminine Desire*. Stanford: Stanford University Press.

Sjöholm, Cecilia. 2010. 'Naked Life: Arendt and the Exile at Colonus'. In S. E. Wilmer and Audronė Žukauskaite (eds.) *Interrogating Antigone in Postmodern Philosophy and Criticism*. Oxford: Oxford University Press, 48–66.

Sjöholm, Cecilia. 2015. *Doing Aesthetics with Arendt: How to See Things*. New York: Columbia University Press.

Slee, Roger. 2018. *Inclusive Education Isn't Dead, It Just Smells Funny.* London: Routledge.
Smith, Anthony Paul. 2016. *François Laruelle's Principles of Non-Philosophy : A Critical Introduction and Guide.* Edinburgh: Edinburgh University Press.
Söderbäck, Fanny. 2010. 'Impossible Mourning'. In Fanny Söderbäck (ed.) *Feminist Readings of Antigone.* New York: State University of New York Press, 65–82.
Sophocles. 1984. *The Three Theban Plays,* trans. Robert Fagles and Bernard Knox. New York: Penguin Books.
Spivak, Gayatri, C. 1988. *Can the Subaltern Speak?* In Cary Nelson and Lawrence Crossberg (eds.) *Marxism and the Interpretation of Culture.* Urbana: University of Illinois Press, 271–313.
Stengers Isabelle. 2008. 'A Constructivist Reading of Process and Reality'. *Theory, Culture and Society* 25 (4), 91–110.
Stengers Isabelle. 2018. *Another Science is Possible: A Manifesto for Slow Science.* Stephen, Muecke (trans.). Cambridge: Polity.
Stevenson, Jacqueline and Baker, Sally. 2018. *Refugees in Higher Education: Debate, Discourse and Practice.* Bingley: Emerald Publishing.
Strawson, Galen. 2004. "Against Narrativity". *Ratio* 17 (4), 428–452.
Sullivan, Richard and Lee, Kimi. 2008. Organizing Immigrant Women in America's Sweatshops: Lessons from the Los Angeles Garment Worker Center. *Signs: Journal of Women in Culture and Society* 33 (3), 527–532.
Taguchi, H. Lenz. 2012. 'A Diffractive and Deleuzian Approach to Analysing Interview Data'. *Feminist Theory* 13 (3), 265–281.
Tamboukou, Maria. 2008. 'Machinic Assemblages: Women, Art Education and Space'. *Discourse: Studies in the Cultural Politics of Education* 29 (3), 359–375.
Tamboukou, Maria. 2010. *Nomadic Narratives, Visual Forces: Gwen John's Letters and Paintings.* New York: Peter Lang.
Tamboukou, Maria. 2013 [2008]. 'A Foucauldian Approach to narratives'. In Molly Andrews, Corinne Squire, and Maria Tamboukou (eds.) *Doing Narrative Research.* London: Sage, 88–107.
Tamboukou, Maria. 2015. *Fighting and Writing: Radical Practices in Work, Politics and Culture.* London: Rowman & Littlefield International.
Tamboukou, Maria. 2016a. 'Feeling Narrative in the Archive: The Question of Serendipity'. *Qualitative Research* 16 (2), 151–166.
Tamboukou, Maria. 2016b. *Gendering the Memory of Work: Women Workers' Narratives.* London: Routledge.
Tamboukou, Maria. 2016c. 'Education as Action / The Adventure of Education: Thinking with Arendt and Whitehead'. *Journal of Educational Administration and History* 48 (2), 136–147.
Tamboukou, Maria. 2017. *Women Workers' Education, Life Narratives and Politics: Geographies, Histories, Pedagogies.* Basingstoke: Palgrave.
Tamboukou, Maria. 2018. 'Rethinking the subject in feminist research: narrative personae and stories of "the real"'. *Textual Practice* 32 (6), 939–955.
Tamboukou, Maria. 2020. 'Traces in the Archive: Re-imagining Sofia Kovalevskaya'. *Life Writing,* doi.org/10.1080/14484528.2020.1771672 (on-line first)

Tamboukou, Maria and *Beatriz* Revelles Benavente. 2020. 'Doing New Materialisms: An Interview with Maria Tamboukou' Matter'. *Journal of New Materialist Research* 1 (1), 155–175.

Tarde, Gabriel. 2012 [1895]. *Monadology and Sociology* (Edited and Translated by Theo Lorenc). Melbourne: re-press.

Tazzioli, Martina. 2015. 'The Politics of Counting and the Scene of Rescue: Border Deaths in the Mediterranean'. *Radical Philosophy* 192, 2–6.

Tedlock, Dennis. 1991. 'Oral History as Poetry'. In Ronald Grele (ed.) *Envelopes of Sounds: The Art of Oral History.* New York: Praeger, 106–125.

Tee, Caroline. 2016. *The Gülen Movement in Turkey: The Politics of Islam and Modernity.* London: I.B. Tauris.

Tihanov, Galin. 2015. 'Whose Cosmpolitanism? Genealogies of Cosmopolitanism'. In Schiller, Nina Glick, and Andrew Irving (eds.) *Whose Cosmopolitanism?: Critical Perspectives, Relationalities and Discontents.* Oxford: Berghahn Books, 29–30.

Theuws, Martje and ten Kate, Gisela. 2016. 'Fact Sheet: Migrant Labour in the Textile and Garment Industry: A Focus on the Role of Buying Companies'. Amsterdam: SOMO. Retrieved from https://www.somo.nl/fact-sheet-migrant-labour-in-the-textile-and-garment-industry/ [Accessed 14-2-2020]

Trinh, T. Minh-ha. 1989. *Woman, Narrative, Other: Writing Postcoloniality and Feminism.* Bloomington: Indiana University Press.

Tsilimpounidi, Myrto and Carasthathis, Anna. 2017. 'The Refugee Crisis': From Athens to Lesvos and back. *Slovenský národopis* 65 (4), 404–419.

Tzoraki, Ourania. 2019. 'A Descriptive Study of the Schooling and Higher Education Reforms in Response to the Refugees' Influx into Greece'. *Social Sciences* 8 (72). doi:10.3390/socsci8030072

Uden, Maria. 2018. 'The Novel Feminist Diffraction Concept: Its Application in Fifty-One Peer Reviewed Papers'. Research Report, Luleå, Sweden: Luleå Tekniska Universitet.

van der Tuin, Iris. 2019. 'Deleuze and Diffraction'. In Rosi Braidotti and Simone Bignall (eds.) *Posthuman Ecologies: Complexity and Process after Deleuze.* London: Rowman and Littlefield International, 17–39.

van den Elzen, Stella Sophie, Maxime. 2021. *Antislavery in the Transational Movement for Women's Rights 1832–1914: A study of Memory Work.* PhD Thesis, Utrecht University, The Netherlands.

Vertovec, Steven. 2009. 'Cosmopolitanism in Attitude, Practice and Competence'. MMG Working Paper 09-08, retrieved from www.mmg.mpg.de/workingpapers [21-3-2020]

Vieten, Ulrike. 2012. *Gender and Cosmopolitanism in Europe: A Feminist Perspective.* Farnham: Ashgate.

Vora, Neha. 2019. 'Review: Stateless in the Gulf: Migration, Nationality, and Society in Kuwait, by Claire Beaugrand'. *Migration Studies,* https://doi.org/10.1093/migration/mny031 [Accessed 26-2-2019]

War on Want. 2012. 'Restricted Rights: Migrant Women Workers in Thailand, Cambodia and Malaysia'. Retrieved from https://waronwant.org/sites/default/files/Restricted%20Rights.pdf [Accessed 14-2-2020]

Weir, Allison. 2017. 'Decolonizing Feminist Freedom: Indigeneous Relationalities'. In McLaren, Margaret, A. (ed.) *Decolonizing Feminism: Transnational Feminism and Globalization.* London: Rowman & Littlefield International, 257–288.

Wittgenstein, Ludwig. 1986 [1953]. *Philososphical Investigations,* trans. G.E. M. Anscombe. Oxford: Blackwell.

Whitehead, Alfred North. 1964. *The Concept of Nature: The Tarner Lectures. Delivered in Trinity College. November 1919.* Cambridge: Cambridge University Press.

Whitehead, Alfred, North. 1967 [1933]. *Adventures of Ideas.* New York: Free Press.

Whitehead, Alfred, North. 1985. [1929]. *Process and Reality* [Corrected Edition], ed. David Ray Griffin and Donald W. Sheburne. New York: The Free Press.

Woolf, Virginia. 1978 [1938]. *Three Guineas.* London: Penguin.

Wuthnow, Julie. 2002. 'Deleuze in the Postcolonial: On Nomads and Indigenous Politics'. *Feminist Theory* 3 (2), 183–200.

Wolff, Janet. 1990. *Feminine Sentences, Essays on Women and Culture.* Cambridge: Polity Press.

Yavuz, Hakan, M. and Balci, Bayram (eds.) 2018. *Turkey's July 15th Coup: What Happened and Why.* Salt Lake City: University of Utah Press.

Yılmaz, Gaye, Karatepe, İsmail Doğa and Tolga, Tören. 2019. 'Introduction: Putting Labor Market Integration in Turkey into its Place—Informality and Refugees'. In Gaye Yılmaz, İsmail Doğa Karatepe, and Tolga Tören (eds.) *Integration through Exploitation: Syrians in Turkey.* Augsburg, München: Rainer Hampp Verlag, 1–11.

Young, Iris Marion. 1990. *Justice and the Politics of Difference.* Princeton: Princeton University Press.

Young, Iris Marion. 2002. *Inclusion and Democracy.* New York: Oxford University Press.

Yung, Judy. 1995. *Unbound Feet: A Social History of Chinese Women in San Francisco.* Berkeley: California University Press.

Yung, Judy. 1999. *Unbound Voices: A Documentary History of Chinese Women in San Francisco.* Berkeley: California University Press.

Yuval-Davis, Nira, Wemyss, Georgie and Cassidy, Kathryn. 2018. 'Everyday Bordering, Belonging and the Reorientation of British Immigration Legislation'. *Sociology* 52 (2), 228–244.

Zavos, Alexandra. 2017. 'Intersections and Cross-Fertilizations between Feminist Research and Refugee Studies'. *Annual Review of Critical Psychology* 13, 1–6.

Zerilli, Linda, M. G. 1991. 'Machiavelli's Sisters : Women and the "Conversation" of Political Theory'. *Political Theory* 19 (2), 252–276.

Zugman, Kara. 2003. 'Political Consciousness and New Social Movement Theory: The Case of Fuerza Unida'. *Social Justice* 30 (1), 153–176.

Index

academic philanthropy, 157, 174, 175
Aegean Sea, 58
aesthetics and politics, 3, 156, 157, 159, 161, 162, 169, 171
affinities, 21, 24, 27, 42, 43, 46, 47, 49, 51. *See also* Mason, Jennifer
agential cut, 13, 69, 70, 110, 204. *See also* Barad, Karen
agential realism, 13. *See also* Barad, Karen
Agier, Michel, 37, 57, 59, 62, 63, 69, 70, 72, 74, 97, 98, 100, 181
agonistic humanism, 129, 134, 135, 140, 143, 144, 207; agonistic politics, 5, 92, 100, 102, 104, 105, 108, 130, 140, 167, 175, 200. *See also* Honig, Bonnie
amor mundi, 64, 159
amphibology, 182,
analytics, 4, 10, 110, 111; assemblage thinking, 10, 11, 13, 110, 111, 131, 198, 199; colonial assemblages, 9; heteropatriarchal assemblage, 197. *See also* heteropatriarchy; memory assemblages, 203; mobility assemblages, 3, 4, 5, 9-11, 20, 39, 57, 60, 71, 97, 98, 182, 189, 199, 202; narrative assemblages, 25; relations of exteriority, 12

Anna, ix, 7, 36–39, 53n11, 72, 75n15
Antigone, 4, 5, 129–37, 144, 145, 199, 203; Antigone assemblage, 131
Anzaldúa, Gloria, 23, 60, 61, 62
archives, 3, 19, 21, 26, 31, 43, 47, 51, 57, 129–31, 144, 157, 158, 161, 162, 170, 172, 192, 202, 204
assemblages, 10, 12–15, 23, 25, 29, 30, 32, 58, 64, 68, 98, 110, 111, 131, 143, 144, 167, 174, 198, 201, 204; agencement, 10; art/education assemblage, 146, 159, 200; assemblage Arendt, Hannah, 3, 19, 22, 23, 35, 41, 49, 64, 75, 130, 131, 134, 137, 140, 144, 156, 158, 159, 161, 162, 170–72, 176, 191, 201, 203
aurality, 29, 47. *See also* orality
Awat, ix, 6, 33, 34, 52n6

Balibar, Étienne, 57–60, 62, 143, 199
Barad, Karen, 12, 13, 69, 99, 110
between-worlds, 70, 74. *See also* Luste, Boulbina, Seloua
Bickford, Susan, 22, 23, 203. *See also* voice
biduns, 5, 180–82, 194
border practices, 92, 167, 201; border situations, 57, 62, 63, 72, 73, 156; border women, 60- 62, 71

221

borders, 2–5, 8, 15, 20, 21, 32, 33, 41, 42, 44, 55–60, 62–68, 70–74, 97, 98, 105, 108, 109, 111, 129, 138, 140–43, 156, 164, 167, 169, 175, 184, 195, 196; borderlands, 55, 58, 65, 70; Braidotti, Rosi, 14, 15, 17–20, 145n10, 187, 189, 190
Butler, Judith, 132, 133, 145n6, 191

carceral humanitarianism, 71, 200
Cavarero, Adriana, 3, 22, 35, 41, 51, 52, 132, 133, 145n6, 191
Christina, ix, 6, 32, 33, 35, 52n4
Click, ix, 6, 129, 138, 139, 140, 145n9, 167–69, 171, 177n22
coloniality of gender, 9. *See also* Lugones, María
coloniality of migration, 9, 100, 102
communicative ethics, 23, 48, 49. *See also* Young, Iris Marion
conatus, 92, 191. *See also* Spinoza, Baruch
cosmopolitanism, 70, 73, 74, 200; banal cosmopolitism, 70, 71, 74. *See also* Agier, Michel

decolonization, 5; decolonial, 46, 145, 196, 201. *See also* Mohanty, Chandra Talpade
Dana, ix, 5, 6, 179–84, 188–90, 194n1
Deleuze, Gilles, 12, 31, 33, 45, 65, 75n4, 159; Deleuze, Gilles and Guattari, Felix, 3, 10, 11, 14–16, 25, 65
Derya, ix, 6, 56, 65, 66, 75n1
deterritorialization, 10, 11, 13, 15, 65, 190. *See also* **Deleuze**, Gilles
diffractions, 21, 36, 46–48. *See also* Barad, Karen; Haraway, Donna
Diotima [Centre for Research on Women's Issues-CRWI], ix, 52n6, 180, 190
dystopias, 5, 156
displacement, 3, 4, 33, 74, 129, 130, 157, 173, 203; forced displacement, 1, 3, 10, 17, 21, 38, 41, 46, 48, 49, 63, 64, 68, 73, 74, 91, 92, 98, 100, 108, 131, 140, 157, 159, 171, 199, 200; poetics of displacement, 92

Elena, ix, 6, 129, 141–43, 177n17
Elina, ix, 7, 164
entanglements, 1, 4, 10, 12, 13, 26, 29, 31, 46, 47, 51, 60, 63, 71, 72, 96, 132, 140, 142, 144, 156, 160, 171, 187, 196; affective entanglements, 26, 31. *See also* Barad, Karen
epistemic gathering, 196. *See also* Pohlhaus, Gaile
Erika, ix, 7, 34, 52n7
errantry/errance, ix, 16, 17, 189, 202. *See also* Glissant, Édouard
ethnopoetics, 28–30. *See also* transcripts

feminisms, 8, 14, 20, 48, 131, 197, 201; feminist geopolitics, 58, 74; feminist narratives, 49; feminist theory of refusal, 203. *See also* Honig, Bonnie; feminism without borders, 5, 196; subject of feminism, 2, 3, 20, 193; transnational feminisms, 196, 197
feminization of asylum, 72
forced choice, 136, 138, 142, 144
Foucault, Michel, 9, 44, 53, 65, 159–61, 171
FRAB-Feminist Researchers Against Borders, 156

garment industry, 80, 91–96, 98, 100–10, 203
gender-based violence, 2, 39, 67, 99, 182
genealogy, 1, 92, 100, 108, 141, 145, 155, 167, 176, 187, 199, 202, 203; feminist genealogies of labour, 91, 100
Glissant, Édouard, 3, 16, 17, 20, 39, 41, 43, 44, 46, 47, 188, 202

Hanielle, ix, 7, 166, 177n20

Hanna, ix, 5, 6, 19, 35, 53n9, 129, 140, 141, 147–53
Haraway, Donna, 47, 48, 173
heteropatriarchy, 197; heteropatriarchal family, 198
heterotopic spaces, 5, 156
Honig, Bonnie, 109, 134–36, 140, 144, 145n2, 145n6n8, 158, 159, 182, 203

Iliaktida, ix, 11, 20n2, 34, 36, 39, 53n13, 67, 75n11, 164, 165, 176n6
Ilya, ix, 7, 196
interludes, 3–5, 46, 53n9n23, 77, 91, 92, 111, 115, 129, 137, 140, 147, 155, 162, 172
intermezzo, 15, 31–33, 39, 48, 61, 188. *See also* **Deleuze**, Gilles
intra-actions, 12, 13, 99, 197, 199. *See also* Barad, Karen

Kolozova, Katerina, 5, 179, 182, 185–87, 189, 191–93. *See also* Laruelle, François; non-philosophy; radical solitude

labour politics, 5; forced labour, 167; modern slavery, 4, 96, 110, 113n4n5, 168, 177n22
language games, 17–19, 193, 202. *See also* Wittgenstein, Ludwig
Laruelle, François, 179, 182, 185–87, 192, 193. *See also* Kolozova, Katerina; non-philosophy; stranger
Lear, Jonathan, 5, 156, 158, 159. *See also* Honig, Bonnie; radical hope
Lefebvre, Henri, 25, 26. *See also* rhythm
Lesvos, ix, 11, 12, 20n3–6, 34, 36, 49, 50, 52n8, 53n11n13n26, 58, 59, 67, 70–72, 75n11n14, 157, 165, 173, 176n6, 177n17–20; Mytilini, 11, 20n3–4, 36, 49, 67, 75n11n14, 176n6, 177n17–20
Linda, ix, 7, 11, 13, 14, 20n4, 71, 72, 75n14

lines of flight, 4, 11, 13, 14, 65, 110, 112, 129, 159, 171, 184, 190, 191, 197, 199, 201, 203
listening, 3, 21–27, 29–31, 33, 35, 41–43, 45, 47, 48, 50, 51, 56, 79, 127, 172, 191, 196, 197, 203; affective listening, 23, 51; art of listening, 21, 23, 43; emergent listening, 33; listening positions, 36; listening practices, 25, 31, 47, 48; listening process, 26, 31; phenomena of listening, 52; political listening, 23; politics of listening, 197; situated listeners, 21, 33
logocentrism, 22
Lugones, María, 63–65, 204
Luste, Boulbina, Seloua, 70, 74

McLaren, Margaret, 200, 204
Mariam, ix, 7, 39, 41, 53n13
Mason, Jennifer, 24, 43, 49. *See also* affinities
Melina, ix, 6, 197, 204n3
memory, 16, 24, 45, 129, 130, 144, 204; counter-memory, 15; memory work, 204; memory writing, 170; mnemonic practices, 45, 204
migrant women, 4, 5, 8n7, 98, 100, 101, 104, 106–108, 112, 114n26, 129, 140, 156
Mohanty, Chandra Talpade, 5, 105, 196, 197, 201, 204n1

Nadia, ix, 4, 6, 19, 20n9, 49–51, 53n23, 77, 90–93, 95–100, 109–11, 112n1, 171, 172, 192, 194n6, 201
narratives, 3–5, 24–29, 32, 33, 36, 37, 39–41, 43, 45, 46, 49–51, 65, 66, 69, 70, 92, 130, 135, 142, 144, 145n2, 156, 179, 182, 190, 198, 204; anti-narrativist thesis, 43; cinematic narrative, 71, 141; circular narratives, 36; episodic narratives, 45; imaginary narratives, 164; and music, 24, 46, 52n2; narrative act,

51; narrative analytics, 13, 21, 25, 40, 53n10; narrative archive, 157; narrative coherence, 41; narrative ethics, 30, 47, 53n12; narrative identities, 40; narrative intermezzos, 33, 39; narrative field, 36, 49; narrative lines, 36, 131; narrative moments, 12, 56; narrative persona, 130, 131, 145n3; narrative phenomena, 13; narrative postscripts, 39; narrative research, 21, 47, 203; narrative rhythmanalysis, 24, 26, 27; narrative sensibility, 49; narrative scene, 24, 26, 27, 29, 47; narratives of displacement, 4, 130; narrative structure, 44; narrative traces, 182; narrative voice, 28; narrative worlds, 38; non-nomadic narratives, 192; oral narratives, 27, 28, 45; political narratives, 129–31, 199, 203; relational narratives, 51. *See also* Cavarero, Adriana; sound of narratives, 29, 41, 52; stanzas, 29, 36–39, 62, 66, 137; as technologies of power, 44; will not to tell a story, 43, 44. *See also* Cavarero, Adriana, interludes, feminist narratives, narrative assemblages, Riessman

nepantla, 61, 62, 65. *See also* Anzaldúa, Gloria

nomadism, 1–3, 5, 14–17, 20, 31, 33, 184, 188–91, 201, 202; arrowlike nomadism, 16, 202. *See also* Glissant, Édouard; circular nomadism, 16. *See also* Glissant, Édouard; geographies of nomadism, 9, 202; nomadic subjects, 1–3, 14, 15, 17–20, 162, 179, 182, 185, 186, 189, 201, 202. *See also* Braidotti, Rosi; nomadic theories, 179, 180, 185, 189, 193, 203. *See also* Braidotti, Rosi; nomadic thinking, 46, 187; nomadisms of escape, 189, 202; nomadology, 3, 15; non-nomad, 5, 179, 185, 187, 189–93, 202

non-philosophy, 179, 185–87, 189, 193. *See also* Kolozova, Katerina; Laruelle, François

new materialisms, 187, 199, 204

Oliver, Kelly, 12, 71, 197, 200, 201. *See also* carceral humanitarianism

opacity, 39, 41, 43, 44, 46, 47. *See also* Glissant, Édouard

orality, 27–30. *See also* aurality

poetics of relation, 16, 17, 46. *See also* Glissant, Édouard

Pohlhaus, Gaile, 196. *See also* epistemic gathering

radical hope, 5, 155, 156, 158, 159, 166, 172, 176, 200, 203. *See also* Lear

radical solitude, 4, 185, 191–93. *See also* Kolozova, Katerina

real, 1, 3, 14, 19, 46–48, 57, 60, 72, 100, 179, 182, 184–93, 202; colonization of the real, 179, 182; real and imaginary, 58, 64, 72; syntax of the real, 187, 191. *See also* Kolozova, Katerina; Laruelle, François

refugee women, 2–5, 9, 11, 12, 17, 20, 21, 23, 25, 29, 31, 33, 34, 39, 46, 48, 49, 51, 52, 65, 71, 74, 75, 92, 107–109, 111, 129–31, 135, 156–58, 160, 162, 166–68, 170, 171, 173, 174, 179, 186, 187, 189, 197–203

refugee camps, 4, 5, 12, 72, 117, 119, 137, 156, 169, 171, 200; Kara Tepe, 12, 20n5, 49, 50, 51, 53n25, 196; Moria, 49, 53n24n25, 157, 158, 164, 165

relational freedom, 199, 200. *See also* Weir, Allison

relational ontologies, 198, 199

rescue politics, 200. *See also* Tazzioli, Martina

Riessman, K., Catherine, 27, 28, 30, 31. *See also* narratives

Riley, Denise, 201
rhizomes, 16, 17, 21, 43. *See also* Glissant, Édouard
rhythm, 3, 21, 24–26, 28–31, 36, 41, 42, 44, 46, 63, 92, 97, 129, 139, 165. *See also* Lefebvre, Henri; narratives, narrative rhythmanalysis

Salvaggio, Ruth, 22, 47, 51. *See also* sounds
scriptural economy, 29, 43
Shachnaz, ix, 7, 164, 165, 177n18
Sima, ix, 6, 44–46, 53n18
Sjöholm, Cecilia, 41, 145n6, 160, 161, 170, 171
Söderbäck, Fanny, 130, 144, 145, 145n2n6
Somi, ix, 4, 6, 72, 73, 75n16, 115, 129, 135–38, 140, 145n1, 162, 164, 172
sounds, 4, 21, 22, 24–30, 32, 36, 41, 42, 45, 46, 49, 52, 92, 143; soundscapes, 3, 27, 30, 129, 197. *See also* Salvaggio, Ruth
Spinoza, Baruch, 14, 38, 44, 58, 75n4, 176, 191, 199
stranger, 185, 192, 193. *See also* Kolozova, Katerina; Laruelle, François; non-philosophy

Tanya, ix, 7, 11
Tazzioli, Martina, 200
territorialization, 10, 13
touching, 51
transcripts, 27–30, 47. *See also* ethnopoetics, Riessman, K., Catherine

transindividuality, 199. *See also* Balibar, Étienne; Spinoza, Baruch
Trinh, T. Minh-ha, 24, 27, 30, 36, 37, 43, 50, 52, 57, 62–66, 69, 192

undecidability of foreigness, 109. *See also* Honig, Bonnie
UAWOG- United African Women's Organization in Greece, 5, 155
UNHCR - United Nations Refugee Agency, ix, 73, 81, 82, 86, 96, 97, 121, 124, 163, 176n9, 177n15
uprooted women, 3, 5, 106, 130, 138, 143, 144, 145n2, 156, 162, 171, 189, 197–204

voice, 2–4, 21–24, 26–31, 41–43, 45, 56, 60, 78, 88, 92, 108, 169; corporeal voice, 21, 22, 191; disembodied voice, 27; politics of voices, 21, 22; recorded voice, 24, 27; transcript/voice debate, 28; vocal ontology of uniqueness, ; voice/logos binarism, 22; voice/text, 21, 27–30, 43, 47. *See also* Bickford, Susan; Cavarero, Adriana; narrative voice

Warda, ix, 7, 66–70, 75n11, 158, 159, 171, 176n6
Weir, Allison, 20n1, 197, 199
Wittgenstein, Ludwig, 17, 18, 20, 193, 202. *See also* language games

Young, Iris Marion, 23, 48, 49, 51. *See also* communicative ethics

Zahra, ix, 7, 11, 12, 20n5, 41–43, 49

Manufactured by Amazon.ca
Bolton, ON